D0113924

THE KEY MAN

THE
KEY
MAN

THE TRUE STORY OF HOW
THE GLOBAL ELITE WAS DUPED
BY A CAPITALIST FAIRY TALE

SIMON CLARK AND
WILL LOUCH

HARPER
BUSINESS
An Imprint of HarperCollins*Publishers*

THE KEY MAN. Copyright © 2021 by Simon Clark and Will Louch. All rights reserved. Printed in the United States of America. No part of this book may be used or reproduced in any manner whatsoever without written permission except in the case of brief quotations embodied in critical articles and reviews. For information, address HarperCollins Publishers, 195 Broadway, New York, NY 10007.

HarperCollins books may be purchased for educational, business, or sales promotional use. For information, please email the Special Markets Department at SPsales@harper collins.com.

FIRST EDITION

Library of Congress Cataloging-in-Publication Data has been applied for.

ISBN 978-0-06-299621-3

21 22 23 24 25   LSC   10 9 8 7 6 5 4 3 2 1

CONTENTS

This book is based on hundreds of interviews with more than 150 people, including 70 former Abraaj employees, business chiefs, politicians, and a Vatican cardinal. All of the men and women who appear in the narrative do so under their real names. Many people who agreed to contribute asked not to be named because they feared it might cause trouble for themselves. These people have been referred to as employees or executives or with other general descriptions.

Quotes attributed to characters in dialogues are drawn from email exchanges, other forms of electronic messaging, videos, or court hearings, or were reconstructed from participants' recollections. We have made extensive use of legal documents and witness statements from the many court cases involving Abraaj, including criminal and civil cases the U.S. government has brought. These documents are identified in the notes section at the end of the book.

We contacted all the main characters in the Abraaj saga and asked them to comment. We have interviewed Arif Naqvi on a number of occasions in the past. Through his lawyer, Arif declined our interview requests for this book, citing his ongoing legal proceedings. He has maintained his innocence of the U.S. charges.

THE KEY MAN

PROLOGUE

"It's a crucial moment in history. It's an opportunity to immutably and absolutely change the course of innumerable lives."

Arif Naqvi, a silver-haired man of soft bearish charm, was giving the biggest speech of his life. Hundreds of business leaders were gathered at the Mandarin Oriental hotel by New York's Central Park to hear him speak on that sunny Monday morning in September 2017. This was his moment. The eyes of the global elite were fixed on him and he knew he needed to make a big impression.

The *New York Times* and *Forbes* had published glowing articles about the tycoon, who socialized with billionaires, royalty, and politicians. Among his associates were Bill Gates, Prince Charles, and John Kerry, the former American secretary of state. Arif was a member of powerful boards at the United Nations and Interpol, the international police agency.

It was no coincidence that world political leaders were meeting at the same time a short walk away at United Nations headquarters. For Arif's objective was to convince his audience that he could solve humanity's biggest problems—hunger, sickness, illiteracy, climate change, and power shortages—better than the politicians assembled across town.

Arif was one of the world's leading impact investors, and his purpose was to do good and make profit—for his investors and for himself.

Two years earlier, the United Nations had announced a hugely ambitious plan, which Pope Francis blessed, to end global poverty by 2030. The plan required $2.5 trillion of annual funding in addition to what governments and companies were already providing.

Arif said he could help.

He was founder and chief executive of the Abraaj Group, a private equity firm based in Dubai. Abraaj managed almost $14 billion and owned stakes in a hundred companies worldwide. Arif was asking investors for $6 billion more, which Abraaj would use to buy and improve companies in poor countries. By doing this he would help the UN end poverty and make profit for himself and his investors too.

"To do good does not necessarily mean to compromise returns," Arif said, pacing back and forth upon the stage. "It is gratifying that we are having this event on morning one, day one and hour one of the UN General Assembly week. And what I hope is that everybody, when they leave from here at the end of today, are going to spend time influencing their networks and spending the whole of the week forcing people not to talk about wars and pestilence and negativity but actually the positive energy that comes out of focusing on impact investing."

A revolution in finance was needed and Arif was going to lead it. He wasn't just harnessing capitalism to make money for the rich but to end the suffering of the poor as well.

"We want to be the beacon and we want others to join us," Arif declared with his calm, reassuring voice. "This opportunity is here. It is now. It is for us to take advantage of and it is for all of us to make collectively the world a better place."

The crowd swelled with applause.

It was a masterful performance, but messages stored on the phone Arif carried told a very different story. Six days before the speech, Rafique Lakhani, a deeply religious Muslim employee who was unflinchingly loyal to Arif, had emailed his boss. Rafique's job was to manage Abraaj's cash, and he was desperate because the firm had run out of money, he told Arif in the email. There was nothing left to pay for promised investments in hospitals in poor countries, Rafique told him.

Arif's sunny optimism on stage masked a deep chaos. Behind the façade of operating a successful investment company capable of improving billions of lives, Arif was masterminding a global criminal conspiracy. Abraaj didn't have any money left because he had stolen it. Arif had taken more than $780 million from his firm and misused money from investors including the Bill & Melinda Gates Foundation, Bank of America, and the U.S., U.K., and French governments.

Now, unbeknown to the audience, Abraaj was on the brink of collapsing with more than $1 billion of debt.

· · ·

Arif was the Key Man. This title, which private equity firms give to their most important executives, had even greater significance in Arif's case because he was offering to solve so many of humanity's problems. He was the charismatic leader of Abraaj and his vision was what investors bought into. He was the reason people gave Abraaj money to manage, and he was trusted with billions of dollars. One adoring investor compared him to Tom Cruise in the *Mission: Impossible* films.

Abraaj was a money machine that had raised a succession of funds to invest in companies and hospitals across Asia, Africa, and Latin America. Arif traveled the world in a private jet and on *Raasta*, his 154-foot superyacht with teak decks and an art deco interior, to do deals with the rich and powerful. He was a fixture at the annual World Economic Forum in the Swiss mountain resort of Davos.

Arif's rise from childhood in Pakistan, a former British colony, to trusted insider of the elite embodied the burst of globalization that began after the Cold War ended. As new forces brought people closer together around the world—from the internet to terrorism—Arif convinced Western investors that he was their expert partner in exploring distant lands.

As global trade intensified at the dawn of the new millennium,

Arif realized that he could pitch his dealmaking skills to politicians as well as investors, as a way to do good by spurring development—all while generating market-beating returns.

In the aftermath of the attacks of September 11, 2001, Arif persuaded Western politicians that he was an ally who could help bring stability to the Middle East by creating jobs in fragile states where terrorism had deep roots.

He was sought out by billionaires and their millennial heirs who enthusiastically adopted the idea of impact investing and the feel-good veneer it gave to the old game of making money.

When China's economic expansion breathed new life into countries along the ancient Silk Road trading routes of Asia, Arif guided Western executives to business opportunities in cities they struggled to find on a map.

Microsoft's founder Bill Gates helped Arif set up a $1 billion fund to improve healthcare in poor countries, and the World Bank and the American, British, and French governments invested in this pioneering fund alongside the Gates Foundation.

Arif won much admiration during his career. A committee of Nobel Prize laureates selected him for an Oslo Business for Peace Award. American academics predicted he might become a brilliant prime minister of Pakistan by 2020 and lead his troubled homeland to prosperity.

"As a charismatic, self-made millionaire and one of the most successful emerging market investors, he was well connected," the academics wrote in 2011. "Naqvi's emphasis on education and self-reliance, along with his self-made personal narrative, untainted reputation and emphasis on fairness and justice resonated well."

• • •

Four months after Arif gave the speech in New York, in January 2018, we received an email from someone who refused to give their name. He or she said they were an Abraaj employee who was afraid that if they spoke publicly they'd lose their job, or maybe worse. They wanted to get a message out and they decided to contact us because we were *Wall Street Journal* reporters who specialized in writing about private equity firms like Abraaj.

"There is a potential fraud investigation," the person wrote. Hundreds of millions of dollars were missing from Abraaj's healthcare fund. "It is all sad but true."

We exchanged hundreds of emails with the nameless source over the next few months. When we contacted Abraaj, they said the allegations were lies.

"Categorically there is no money that disappeared," an American executive at Abraaj said. "Why would such a successful firm do something like that?"

The source often went silent without warning, only to reappear days later using a new email address. After four months, the messages stopped altogether. We felt like we'd lost a friend.

This was a big story if we could prove it was true. We called dozens of people on five continents to find out what was going on. Working with Nicolas Parasie, a *Wall Street Journal* colleague in Dubai, we interviewed Abraaj employees, investors, and advisers. They shared emails and details with us that added to a vast collection of documents gathered from court cases and regulatory filings. With the notes we took during telephone conversations and messages exchanged with sources on WhatsApp, Signal, and Telegram, we collected enough pieces of the jigsaw puzzle to gain a clear picture of events at Abraaj. We spoke to so many people that Abraaj employees began calling us to find out what was happening.

Then we made a crucial breakthrough. A chain of trusted sources put us in contact with a person who claimed to have proof of massive theft and fraud at Abraaj. After repeated telephone calls and false starts, this person finally agreed to meet in a café near the Tower of London, an ancient fortress in the heart of the city's financial district.

The person pulled a laptop computer from a travel bag and opened files showing Abraaj bank statements, emails, and documents. Fraud, theft, and attempts to bribe Pakistan's prime minister had taken place, the documents showed. We photographed the documents and walked back across London Bridge to the newsroom, firmly clutching the evidence. Our front-page investigation was published in the *Wall Street Journal* on October 16, 2018. Arif insisted he had done nothing wrong.

Six months later, a British police officer arrested Arif as he stepped off a commercial passenger flight arriving at Heathrow Airport in London from Pakistan. The policeman told Arif that he was wanted for extradition to stand trial in the United States, where New York prosecutors accused him of operating a criminal organization. He had stolen for personal gain and to prop up Abraaj, his renowned private equity firm and a darling of the global financial elite.

On the day of his arrest in April 2019, Arif was carrying two Pakistani passports, a Saint Kitts and Nevis passport, and an Interpol passport. He told the police officer that he was surprised he was arresting him because he'd checked before flying to see whether there was an Interpol "red notice" arrest warrant in his name and there wasn't one. The police officer told him he didn't need one. Arif was being charged under an American law created to prosecute criminal gangs like the mafia.

The story of Abraaj that Arif wanted people to hear was the triumph of capitalism over poverty, of the future over the past, of a global vision regaled from Washington to Davos, Dubai, and Beijing. The only problem, according to the U.S. Department of Justice, was that Arif was a liar and a thief motivated by criminal ambition.

After years in which Arif took the world by storm, as Bill Gates entrusted him with money and Warren Buffett and other billionaires welcomed him into their exclusive club of rich philanthropists, he stood accused of swindling investors out of hundreds of millions of dollars, breaking laws and offering bribes, all to keep his billionaire lifestyle afloat.

The dark side of globalization—a shadowy hinterland of political intrigue and illicit offshore money flows—lurked behind the bright vision of the future Arif championed in public.

His investments, in truth, were too good to be true, and his firm had been insolvent for years. Stolen cash propped up Abraaj in what the famed Bernard Madoff investigator Harry Markopolos described to us as a Ponzi scheme with leverage. Abraaj had become one of the largest corporate frauds in history, and Arif, accused of wrongfully holding on to $385 million of the funds he had taken, faced 291 years in a high-security jail.

Abraaj employees who naively believed in Arif and his mission of making money and doing good were at a loss to explain what went wrong. They debated whether he was a narcissist, sociopath, psychopath, or all three.

"There is no one so compelling as a mad man or a con man. He was brilliant and he was devious," said a former Abraaj executive. "He was so selfish and so greedy that he essentially undercut everything he was saying."

As Abraaj crumbled, Arif told a colleague that he wanted to walk away with three things intact: his wealth, dignity, and reputation.

This is not the story Arif wanted to be told. It is the true story of how one of global finance's most celebrated companies turned out to be little more than a capitalist fairy tale.

CHAPTER 1

THE BOY FROM KARACHI

The young boy stared in wonder at the grainy black-and-white images on the television screen. The pictures of the first men walking on the moon pierced earth's atmosphere in July 1969 and entered the homes of 600 million people around the planet, including in Karachi, a bustling port city on Pakistan's Arabian Sea shore.

"Wow," Arif thought. "How privileged am I to be watching this."

Like millions who witnessed the space odyssey as it happened and billions who saw it later, the realization that people were on the moon and looking back at our world gave Arif a whole new perspective on who and where he was. He wasn't merely alive within the walls of his house or the streets of Karachi or even the planes and mountains of Pakistan. The whole world was his stage.

Globalization was shaping Arif's world long before the moon landing. His school in the sweltering city of Karachi was built more than a century before he was born by foreigners who had set sail from a cool and rainy island four thousand miles away. Karachi Grammar School was founded by the Reverend Henry Brereton, the first British chaplain of Karachi, in 1847 to educate the white offspring of missionaries, merchants, and the military. By the time Arif enrolled, the school was part of the newly independent nation of Pakistan and the students were mostly local children like him.

An intelligent, cocky boy with sharp features and thick black hair, Arif had an answer for everything. Teachers found him both likable and divisive because there were two distinct sides to his personality. Some students admired his lively sense of humor but others were hurt by his lack of sensitivity. He was a scholar and a risk-taker who pushed school rules to the limit. His name was painted in gold letters on a wooden panel memorializing first-class students, many of whom went on to become politicians, generals, and corporate chiefs. But Arif wanted to leave a mark on the school on his terms too, so he carved his name into a stone porch near a bell that was the symbolic heart of the old institution. Teachers, unsurprisingly, were less than impressed but the brazen act ensured they remembered him long after he left.

Arif learned to sing the school song lustily in a hall with a corrugated iron roof called the Shed, which became unbearably hot in summer but was useful in winter for assemblies and prize givings.

"God, whose mercy long has kept our school from age to age, hear as we offer up to thee our fair and splendid heritage," Arif sang. "Help us to keep our ideals pure, whatever else may change."

The Christian God of the British songwriters had been replaced in the minds of the Pakistani students with Allah, the God of Islam, but ambition and idealism burned just as intensely in them as in their colonial predecessors. The school was infused with the legacy of the British and their recently expired empire. Discipline was strict. Teachers in long black gowns struck disobedient students with canes, and boys who let their hair grow long over their white shirt collars were sent straight to the barbershop.

Lessons were taught in English rather than the local Urdu language. Students learned by heart the works of William Shakespeare, the English playwright who first described all the world as a stage and wrote *Macbeth*, the tragedy of an ambitious general, and the comedy *Much Ado About Nothing*. Arif acted in four school plays and was vice president of the drama society.

The mighty stone school stood at the center of Karachi, among other imposing buildings erected by the British colonizers. The clock tower of the Empress Market was nearby. Named after Queen Victoria, Empress of India, the market was built in the 1880s on a plot of land where British soldiers executed local freedom fighters by blowing them to pieces with cannonballs.

When the British gave up the empire at midnight on August 14, 1947, they divided the land into two new nations: the Islamic Republic of Pakistan and the Republic of India. The pacifist politician Mahatma Gandhi had dreamed of creating one free and united India for citizens of all religions but his vision didn't come true. Pakistan was made for Muslims, and India was dominated by Hindus. People migrated by foot, ox cart, and train across the new border—to or from Pakistan depending on their religion—with millions suffering injury, rape, or death in the violent transition.

Arif's family was part of the exodus, moving from northern India to Karachi to start a new life. Karachi's population doubled to 1 million soon after independence and kept growing rapidly to reach 16 million in the twenty-first century, almost double the size of London.

The British left behind railways, ports, power stations, and elitist values. On the manicured green lawns of Karachi's members-only Sind Club, white army officers were replaced by a new upper class of Pakistanis who talked in English about business and politics while sipping gin and tonic. They sent their children to Karachi Grammar School and frequently looked down on parents who weren't wealthy or well-connected enough to join their exclusive club.

Arif's father wasn't a Sind Club member but he was still able to pay the Karachi Grammar School fees to make his children part of the English-speaking elite. For most people in Karachi the grammar school was unreachable. It was a price worth paying, parents reckoned, because in a country with a rigid class system, attending the exclusive school brought them closer to the orbit of prime ministers, judges, and the owners of industry.

Arif's father fell on hard times in his business dealings, making life tougher for Arif and his three sisters than it might otherwise have

been. Arif had a fiercely competitive streak and the setbacks of his
father wounded his pride. He was acutely aware of the difference between himself and the sons and daughters of the extremely wealthy.

Arif was determined to advance his family's fortunes. He mastered
the art of networking and won the loyal support of fellow students
who stayed close to him in later life. Wahid Hamid, a Karachi Grammar School pupil who befriended Barack Obama at college in the
United States, would go on to work closely with Arif at Abraaj some
thirty years later. Javed Ahmed, a fellow school prefect and lifelong
friend, served as chief executive of the British sugar company Tate &
Lyle and provided money for a bond to help get Arif out of jail after
his arrest. Arif also kept in touch with Samir Fancy, a boy with important family ties through his mother's prior marriage to the sultan
of Oman. Samir captained the school cricket team and Arif never
forgot when he didn't select him for a match.

Karachi was a peaceful place during Arif's school days. Children
swam at Sandspit Beach and bought ice cream near the port. Fishermen told tales of local adventurers such as the Bhatti cousins, who
smuggled gold into Karachi from an area of Arabia Europeans once
called the Pirate Coast. Today it's known as the United Arab Emirates. The smugglers were so prolific that the price of gold in Karachi
would rise and fall as they delivered shipments of the precious metal
to the city. They won the allegiance of the city's poor by paying for
food and education and, in return, people provided the cousins with
information to help them stay a step ahead of the police.

Arif's classmates pored over newspapers and magazines filled with
tales of glamorous members of the elite like Prince Shah Karim Al
Hussaini, otherwise known as the Aga Khan. The wealthy prince's
father claimed to be a direct descendent of the Prophet Muhammad
and his mother was a British aristocrat. The Aga Khan's ancestors
were weighed in gold by religious followers who gifted the riches to
their leader. The Aga Khan impressed Pakistanis with gossipy news
about his glamorous life and philanthropic acts, which would include
building a renowned university hospital in Karachi.

School infused Arif with the ambition to do more than leave his mark on the stone bell porch. As the school song put it, like the "generations that have trod this path before" he would "strive whatever betide, to learn to play the game."

He was determined to play the game of life and win.

Arif honed his acting, public speaking, and leadership skills. He was a member of the debating team, captain of the general knowledge team, editor in chief of *Pulse*, the school newspaper, and co-editor of *The Grammarian*, the school yearbook. He was a runner-up in an inter-school oratory competition and won awards for journalism and for being the most outstanding student of the year in 1978. In his last September at school he participated in a big debate, speaking for the motion that the most valuable member of society is the rebel. Arif's team won by arguing that rebels are reformers rather than destructive forces. Arif gained "more points for the delivery rather than for material," according to *The Grammarian*.

He was never shy about success and claimed to have transformed *Pulse* during his editorship. "We, the Editors, unabashedly accept all credit, which the avid reader may wish to confer on us," he wrote in the yearbook.

Ever the optimist, Arif liked to say there were two types of people in the world—those who wake up in the morning, open the window, look out, and pessimistically say "Good God, it's morning," and those who open the same window and optimistically say "Good morning, God!"

The place for such an ambitious son of Karachi to go next was the old imperial capital, London. It was a journey many privileged children from former British colonies took and in 1979, at the age of nineteen, Arif started studying for a university degree at the London School of Economics. Life in Britain was a sobering introduction to the vast inequality in the world. A relatively well-to-do boy in Karachi, Arif was comparatively hard-up in the vastly more expensive British capital. Fellow Pakistani students walked everywhere and avoided taking buses or the London Underground to save money.

He took pleasure in his academic success in London. It was one way of striking back at the racism he experienced. There were also mild acts of rebellion, like smoking in a common room, for which he was reprimanded.

Arif was taught by a British professor who specialized in Soviet economics and studied the ideology of communism, which promised to elevate the poor people whom globalization left behind. The tensions of the Cold War between the United States and the Soviet Union were building at the time, and the Americans were supporting a military dictator in Pakistan who, with U.S. assistance, armed Mujahideen fighters in neighboring Afghanistan in a bid to oust occupying Soviet troops. Osama bin Laden fought among the Afghans against the Russians.

Arif made friends in London and widened the foundations of his global network, which served him well in life. He also found love, falling for a fellow former Karachi Grammar School student. Fayeeza Chundrigar was related to a past prime minister of Pakistan who had given his name to Chundrigar Road, Karachi's equivalent to Wall Street. A conscientious student, Fayeeza professed a strong concern for her poorer fellow citizens as well as an interest in finance, which led to a job at Pakistan's Bank of Credit and Commerce International. They got married after graduating in 1982.

Arif's priority was to get rich, but there weren't many opportunities for a young Pakistani in London's financial district, known as the City, in the early 1980s. The City was still a stuffy club reserved mainly for rich white men from English private schools like Eton College. Prime Minister Margaret Thatcher's reforms, which opened the City to international competition and foreign workers, hadn't yet taken root.

Arif was training as an accountant at Arthur Andersen in London in October 1985 when an advertisement appeared in the *Financial Times* for an exciting job back in Pakistan. A new advisory firm called Financial and Management Services had been set up in Karachi by British investment bank Morgan Grenfell, U.S. advisory firm Booz

Allen Hamilton, and the Pakistan Banking Council. They were looking for dynamic Pakistani professionals with international experience and qualifications who wanted to return home to work. Arif applied and was hired.

British managers at the advisory firm found Arif charming, intelligent, and energetic but Pakistani colleagues saw a different side to his personality. Arif was friendly when he wanted something and ruthless when he didn't. Colleagues described him as aggressive and bumptious, a hypercompetitive chancer with an enormous sense of entitlement and ego. His stint as a consultant based in Karachi's Avari Towers ended as a rumor spread through the office that he hadn't completed all his accounting exams in the U.K. Arif left the company soon after a letter arrived from London confirming that he hadn't qualified.

He moved to an office in the city's upscale Clifton district to work for Firoz Shroff, a real estate developer and one of the Aga Khan's Ismaili followers. Ismailis are renowned as savvy business operators, a characteristic Firoz attributed to hard work and—as the old British saying goes—to carefully counting pennies rather than pounds. Firoz told Arif that a bar of soap and tube of toothpaste could last him six months but Arif wasn't impressed by his boss's frugal ways.

Firoz liked Arif and thought he was smart but soon discovered characteristics that troubled him. Arif had a big ego and wanted to use debt to finance deals, but to Firoz debt was like a drug and ego was a disease. It seemed to him that Arif was on a mission to prove he could be more successful and richer than Pakistan's dominant industrial families—the Dawoods, the Adamjees, and Agha Hasan Abedi, who was busy building the Bank of Credit and Commerce International, where Fayeeza worked, into a global company.

"Good luck," Firoz told Arif. "I don't want to be above anybody. I would rather be under the carpet."

Reflecting on Arif's ambition, Firoz thought something must have happened to him at school—he was in a hurry to gain status to impress former classmates at Karachi Grammar School.

Arif worked with Firoz for a few months and then joined American Express, where he served a brief stint in the U.S. credit card company's Karachi office.

A big break came in 1990 when he applied to join Saudi Arabia's Olayan Group. The company belonged to a wealthy Saudi family that had interests in consumer goods, logistics, and banking in the oil-rich homeland of Islam. A job at Olayan would open doors to important people across the Middle East.

Arif made a positive impression on Imtiaz Hydari, a Pakistani who had risen through the ranks to become president of Olayan. Imtiaz saw something special in the infectiously positive, intelligent, and well-spoken thirty-year-old, and hired Arif as a business analyst. Imtiaz later described Arif as having far-reaching ambitions, and an ego to match.

As a technological revolution supercharged a world collecting on the peace dividend of the Cold War's end, Arif moved to the Saudi capital, Riyadh. The workforce was international and he met ambitious Indians, Lebanese, Palestinians, Egyptians, Europeans, and Americans.

Arif's job involved regular meetings with his brilliant billionaire boss Suliman Olayan, but soon he grew restless. It wasn't enough for the young man to work for the rich and powerful, because he himself wanted to be rich and powerful.

"I want to leave," Arif told Olayan one day.

"Well, I think you are being a bit presumptuous," Olayan replied, according to an account of the meeting by Arif. "You are very young. You can have any job in this group you want. Which one would you like?"

"Well, chief, you can't offer me what I really want," Arif said.

Olayan bristled and asked why.

"Well, I want your job," Arif said.

"He was too ambitious," recalled Zahi Khouri, a former Olayan executive. "To be an employee was too small for him," he said. "The shirt he was wearing was too tight on him and he needed a bigger size."

At a poker game in Riyadh, Arif asked a group of wealthy Pakistanis for money to help him start his own company. At first they didn't take him seriously and laughed at the request. One poker player snobbishly thought Arif wasn't well-dressed enough for the big role he wanted to play in finance, but Arif persisted and his plans eventually won over a poker player called Izzat Majeed. He was a Pakistani financier who managed money for a Saudi businessman called Abdullah Basodan, who in turn had connections to a Saudi billionaire called Khalid bin Mahfouz.

It wasn't possible for a Pakistani to start a company in Saudi Arabia because only Saudis could control companies and it was important to speak Arabic, which Arif couldn't. Besides, Pakistanis were frequently looked down on in the kingdom as natives of a country that provided a big supply of poor manual laborers.

So in 1994 Arif crossed the border and entered the UAE, the desert country formerly known as the Pirate Coast. The ruling family of the city-state of Dubai was welcoming foreigners as it vied to transform its realm into a global center for trade and finance. English, which Arif spoke better than many Englishmen, was the language of business in Dubai.

With $50,000 in savings, which Arif told some people he'd made by selling a car he won in a raffle, he started his own investment firm called the Cupola Group and convinced the poker-playing Izzat Majeed to invest. Izzat brought in his Saudi client Abdullah Basodan.

Arif started with a string of modest investments that were largely unsuccessful. He built a credit-card factory in Dubai and bought local franchises of Western companies such as the TGI Fridays restaurant chain. He created a magazine targeting expat Pakistanis, which one of his sisters edited, and he invested in a supermarket project in Lahore, Pakistan, involving Imran Khan, the celebrated former captain of Pakistan's national cricket team.

In spite of the indifferent deals, Arif made an outsized impact in Dubai with public relations blitzes and a grand annual ball. "It all looked very, very glamorous," one guest recalled.

In the summer of 1998, Arif visited London and met up with Imtiaz, who had by then also left Olayan. Imtiaz told him about an exciting opportunity. He said that Inchcape, a company founded in the days of the British Empire to ship goods between London and India, wanted to sell its Middle Eastern grocery stores and liquor chains to focus on its main business distributing cars.

Inchcape's grocery and liquor business was profitable and had annual sales of more than $600 million but potential bidders including Olayan had ruled out making an offer because of a problem. Inchcape had more than a hundred local Arab partners in its Middle Eastern business, and reaching an agreement with all of them about a takeover was impossible. Besides, these Arab partners wanted to buy the Inchcape business for themselves.

Arif saw opportunity where Olayan saw complexity.

"This is exactly what I am looking for!" Arif said to Imtiaz, who was trying to find a buyer to make an offer. "Can you give me some idea of what I need?"

"Show me one hundred and fifty million dollars," Imtiaz replied.

Arif didn't have anywhere near that kind of money and Imtiaz knew it, but Arif said he would return to Dubai to find investors. Imtiaz gave him a week to raise the money.

It took weeks, rather than a week, but Arif secured $27 million of funding from the Saudi investor Abdullah Basodan. Then he returned to London to meet bankers at ANZ Grindlays, who agreed to lend $60 million secured on the Inchcape assets Arif planned to buy.

Arif, still short of his $150 million target, pressured Imtiaz with requests to help. He called Imtiaz his dear friend and described himself as his *chota bhai*, an Urdu phrase that means "younger brother." Imtiaz has called the phrase "a form of emotional blackmail commonly used in Eastern culture" because the assertion of a family connection implied there was an obligation to help. Arif's determination paid off. Imtiaz decided to throw in his lot with Arif and persuaded Inchcape to accept an unfunded $150 million offer. Inchcape's executives warily accepted the bid. They were suspicious of the sources of

Arif's money, and one later described him privately as a charming swindler.

A rival bidding group made up of Inchcape's Arab partners also put in an offer. The group included some of the most powerful families in the Middle East, but they offered less than Arif.

Arif won the auction. Now he had to find a way to pay.

Upon learning of Arif's victory, Inchcape's Arab partners flew into a rage because losing to a Pakistani upstart they'd never heard of was insulting for them. They mutinied and refused to work with Arif on the deal.

Arif turned the situation to his advantage by using their rebellion as a bargaining chip with Inchcape. He demanded a discount to the $150 million price for the business and the right to pay in installments. Inchcape executives were eager to get rid of the business and their irate Arab partners so they cut the price to $98.5 million and allowed Arif to pay in installments.

Arif, still short of money, then made a move that revealed rare flair for dealmaking. He offered to sell part of the Inchcape business to the Arab partners for $18 million even before he owned it. The Arabs agreed, made the payment, and Arif used their cash to fund his first installment to Inchcape.

Operating the grocery stores and liquor chains was clearly going to be impossible because of the opposition from the Arab partners, so Arif changed his strategy and decided to break up and sell most of the assets within two years for far more than the sum of the parts. After repaying the loan to ANZ Grindlays he was left with a profit of $71 million.

News of Arif's success spread through Dubai's palaces, clubs, and restaurants and earned him grudging respect from Arabs who had stood in his way. Some became investors in his later adventures. The audacious takeover of a company Arif couldn't afford to buy had succeeded, and his hard work and quick thinking were paying off.

Now in his early forties, Arif used his new wealth to buy a large apartment in a gated mansion block set back from Exhibition Road in

London's opulent South Kensington district. Samir Fancy, the former Karachi Grammar School cricket captain who as a boy Arif believed kept him out of a game, owned an apartment in the same building, which was near the Aga Khan's palatial Ismaili Centre. Grand Victorian buildings surrounded Arif's London residence, just as they had during his school days in Karachi. The Albert Memorial, which Queen Victoria adorned with statues of colonized peoples to honor her husband, loomed over Arif on walks in nearby Hyde Park.

"God has been kind to me in that I have been blessed with all the good things globalization has to offer," Arif said.

The boy from Karachi had made his mark in London.

CHAPTER 2

A GLITTERING OASIS

Dubai was the ideal place for Arif to pursue his dreams. In 2001 the city on the shore of the Arabian Desert was midway through transforming itself from an impoverished beach town inhabited by pearl divers and fishermen into the futuristic metropolis of glistening skyscrapers, lush green parks, and six-lane highways of today. An explosion of commerce had made fortunes for the grandchildren of pirates and merchants who once sailed goods and contraband in wooden dhows across the Arabian Sea to Karachi and beyond. Dubai was emerging as a global financial center, with vast inflows of money for legitimate investment purposes, as well as the illegitimate proceeds of crime and corruption from Asia, Africa, and the West.

Construction of the giant Burj Khalifa tower—twice the height of the Empire State Building—and the famous palm-shaped islands off the coast hadn't yet begun, but the Burj Al Arab, a 1,053-foot-high hotel shaped like a giant sail, indicated the scale of things to come. Dubai was growing up around its man-made deepwater port, free-trade zones, world-class airport, and sterling Emirates airline, owned by the ruling family of royal sheiks.

In a burst of ambition, Dubai was striving to assert its dominance over Bahrain and Qatar to become the undisputed center of Middle East business and the vital hub connecting East and West. The motive was simple. Dubai lacked oil, the source of the region's vast wealth. Its ruler, Sheik Mohammed bin Rashid Al Maktoum, was determined to build a city of riches by creating a welcoming environment for people to work and play hard in. Western executives and their families were welcome. Alcoholic drinks—traditionally a strict taboo on the Arabian Peninsula, where the Prophet Muhammad lived—were permitted in Dubai. Prostitutes waited for clients in bars and hotels.

Dubai was a melting pot of nationalities. Asians with university degrees like Arif mixed with Europeans and Americans pursuing lucrative careers in finance, education, and healthcare. Meanwhile, thousands of impoverished Pakistanis and Indians toiled in terrible conditions on construction sites, and poor female migrants from the Philippines cooked and cleaned as maids. Foreign residents outnumbered locals eight to one.

Arif was becoming a local legend. Gossip swirled about the origins of his cash—Pakistani politicians and drug money were rumored to have funded his early investments—but there wasn't any doubt about his triumph in profiting from the sale of the Inchcape businesses that supplied Dubai with food and liquor. Arif was seriously wealthy for the first time in his life but he wanted more. Unsure what to do next, he visited Kito de Boer for advice. The tall, friendly Dutchman was setting up the Middle East operations of McKinsey & Company, the American management consulting firm. Arif's and Kito's wives, who shared a passion for art and interior design, had become good friends.

Kito was passionate about promoting business as a modernizing force in developing countries. He saw Dubai as a hub for a new wave of entrepreneurs from emerging markets who he could turn into lucrative clients, but the region needed investment and expertise to help new companies grow.

Who am I? Arif asked Kito.

Kito recognized Arif's ability to make big profits from buying and selling companies. He told Arif to start a private equity firm.

Private equity was pioneered in the 1980s by American dealmakers at investment firms like KKR, Blackstone, and Carlyle who figured out how to buy businesses using little of their own money. Instead, they used the companies they intended to buy as collateral for loans, or leverage, which they used to fund the takeovers. Profits from the acquired companies were then used to repay the loans. These acquisitions were called leveraged buyouts.

The American private equity founders became rich and famous billionaires who were celebrated in business circles—men like Henry Kravis and George Roberts, the cousins who started KKR; the Blackstone cofounder Stephen Schwarzman; and Carlyle's cofounder David Rubenstein. As they grew in wealth and influence, they hired former presidents, prime ministers, and generals to work for them. At various times private equity firms owned and controlled some of the world's most famous companies, including Hilton Hotels, Dell computers, and Burger King. Private equity tycoons were often viewed less favorably by society at large, and labor unions and left-wing politicians frequently accused them of asset stripping, avoiding taxes, and firing workers to cut costs and increase their own profits. A German politician once described them as locusts.

Such criticism was rare in Dubai, a city dedicated to making money. Business success was all that mattered, and Arif now had bragging rights because he had completed the first-ever leveraged buyout in the Middle East with the Inchcape deal.

Restaurants sprang up across Dubai to serve cuisine from every corner of the world. Arif dined at Sho Cho, a Japanese restaurant on the city's shimmering waterfront that was a favorite for international residents. He got to know a crowd of similarly ambitious dealmakers. Prominent among them was Shirish Saraf, a fast-talking young Indian who was obsessed with parties, women, and sports. Shirish was an exuberant character with a big smile, an athletic build, flowing hair, and an aquiline nose. He had led takeovers of Middle Eastern companies including Memo Express, a parcel courier.

The friendship that bloomed between Arif and Shirish reflected a special quality about Dubai—the city enabled people from regions torn by conflict to overcome traditional rivalries and work together.

Shirish was a proud Hindu whose family hailed from Kashmir, the mountainous region of northern India that Pakistan and India intermittently fought each other to control.

Shirish and Arif bonded in Dubai over a shared enthusiasm for deals and making money. They also discovered that they came from similar backgrounds. Both attended elite schools that British colonialists had built in their countries—Shirish attended Mayo College in Rajasthan, whose founder intended it to be the Eton of India, and then went to Charterhouse School in England. Both Shirish and Arif graduated from the London School of Economics and were obsessed with cricket and Shakespeare. They drank, joked, and brainstormed about companies to buy. Shirish loved Arif's grand plans and easy charm. He thought some people mistook Arif's cockiness for arrogance, and he liked him for that, because he thought that he, too, was sometimes misunderstood for the same reason.

Shirish became a regular guest at Arif's home in Dubai. He thought Fayeeza, Arif's wife, was a lovely human being—as straight as an arrow. Fayeeza and Arif were welcoming and stylish hosts, warm but not flashy. Arif treated Shirish like a younger brother and they introduced each other to their parents. Shirish's father and mother were wary of Pakistanis but they soon warmed to Arif. The two dealmakers agreed to explore ways to work together.

• • •

Arif joined the Young Presidents' Organization to widen his network in Dubai. The organization for chief executives was founded in Rochester, New York, in 1950 and was expanding globally to spread the gospel of American entrepreneurialism. Arif became chairman of the Dubai chapter.

It was at a Young Presidents' Organization event that Arif first met Fadi Ghandour, who turned out to be a crucial connection. The tall, thin entrepreneur from Jordan was the founder of Aramex, a courier company known as the FedEx of the Middle East. Fadi's cool, professorial appearance belied a passionate nature. Arif met Fadi during a team-building exercise in which they both had to pretend to be stranded on a mountaintop after a plane crash. Arif played the part of an injured passenger and Fadi was supposed to help him.

"Let's just kill him," Fadi told other members of the role-playing exercise. "We are going to need meat for the way down."

The joke about Arif's stocky figure appealed to his sharp sense of humor and the two became great friends. Fadi grew to consider Arif as a fellow Arab rather than a Pakistani outsider—"One of us," as he put it.

Fadi was the epitome of the Middle Eastern entrepreneur that Kito had identified as a change maker, and Arif wanted to invest in his company. Fadi had started Aramex in 1982. Before then, sending a letter from New York or London to the desert cities of the Middle East was extremely difficult because state-owned postal services were unreliable and there were few alternatives. Fadi spotted an opportunity to build a useful and profitable company. He became an expert at getting letters to homes and offices across Egypt, Turkey, Lebanon, Syria, and occupied Palestine, even as wars raged in the region. During the bloody Lebanese civil war in the 1980s, shooting paused to allow Aramex trucks through, and the company was still delivering in Kuwait when Saddam Hussein invaded in 1990. When necessary, Fadi's employees used donkeys to deliver the post over rocky paths.

Fadi's family history was shaped by wars and revolutions, so he knew that opportunity and disaster were never far away. His father became wealthy by founding Jordan's national airline after fleeing Lebanon, where he had played a part in a failed coup.

Fadi spent his childhood in Jordan and then studied engineering at George Washington University in the United States. He returned home to start Arab American Express—Aramex for short—with an American friend. Aramex won contracts from the U.S. companies Airborne Express and Federal Express to deliver parcels and letters in the Middle East. Fadi learned from his American clients how to build a formidable business.

In 1997, Aramex became the first Arab company to sell shares on the Nasdaq stock exchange in New York. But the shares languished, even though Aramex's profits grew year after year. American stock market investors were wary of buying shares in a company so exposed to Middle Eastern risks—by Aramex's own admission the challenges it faced included expropriation, nationalization, war, insurrection, terrorism, and civil disturbance.

When Arif met Fadi, the Jordanian entrepreneur was already in talks to sell Aramex to a major American courier. Flush with cash, Arif was looking for a new deal and Aramex fit the bill perfectly. He thought Aramex would be better off owned by people who really understood it, people who believed in it—people from the Middle East who weren't prejudiced against Middle Eastern companies.

On September 2, 2001, Arif sat down with Fadi to discuss a takeover of Aramex. Nine days later, Middle Eastern terrorists flew passenger planes into the twin towers in New York, changing the world forever. The attacks scared off Aramex's American suitor. Americans had long associated the Middle East with conflict, but the fear and mistrust spiraled as the region's deadly tensions stained New York's streets with blood and dust.

Once again Arif saw opportunity where others saw chaos and complexity. Now was the time to buy Aramex, because Nasdaq was not the right place for an Arab company. Less than twenty-four hours after the planes hit the towers in New York, Arif signed a confidential agreement with Fadi to explore a takeover of Aramex. He was ready to do business even as the American war machine started to move in response to the terror attacks.

Following Kito's advice, Arif planned to create a private equity firm and raise a takeover fund with money collected from wealthy local families to buy Aramex and other Middle Eastern companies. Arif's timing was good. Wealthy Arabs feared they were no longer welcome in America. Their U.S. bank accounts might be frozen even if they had done nothing wrong, so rich Arabs decided to invest money closer to home. Investing in a Middle Eastern private equity fund had suddenly become more appealing.

Despite the favorable conditions, Arif still lacked the credentials to raise enough money quickly to buy Aramex. Besides, he was unknown in the United States and his firm, Cupola, was unregulated. A mysterious Pakistani dealmaker from Dubai would raise too many red flags with American investors and regulators if he bid for Aramex.

Kito saw the makings of a world-class investor in Arif. Maybe he could become the Henry Kravis or Stephen Schwarzman of the Middle East. Kito advised Arif to team up with Ali Shihabi, a Saudi businessman who had the credentials Arif lacked. Ali had good pedigree—he had chaired a Saudi bank and was equally at home in Riyadh dressed in flowing, traditional robes, and navigating Washington in a tailored suit. Ali's father was a Saudi diplomat who had served as president of the United Nations General Assembly, and his mother was Norwegian.

In certain Middle Eastern circles there was a distinct hierarchy of nationalities. Saudi Arabia, the home of Islam's holiest places, was at the top and Pakistan was closer to the bottom. Ali was the yin to complement Arif's yang, Kito thought.

Ali had an investment company in Dubai called Rasmala Partners and his investors included members of the Saudi royal family and Deutsche Bank, Germany's largest and most prestigious lender. Rasmala was regulated by Britain's Financial Services Authority, one of the main global watchdogs for the finance industry.

Ali and Rasmala could supply the blue-chip investors and regulatory approval that Arif needed to bid for Aramex, and Arif had something Ali needed too—a gut instinct for a good deal. Ali knew he wasn't the best dealmaker—he thought he was better at cultivating relationships with investors and managing operations.

Arif and Ali agreed to team up and use Rasmala to bid for Aramex. Arif brought in Shirish, Imtiaz, and an Indian dealmaker called Salman Mahdi to complete the new partnership. The combination of two Pakistanis, two Indians, and a Saudi-Norwegian epitomized the spirit of Dubai. They were planning to buy a Jordanian entrepreneur's company back from American investors to help it prosper in the Middle East. Fadi agreed to invest alongside Rasmala Partners and to continue managing Aramex if the takeover succeeded.

Ali chaired Rasmala and controlled the financial, legal, and compliance departments. Arif became Rasmala's managing director and was responsible for dealmaking.

Ali received skeptical feedback from friends who warned him that he was making a mistake by getting into business with Arif because he wasn't trustworthy, but Ali was confident that he could benefit from Arif's strengths and manage his weaknesses. Arif told Ali that doubts about his reputation were partly due to people confusing him with another Naqvi—Swaleh Naqvi, a banker convicted of fraud in the collapse of the Bank of Credit and Commerce International in the 1990s. Arif had nothing to do with the bank other than his wife had worked there and wasn't related to Swaleh.

When Shirish, Arif's party-loving Indian business partner, told local Arab friends about the plan to build a new private equity firm they also laughed and said such an ambition was impossible for a bunch of Pakistanis and Indians to pull off.

Bidding for Aramex was completely different from anything Arif had attempted before. Publicly traded American companies were notoriously difficult to take over because an array of financial and legal requirements had to be satisfied to ensure shareholders were treated fairly. Regulators had to be convinced the buyers were credible and that the source of their money was legitimate.

Working out of an office in Emirates Towers, twin skyscrapers in the heart of Dubai, the Rasmala team laid the groundwork for their offer. Ali arranged the legal documents and tapped his connections to raise loans. This took longer than expected because banks were wary of lending to the eclectic team but Ali secured a loan from a Jordanian bank partly owned by one of his Saudi investors.

The Middle East was at an inflection point. War was coming and the sweep of globalization was slowly filtering through to a region that had a deep-rooted mistrust of the West.

On January 9, 2002, the five partners met for dinner at Arif's house in Dubai. Over plates of spiced biryani, they talked excitedly about the adventure ahead. Arif pulled out a pen and scribbled down on a piece of paper what he called a partnership charter for Rasmala. The guiding principles were respect, trust, and one man, one vote. He jotted down rules: no finger-pointing, absolute frankness, and no disagreements in public or in print.

"All for one, one for all," Arif wrote optimistically, invoking the spirit of the French novelist Alexandre Dumas's three musketeers. "Violations of the above, the other partners crap on the violator irrespective of status," he added.

The five partners all signed the piece of paper, and on the following day their $65 million takeover bid for Aramex was announced in New York.

CHAPTER 3

NOW WE RULE

With news of the Aramex takeover offer now public, Arif, Ali, Shirish, Imtiaz, and Salman found themselves in the eye of a storm, with bankers, lawyers, regulators, and journalists all demanding answers to urgent questions about the deal. Under pressure, Arif and Ali's relationship began to buckle. As Ali got to know Arif better he started to worry, and the more he worked with Arif, the more worried he became.

First there were small things, like Arif's insistence on flying first-class. Then Ali started wondering whether Arif had a personality complex.

"You are intimidating me with your height," Arif said to him one day.

It seemed to Ali that Arif was always trying to aggrandize himself. He claimed to one company that he represented Saudi royalty because a handful of Ali's investors were members of the vast royal dynasty. A slick marketing move maybe, but Ali thought it was a step too far.

One day while Arif and Ali were working together on some documents Arif began talking about a Pakistani member of his team.

"This guy will be loyal to me unto death," Arif said.

"How do you get that sort of loyalty?" Ali asked.

"He skipped bail in America after he was charged with rape," Arif said. "I helped him out in Pakistan with his passport and hired him in Dubai."

Ali was horrified that Arif took pride in the loyalty of this man. It was a mafia mentality and part of a pattern of boasting about controlling people, Ali thought. Arif had also said he could get inside people's minds and bragged about having people in his pocket, including a senior officer in the Pakistan Army.

Soon Arif and Ali were fighting all the time. The last straw for Ali came in the summer of 2002 when Abdullah Basodan, the Saudi investor who helped fund Arif's takeover of Inchcape, contacted Ali. Basodan was furious. He claimed Arif had ripped him off after the Inchcape deal and owed him millions of dollars. He said that he was suing Arif for fraud. Basodan hadn't received profits from the Inchcape deal and he'd heard that Arif was living the high life, buying expensive property in London.

When the conversation with Basodan ended, Ali asked Arif for his version of events. There was a misunderstanding, Arif told him, and he was resolving the situation. Ali wasn't satisfied with the answer and became convinced that Basodan was telling the truth.

Ali was increasingly at odds with Shirish, too.

To create the Rasmala partnership, Shirish and the others had bought into Ali's company in a hurry so they could make the offer for Aramex. In doing so they had acquired shares in Ali's prior investments, but because time was short, Shirish felt he hadn't properly analyzed those investments before buying into them. Now Shirish had looked at the investments and concluded they were duds. He was angry with Ali for not warning him and the others before they bought into Rasmala. Shirish confronted Ali one evening in the Emirates Towers office and asked for his money back.

"Caveat emptor," Ali said, according to Shirish.

Shirish was furious.

"That's a great way to start a partnership," Shirish said.

Ali refused to return the money.

Late one evening Shirish walked out of the office and took the elevator down. As he walked into the warm Arabian night he met Arif, who was waiting for the doorman to drive his car around to the front of the skyscraper. Shirish complained bitterly to Arif about Ali and said he was ready to quit the Rasmala partnership.

"I'm done," Shirish said. "I would rather set up my own company."

"Are you prepared to walk away from your money?" Arif asked.

"Yes," Shirish said. He had invested about $300,000 of his savings in Rasmala.

Arif started to sob uncontrollably. The partnership they had put together with so much enthusiasm just a few months earlier was falling to pieces. Arif couldn't work with Ali, and now Shirish wanted to leave. Arif rested his head on Shirish's shoulder and wept.

Arif also broke into tears during a discussion with Ali one evening. Ali had never seen a grown man weep so much and tried to console Arif with a hug. He was at a loss for how to handle Arif. Ali had thought he could manage his brilliant, unpredictable partner but that turned out not to be possible. In August 2002 Ali emailed Arif to say he had had enough of his *qasams*, or promises.

Arif, my problem, today, is that after 9 months of partnership and numerous qasams and emotional meetings etc I still find it difficult to trust you.

This, despite desperately wanting to trust you to make this partnership work. You are not transparent with me, your style is not to deal with a difficult issue head on but in an underhand way, or through proxies. Your "past," your perpetual insecurity, your clinical inability to accept gracefully my contributions to the business, particularly when you feel that might put you in a negative light, is just getting too much for me.

At considerable personal reputational risk, I have assumed the role of your public supporter, yet have to keep looking over my shoulder at you in Rasmala.

Arif, I like you and your family a lot. You can either look at me as an obstructionist prick, and then can take your business elsewhere or can look at me as a sincere, straightforward friend and ally that has an obvious vested reason in your and my success. Your brilliance and energy are mixed with some serious flaws. You either let me help you, be completely honest, straightforward and correct with me or we split.

They split.

Ali left, and Arif and the others stuck together. Ali took back ownership of Rasmala and Arif took control of the fund they had created to buy Aramex. Although Arif and Ali's partnership was over it had served a vital purpose for Arif by providing him with the credentials he needed to buy Aramex. Rasmala laundered Arif's reputation, a banker later told Ali. Arif vowed never to mention Rasmala again and referred to the partnership as the "nameless predecessor firm" whenever he was compelled to mention it.

Arif now controlled Aramex through a private equity fund with no name. Who came up with the name Abraaj is a point of contention among the partners. Arif has credited Salman with the idea. Shirish said he gained inspiration when he arrived at work one morning at the Emirates Towers in his new Audi A8 and the doorman welcomed him into the building using its Arabic name, Abraaj Al Emarat—*abraaj* means "towers" in Arabic. Shirish said he talked it over with Arif, who considered the meaning first in Arabic and then in Urdu. *Ab* means "now" in Urdu, and *raj* means "rule," so *ab raj* can be translated as "now we rule."

. . .

Imtiaz and Salman soon followed Ali out the door. They left Arif and Shirish with three urgent tasks to complete to get Abraaj up and running. They had to hire a team; raise money from investors for the fund to buy more companies; and help Fadi expand Aramex and sell it for a big profit within five years. Success required all these objectives to be reached.

Shirish played an important role in setting up Abraaj by bringing money from his network of wealthy sheiks and merchants into the firm. Arif's enormous confidence won him allies as he scoured the region for new employees and investment.

"If you believe you can walk on water, people around you will believe you can walk on water," he told Khaldoun Haj Hasan, a young Jordanian who joined Abraaj from a sleepy UAE government investment fund.

The Jafar family, a member of which had advised Iraq's Saddam Hussein on nuclear policy, agreed to invest in Abraaj. So did Fahad al-Rajaan, the head of a deep-pocketed Kuwaiti government pension fund called the Public Institution for Social Security. The relationship with al-Rajaan would prove invaluable to Arif as the Kuwaiti pension fund invested more than $700 million in Abraaj in subsequent years. A Kuwaiti court later convicted al-Rajaan in absentia of embezzling money from the pension fund he had led.

The new investors committed money to the Abraaj fund that owned Aramex, gaining stakes in the courier company and providing cash for new deals.

The Abraaj pitch was standard for private equity. They charged investors an annual fee of around 2 percent and used the money to buy companies and fix them up. Abraaj kept 20 percent of the profits generated from selling the companies and was supposed to return the rest of the gains to investors.

Middle Eastern governments, royals, and traders pledged millions of dollars to Abraaj. Arif and Shirish's first fundraising was boosted by oil prices, which rose as U.S. forces invaded Iraq in 2003, filling the bank accounts of their investors, many of whom profited from producing and selling oil.

As they were completing raising the fund in June 2003, Arif and Shirish flew to a World Economic Forum meeting in Jordan. In a conference center by the Dead Sea, Arif discovered an intoxicating new world of networking opportunities where investors and politicians met. U.S. Secretary of State Colin Powell, UN Secretary General Kofi Annan, and Queen Rania of Jordan were attending the meeting. They talked about how companies could help solve Middle Eastern problems like unemployment and chronic water shortages. The combination of money and politics fascinated Arif. He rushed around the conference, hustling attendees and drumming up support for Abraaj. He and Shirish finished raising $118 million for Abraaj's first fund soon after.

The bond between Arif and Shirish strengthened as they spent so much time working together. For lunch at the office in Dubai they ate Pakistani food that Fayeeza sent. Shirish stayed at Arif's London home when he traveled to the British capital, and he later bought his own South Kensington apartment just around the corner. They were ultracompetitive, and betting against each other was their main form of entertainment. On business flights they played Who Wants to be a Millionaire and Trivial Pursuit, with the stakes rising to hundreds of dollars. They even bet on Shakespeare.

"I'll ask you five soliloquies and you have to tell me which play, which act, and which scene they're from," Shirish said.

"Oh, I can do that," Arif replied.

Shirish had brought his secretary to Abraaj, a highly capable young Algerian woman called Ghizlan Guenez. Arif took an interest in Ghizlan and wanted her to be his secretary.

"Let me go on holiday, bro, you can have Ghizlan," Shirish said lightheartedly.

So that's what happened. A visitor to Abraaj in its early days was so struck by Ghizlan's beauty that he wondered how Arif ever got any work done without being distracted by her.

The hypercompetitive relationship between Arif and Shirish infused the spirit of Abraaj, and a pool table in Abraaj's common room became a place for high-stakes games. Arif was a lousy pool player and his enthusiasm for the game evaporated as his losses mounted, so he decided to ban betting on the sport. Shirish and Khaldoun, the young Jordanian employee, kept up their pool rivalry in secret. One evening, they became locked into a spiral of double-or-quits games that resulted in Khaldoun winning thousands of dollars from Shirish.

Shirish figured he could get out of paying his debt on a technicality, Khaldoun recalled years later. Shirish told Arif about the giant bet, reasoning that Arif would say he didn't have to pay because he'd banned betting on pool. Arif called Khaldoun and Shirish to his office and told them that all payments had to be honored but since they had both broken the gambling rule, he, on behalf of Abraaj, would take a cut of the payments too.

"Each person was trying to outsmart the other in a playful way," Khaldoun said. "They were dealmakers. They loved bets. They loved competition."

The competitive, alpha male behavior also seeped into the private lives of many Abraaj employees.

"We used to work and we used to fuck," a senior executive said about the mindset in the early years.

New deals began to flow.

Abraaj snapped up a water treatment company in the UAE, an insurer in Oman, a financial services company in Qatar, and an internet company in Jordan. The four companies were quickly sold on, generating $81 million, more than triple the amount Abraaj invested to buy them.

There was one particularly controversial takeover in the early years. Abraaj bought the Spinneys supermarket chain in Lebanon from Arif's old firm, Cupola. The deal raised red flags because Arif was both the seller and the buyer of Spinneys. He had a duty to protect the interests of the investors in Abraaj, but since he was selling them a company he owned he also had an incentive to make as much money as possible for himself. Arif used the proceeds from the Spinneys sale to repay a loan he'd taken out to pay off Basodan, the angry Cupola shareholder. When Ali Shihabi heard about Arif selling Spinneys to Abraaj he was shocked.

"This fellow is going to end up in jail," he told his wife.

. . .

At Aramex, Fadi was planning a massive reorganization to enable the company to deliver millions more letters to the desert cities of the Middle East. He still owned about a quarter of Aramex's shares and was just as motivated as Arif to make a success of it. To incentivize employees, Fadi and Arif made the enlightened decision to allocate about 10 percent of Aramex's shares to staff. If the company prospered, employees would prosper too.

Arif and Fadi moved Aramex's headquarters from Amman to Dubai to benefit from the city's vast airport and a flight network that spanned the world. They built a $5 million processing center in Dubai and expanded operations in other countries through acquisitions of smaller competitors, including buying Memo Express from Shirish and his investors.

In 2003, Fadi made a move to grant Aramex full control of its destiny when he created a proprietary tracking system for letters and parcels. Until that moment Aramex had relied on a tracking system provided by the Seattle-based Airborne Express, but when DHL bought Airborne Express in 2003 it cut off Aramex's access to the system.

Fadi employed Arab software engineers to create the new tracking system. Then he called a meeting in London and offered the system to forty other couriers around the world that had previously relied on Airborne. They accepted. The system was a triumph and put Aramex in the control seat of a global network of couriers using its tracking system.

Aramex grew rapidly under Abraaj's ownership. Sales doubled to $232 million and profit quadrupled to $20 million within four years, proving that Arif's ambition to create global companies based in the Middle East was achievable. Arif was triumphant.

"Globalization is not a Western term," he declared to investors. "We can globalize quality firms outwards too, not just be the recipients of that philosophy from Ford or Nestlé or Toyota."

The bet on Aramex paid off for Arif in 2005 when Abraaj sold its shares in the courier company on the Dubai stock exchange. Abraaj received $86 million, more than five times the $15 million it had invested. On the back of the success, Arif quickly raised $500 million for Abraaj's second private equity fund in 2005.

But it wasn't just wealthy investors who profited. Hundreds of Aramex employees owned stock options and shared a $14 million payout. The money helped the employees to buy homes and pay for their children's education. In a region where the traditional routes to prosperity were inheritance or government patronage, Abraaj had spearheaded a new way to create well-being for workers.

Arif and Fadi remained close after the sale, and Fadi became a director of Abraaj. The duo became evangelists for private equity in the Middle East and talked enthusiastically at business conferences about Aramex and Abraaj as successful role models. They courted the media to spread their message, and one particularly influential journalist was listening.

Thomas Friedman was a high priest of globalization who wrote for the *New York Times*. He had nothing but praise for Aramex in *The World Is Flat*, his book about how the global expansion of business practices and the internet was creating unprecedented opportunities for entrepreneurs in developing countries.

"It is the example that is worth a thousand theories. It should be the role model of a self-empowered Arab company, run by Arab brainpower and entrepreneurship, succeeding on the world stage," Friedman wrote.

The American journalist saw something of profound importance in the wealth Abraaj had helped create for Aramex employees. He saw an antidote for the terrorism for which the Middle East was notorious.

"It is no accident that the three thousand Arab employees of Aramex want to deliver only packages that help economies grow and Arab people flourish—not suicide bombs," he wrote. "Give me just one hundred more examples like Aramex, and I will start to give you a different context—and narrative."

CHAPTER 4

THE GREAT SHOWMAN

Arif drew on the acting and debating skills he developed from school onward to speak with conviction at hundreds of financial conferences staged in the ballrooms of luxury hotels around the world. Each of these choreographed gatherings was like a form of corporate theater where Arif was a master actor. Grabbing the attention of the audience at these events could unlock billions of dollars in investment, and Arif's grandiose claims often woke people from slumber.

"What do Alexander the Great or Genghis Khan or Newton or Einstein or Marx have in common with Sam Walton, or Rockefeller or Olayan or Bill Gates?" Arif asked investors. "They broke from the ranks, took risks, and achieved great things. They were agents of change."

He flew from city to city in his Gulfstream jet with a personalized tail number—M-ABRJ—and sailed on yachts from port to port to meet new investors who could help increase his fortune. One year, the World Economic Forum hosted a meeting for ultrarich families at the Hôtel Hermitage in Monaco. Arif was determined to put on a show of his own, so he invited some of the conference attendees for cocktails on his boat in the harbor of the Mediterranean principality. As the guests boarded the boat Arif proudly pointed to the dark green Pakistani flag with its white crescent moon and star fluttering from the stern. Among the guests was Matthew Bishop, the *Economist* journalist who had written a book called *Philanthrocapitalism* about how rich people could save the world with the power of their money.

Arif's talent for telling tales was even greater than his skill for cutting deals. He compared himself to Sinbad, the mythical adventurer in the Arabian *Thousand and One Nights* folk stories who traveled to distant lands on treasure quests and encountered strange beasts.

Telling compelling stories has always helped to attract attention and funding in the finance industry—but stories that turned out to be fictional usually ended badly. Investors had thousands of fund managers to choose from around the world, so they needed convincing to pick a firm led by a largely unknown outsider from a region renowned for corruption.

As money flowed into Abraaj from new investors and from profitable deals, Arif used his new wealth to buy his way further into the global elite. Unlike in the past, when belonging to certain families or religious groups was a vital marker of status, the price of entry into the twenty-first century's global financial aristocracy was simply control of vast amounts of money.

Arif spent heavily on public relations campaigns for Abraaj. Onstage, on-screen, and in print he regaled bankers and academics with tales of his investing skills and presented himself as a reliable guide to unfamiliar lands where untold riches could be discovered. His stories recast poor developing countries where Western empires had crumbled and faded as places of excitement and opportunity.

He recruited celebrities to impress investors. Buzz Aldrin, the second man to walk on the moon, dined with Abraaj investors, and former U.S. President Bill Clinton spoke to them. Tina Turner sang for Arif and his investors at a party in Dubai. As the American pop legend belted out "Simply the Best," guests sipped vintage champagne served from an ice bar that was melting slowly into the Arabian sand on the beach, fire dancers performed and cigar rollers flown in from Cuba handed out their aromatic wares.

News of Arif's parties leaked to the press through Dubai's gossipy social scene but that was fine because, unlike many private equity tycoons who shunned publicity and enjoyed their wealth in private, Arif craved media attention—on his terms, of course. *Desert Capitalists*, a book by a former *Financial Times* journalist, cast Arif as the pioneer of Middle Eastern private equity. His growing fame in business circles was spurred on by editors of business magazines who awarded him prizes and flattering coverage, and received advertising and conference sponsorship fees from Abraaj.

Ostentatious philanthropy played a big part in Arif's pageantry. Whether he learned this from the example set by the Aga Khan or Western billionaires or the Karachi gold smugglers who fed the poor, Arif recognized that charity was important, and an important way to signal status and influence.

He became a patron of the arts and sponsored Dubai's most prestigious exhibition each year. He awarded a coveted $100,000 annual prize to young artists and developed an extensive collection by acquiring the winning artworks.

He built a mosque in Dubai and supported charitable initiatives by the ruler, Sheik Mohammad bin Rashid. He was rewarded for his efforts when the sheik acknowledged him in public. One time, there was a choreographed encounter between Arif and the sheik at an exclusive Dubai restaurant where Arif was dining with investors. Sheik Mohammed's greeting was a very public sign of royal approval.

Arif gave millions of dollars to universities around the world, including Johns Hopkins University in the United States, and the London School of Economics, which named a professorship after Abraaj.

Following in the footsteps of billionaire philanthropists like Bill and Melinda Gates, Arif and Fayeeza started a $100 million charitable organization called the Aman Foundation to improve healthcare and education in Pakistan.

Accolades followed. Pakistan awarded Arif the Sitara-i-Imtiaz, or star of excellence, one of the country's highest civilian honors, and Prince Charles welcomed Arif and Fayeeza into one of his charities, the British Asian Trust.

Royalty, artists, astronauts, and academics were to Arif like the dazzling feathers of a peacock—a splendid show designed to impress. And any skeptics troubled by the gaudy display could be reassured by Arif's humility. "Today's peacock is tomorrow's feather duster," he liked to repeatedly say.

A psychological trick was at play in the ostentatious behavior. People saw and heard about Arif spending millions and believed him to be extremely wealthy and successful—even more wealthy and successful than he really was. The grandeur was the proof of his substance and influence but some people did wonder how he afforded it all. An employee who organized alcohol-fueled, million-dollar Abraaj parties that sometimes went on for days liked to joke that Arif paid for them by shaking the Abraaj money tree.

"You would have to think that he had more money than God," said another employee.

• • •

The World Economic Forum's main meeting took place in January each year in the Swiss Alpine ski resort of Davos. The gathering was the nerve center of the global elite, where billionaires and politicians from East and West met. Davos was the central incubator for the surging globalization zeitgeist—a place of high-minded public rhetoric and behind-the-scenes dealmaking. Duplicity was baked into the very fabric of the forum. Tickets cost thousands of dollars each and access was tightly controlled by armed guards. But Klaus Schwab, the founder of the forum, insisted that his goal was to improve the world for every citizen and not just for the ultrarich who could afford tickets.

Executives delivered noble-sounding statements made for public consumption from the main stage. Then, inside hotel suites rented out for thousands of dollars, they bargained with politicians and struck secretive deals that generated profits for them and consequences that would shape the future of humanity.

Arif was in his element.

He made it a point to be a regular Davos attendee, paying millions of dollars to put himself and Abraaj front and center. He hired a World Economic Forum executive, a Frenchman called Fred Sicre, to ensure he got maximum exposure for his money.

A symbiotic relationship was at play. Arif got access to the Davos network, and Davos got access to his network. Davos offered Arif credibility and new sources of money, and Arif offered Davos attendees insights into developing countries they knew little about but which contained billions of potential new customers. With rigor and vigor, Arif systematically embedded himself in the elite as an authentic, reliable representative of these new markets. He spoke the language of the elite: the language of money.

Western executives and investors were interested in what Arif had to offer because, even as American troops battled in Afghanistan and Iraq during the early years of the new millennium, they were seeking to expand in emerging markets, including more peaceful Middle Eastern and Asian countries. Populations were booming in India, Pakistan, Jordan, Turkey, and Egypt, and Westerners wanted access. Arif presented himself as their partner. His pitch was simple. Most people in emerging markets were extremely poor but they were rapidly acquiring more purchasing power and economies were booming.

A fashionable new business theory supported Arif's pitch. Put simply, the new idea was that investing was a way to do good as well as to make money. The Indian academic C. K. Prahalad was a prophet of this theory. His 2004 book, *The Fortune at the Bottom of the Pyramid: Eradicating Poverty Through Profits*, was a seminal articulation of the creed. Prahalad's ideas percolated through universities and governments and were enthusiastically embraced by global business leaders including Paul Polman, a Dutchman who considered training to be a priest and a doctor but went on to become chief executive of Unilever, the consumer goods maker.

Emerging markets were notorious in the West as places of hunger, war, and poverty. The new theory about doing good and making profit at the same time appealed to Western executives because it provided a rationale for exploring these markets and a defense against accusations of exploitation.

Business leaders were better placed to solve poverty than politicians, according to the theory. Governments in developing countries didn't have enough tax revenues to build schools, hospitals, and transport and communication networks, so investors would provide these services instead and earn profits, too. In places too poor to make profits, billionaire philanthropists would step in and use their business skills to craft welfare projects better than any government could.

Arif talked constantly about improving the world, and it felt good to believe in him because he was a self-proclaimed agent of change who came from a country that needed help. His performances on stage and in the side rooms at Davos were enthusiastic and inspirational.

Slowly but surely, Arif's network widened as he made and consolidated friendships at Davos and dozens of conferences like it. His circle grew to include Bill and Hillary Clinton, Bill Gates, and a Deutsche Bank executive called Anshu Jain.

· · ·

Anshu was an important man.

An Indian with a British passport who worked for a German bank, he was the quintessentially multicultural executive that globalization created and Davos celebrated. As co-head of Deutsche Bank's investment bank, he could help unlock billions of dollars of equity and loans for Abraaj and open access to useful business contacts across the world.

Anshu was obsessed with cricket, and it was through this sporting passion that Arif got a chance to deepen his relationship with the banker. Days after the Davos forum ended in 2006, Arif flew Anshu on a private jet to Pakistan to watch an international cricket match against India. It was a risky trip for an Indian to make at the best of times. India and Pakistan had fought four wars against each other and just a few years earlier their troops had massed at the border, but Anshu was eager to see the game. After they touched down in Karachi, Arif ushered Anshu into a box at the National Stadium and introduced him to local business leaders.

Pakistan won the day and a great time was had by all, but the danger of doing business in the country was made apparent soon after. Shirish, who also made the risky journey to Pakistan to watch the game, got caught up in an angry mob wielding sticks while visiting the city of Lahore. They were protesting about a Danish newspaper cartoon that depicted the Prophet Muhammad with a bomb in his turban. Shirish thought he was going to die, but he managed to escape the furious crowd, never to return to Pakistan.

Pakistan fascinated many Western bankers. The country of more than 150 million people could be a valuable market but it was largely off-limits without the help of friends like Arif, the middleman with a firm capable of receiving money to invest in companies and projects in the large Muslim nation.

The mutually beneficial business opportunities that might spring from the Karachi cricket trip for Arif and Anshu reflected precisely the kind of win-win relationship the Davos elite loved to cultivate with one another.

Arif had inherited Deutsche Bank as an investor from Ali Shihabi's Rasmala. After Arif and Ali split, Arif lobbied Deutsche Bank hard to stay with him as an investor. Salman Mahdi, the fifth Rasmala partner, had attended Delhi University at the same time as Anshu and joined Deutsche Bank after he left Abraaj. Ali said he warned Deutsche Bank executives against doing business with Arif and told them about Basodan's claim that Arif tried to defraud him but Deutsche Bank didn't listen. Ali suspected that Arif had told Anshu that critics like him were racists who disliked Indians and Pakistanis.

"With the Indian and Pakistani crowd, Arif plays this role of the poor person who has to face prejudice and succeed," Ali said. "Arif plays a lot on the 'we are discriminated against—the Arabs are racist, the Americans are racist, the Brits are racist.'"

• • •

Deutsche Bank's support for Abraaj proved crucial soon after the Karachi cricket match. In June 2006, Arif hired an ambitious young Egyptian dealmaker called Mustafa Abdel-Wadood, who he'd been wooing for years.

"I have a theory in life," Arif had told Mustafa when they first met at a World Economic Forum event. "All good people should work together."

Arif's persistence finally paid off when Mustafa agreed to give up a well-paid job at the Egyptian bank EFG Hermes and join Abraaj. The son of an Egyptian diplomat, he had led a gilded life. His childhood was spent mixing with the cream of Egyptian society, and he had expanded his network by studying at university in Cairo and then completing a master's degree in business administration at Georgetown University in Washington. Mustafa's friends included an ambitious young Emirati called Yousef Al Otaiba, who later became the UAE's ambassador to the United States.

Affable and smart, Mustafa put the advantages he was born into to good use. He spent his early career working for Egypt's billionaire Sawiris family, helping them build a vast telecoms empire across Africa. After making his first fortune working for them, he set up his own firm, which he quickly sold. Then he joined EFG Hermes, where he led its investment banking unit before moving to Dubai to build out its operations there. After nearly three years in that job he'd tired of his managerial duties and was keen to do deals again.

Arif had no experience leading very big takeovers and had little knowledge of the Egyptian market but he wanted to buy EFG Hermes, and with Mustafa on board this became possible. For Mustafa, investing in EFG Hermes was a chance to earn his stripes and prove to his new boss what he was capable of. Mustafa pulled together a small team of Abraaj executives and they began laying the ground-work for a deal. He smoothed over regulatory and political hurdles in Egypt that Arif, as a Pakistani outsider who didn't speak Arabic, would have struggled to negotiate.

First though, Abraaj needed to raise the cash to pay for the deal.

Arif and Shirish spent the summer of 2006 in London to escape the unbearable heat in Dubai. One evening in the bar of the Mandarin Oriental hotel near Harrods department store they discussed how to raise money to buy the Egyptian bank.

On napkins, Arif and Shirish scribbled the names of investors who they thought would help fund an offer. They wanted to raise the money very quickly and the easiest way to do this was by offering to sell shares in Abraaj, instead of raising a new fund.

Arif wrote *Deutsche Bank*.

Shirish wrote *Citibank*, where he knew a senior banker who, like him, had attended Mayo College in India. They called their contacts. Deutsche Bank, Citibank, and a handful of wealthy Middle Easterners agreed to invest about $500 million for a 50 percent stake in Abraaj.

Arif used the money to buy a quarter of EFG Hermes in July 2006 for $505 million. It turned out to be a bargain. EFG Hermes had a big business in Lebanon and its share price had collapsed after Israel invaded the country. As Israeli rockets pounded Lebanon, Abraaj was the only investor willing to take the risk. Arif's initial plan was to gradually combine Abraaj and EFG Hermes into a Middle Eastern investment bank capable of lending and advising on all kinds of business, like Goldman Sachs. But Arif struggled to get on with the leaders of EFG Hermes. As the Egyptian bank's shares soared on the stock exchange in Cairo in 2007, Arif changed tack. He decided to sell the shares a little more than a year after he'd bought them to a company owned by Dubai's Sheik Mohammed for $1.1 billion, double the price he'd paid.

The massive profit rocketed Arif into the premier league of global finance. He paid out a $600 million dividend to his investors, leaving him $500 million to play with. It was the biggest of a number of successful investments Abraaj sold in 2007. Others included shares in Arabtech, the construction company building the mighty Burj Khalifa tower in Dubai.

Five years after he'd started Abraaj, Arif was now a millionaire many times over and basking in adulatory media coverage. *Institutional Investor*, an important magazine in the financial world, crowned Arif the Gulf's Buyout King in a long profile. The article was one of the first that many wealthy investors in North America and Europe read about Arif.

But Shirish noticed a troubling change in his old friend around this time. Arif believed he was singlehandedly responsible for the success of the EFG Hermes deal. He stopped listening to Shirish and began demanding a level of deference that Shirish refused to give. Shirish had thought that he and Arif were partners at Abraaj but Arif apparently saw things differently.

"I started realizing that for him there was no real friendship. It was a game where we were all part of that game. When he needs you he will charm you. When he doesn't he'll discard you," Shirish said. "That's how it works for him."

In the summer of 2007 Shirish got into a scrape with the police in Dubai and was arrested and thrown into jail for a few days. Shirish said that he was arrested after a minor traffic incident with his car but wild rumors circulated in Dubai about his partying and high living finally catching up with him.

Shirish quit Abraaj and sold his shares in the firm to Arif and the company for tens of millions of dollars.

With Shirish gone, Arif assumed absolute control of Abraaj. He was the last man standing among the five original partners, and no one could tell him when he was wrong anymore. That had been Shirish's job. Arif surrounded himself with yes-men and yes-women who did his bidding without question. He appointed Waqar Siddique, his brother-in-law who had worked with him since the 1990s, to oversee risk management.

Shirish started his own firm and described himself to investors as a co-founder of Abraaj. But Arif was determined to airbrush Shirish out of the Abraaj story, just as he had done with the other three men whom he'd once called his equals in the Rasmala partnership agreement.

Shirish's firm received an email from one of Arif's new employees who complained about Shirish describing himself as a founder of Abraaj. The claim was false and potentially harmful to the reputation of Arif and Abraaj, the employee wrote. Shirish was merely an early employee of Abraaj and not a founder, the employee wrote.

Shirish was furious. It was easy to disprove the accusation because Arif had repeatedly described Shirish in writing as a fellow founder. Shirish felt used and betrayed. He had raised hundreds of millions of dollars for Abraaj and completed deals that helped create the stellar track record that Arif was using to promote Abraaj.

Shirish met again with the man he once considered his older brother, a few years after leaving Abraaj. By then Arif had moved into a palatial new mansion in Dubai's luxurious, gated Emirates Hills district. The neighborhood was known as the Beverly Hills of Dubai and was home to wealthy people from all corners of the world. The family of the Zimbabwean strongman Robert Mugabe had a house there, as did Thaksin Shinawatra, a former prime minister of Thailand who fled his country to escape a jail sentence for corruption.

Arif's new house was a stylish mix of modern and traditional architectural styles inspired by the Haveli mansions of India and Pakistan, which are built around a central courtyard with a fountain. It was a treasure trove of art from the Middle East, Africa, and Asia, with ornate works from Lebanon, Syria, India, and Pakistan adorning the high walls.

The meeting was brief.

Shirish yelled at Arif and accused him of surrounding himself with sycophants. Arif was using his egotism as an anesthetic to dull the pain of his stupidity, Shirish said.

"You remind me of the rooster that thought the sun rose in the morning to hear him sing," Shirish said.

• • •

We first interviewed Arif a few months after he made the giant profit from selling EFG Hermes shares in 2007. Simon Clark traveled 3,400 miles from London to Dubai to interview Arif at Abraaj's headquarters in a gleaming skyscraper. Arif was the epitome of the self-made entrepreneur who was emerging from the city onto the global stage and the obvious person to speak to for a feature about the rise of Dubai. But after arranging the meeting weeks earlier, Arif refused to talk when Simon entered his office. Simon was shocked by this and faced the humiliating prospect of returning to London without the big interview. Simon turned to the photographer who had accompanied him to the interview and said they might as well go to the next meeting, with an important adviser to Dubai's ruler, Sheik Mohammed.

"You're seeing him?" Arif asked.

"We're going there now," Simon replied.

"Let's sit," Arif said.

Arif turned on the charm and told the story of his success. Knowledge of who Simon planned to meet next had prompted him to change his mind about the interview. The perception of access to powerful people apparently made all the difference to Arif.

The interview also brought us closer to the vast inequality in Arif's world. Arif's office overlooked construction sites where immigrants toiled in tough conditions, building skyscrapers under the boiling sun. Abraaj had owned shares in one of the largest construction companies employing those workers. After the interview, Simon walked onto a dusty building site where the tallest building in the world was going up. He talked to ditch diggers from Pakistan and India who occupied the lowest rung of Dubai's social order because he wanted to write an article that included the lives of the city's poor residents as well as the rich. The ditch diggers lived in crowded dormitories and many were hopelessly indebted to the middlemen who had arranged their jobs and travel to Dubai.

Simon had once worked as a teacher in Pakistan and had a keen interest in the beautiful, chaotic country where Arif and many of the construction workers came from. Pakistan had a spectacularly corrupt elite but the mostly friendly populace frequently humbled visitors with great hospitality even when they had little money or food for themselves.

Arif liked to give the impression to journalists that his rise to prominence in Dubai represented the promise of a better future, not just for himself but for all Pakistanis and people striving in developing countries across Asia, Africa, and Latin America. Yet for all the promises Arif made about building a fairer and better world, Simon found him to be unusually preoccupied with status, power, and control. The article he wrote told Arif's story and the stories of the ditch diggers, too. Dubai wasn't a city of riches for everyone.

．．．

After Shirish left Abraaj, Arif went on a hiring spree that added dozens of employees—Lebanese, Turks, Indians, Iranians, Palestinians, Jordanians, Syrians, Americans, Britons, and Italians—a United Nations of finance. Arif's self-proclaimed integrity and ambition made a big impression on new employees. Mustafa was in awe of his boss, and one particular episode in Cairo stayed with him. Mustafa and Arif were in the city to negotiate the $1.59 billion sale of Egyptian Fertilizers Co., one of Abraaj's biggest investments, to Nassef Sawiris, a member of the family Mustafa used to work for.

As Arif and Mustafa checked out of the Four Seasons Hotel, Mustafa noticed that Arif was paying his bill with a personal credit card. Mustafa offered to pay for them both with his company credit card but Arif refused, saying that he never used Abraaj's money for his own expenses.

"Wow," Mustafa thought. The display of wealth impressed him, even though he thought Abraaj should pay Arif's professional expenses. "Wrong, but wow."

• • •

Arif's great showmanship hid a darker side to Abraaj's operations. The inner workings of Abraaj's finances were a mystery to most employees. Hidden deep within the firm's Dubai headquarters was a secretive treasury department, which Waqar, Arif's brother-in-law, oversaw with Rafique Lakhani, a Pakistani accountant who had worked for Arif since the 1990s.

Arif was misusing money from early on. He boasted that Abraaj was the first private equity firm to choose to be regulated by the Dubai Financial Services Authority, the watchdog for the city's international financial center. To comply with the regulator, Abraaj was required to keep a few million dollars in a Dubai bank account at all times, in case the firm ran into financial difficulty. What Arif didn't brag about was that Abraaj was really made up of a tangled web of more than three hundred companies based mostly in tax havens around the world. The company that was regulated in Dubai—Abraaj Capital Ltd.—was just a small piece of this global network. The two most important Abraaj companies were incorporated in the Cayman Islands and weren't regulated by Dubai's watchdog. They were called Abraaj Investment Management Ltd. and Abraaj Holdings Ltd.

Abraaj Capital—the unit based in Dubai—was constantly in breach of the Dubai regulator's rules. Instead of always keeping a few million dollars in Abraaj Capital's Dubai bank account, Arif mostly kept the account almost empty. But just before the end of each quarter, when Abraaj Capital had to report how much money was in its bank account to the regulator, Arif and his colleagues moved money into the account to make it seem like it contained the required amount of money. A few days after the end of the quarter, they emptied the account again. They were deceiving the Dubai regulator by making it seem like the account had enough money when in fact most of the time it didn't. This financial sleight of hand, known as window dressing, became a very bad habit at Abraaj. But all these financial maneuvers were invisible to most employees. All they saw was what

Arif wanted them to see, and what he wanted them to see was a great show.

In late 2008, as the worst global financial crisis in decades struck, Arif hired a jet and flew all his staff to Istanbul for a weeklong party. He was in the mood to celebrate after raising $2 billion for Abraaj's third takeover fund, and Istanbul was a convenient place for employees to assemble. The Turkish city was an intoxicating mix of East and West, straddling the Bosporus, the narrow strait of water where Europe and Asia meet. Arif booked out the Ciragan Hotel, a former imperial Ottoman palace where the Sultan Suite cost $33,000 a night. One evening, employees took turns to sing at a party by the Bosporus. Confronted with the prospect of making fools of themselves, some downed alcoholic drinks to boost their courage as Arif filmed the performances.

For the grand finale, Arif walked on stage wearing a fedora and belted out Frank Sinatra's "My Way." As he finished, adoring employees gathered around like fans mobbing a celebrity, jostling one another for photos with him.

"This is unbelievable!" a new employee said to a colleague. "Why is everyone cheering?"

"People say that Abraaj has a strong culture," the colleague replied. "Look at this. This is not a culture, this is a cult."

CHAPTER 5

KARACHI ELECTRIC

Brimming with confidence and cash, Arif embarked on his most audacious acquisition in 2008 when he took control of Karachi Electric, the failing electricity utility in his home city.

"You could not have designed a more troubled company if you had set your mind to it," Arif recalled years later. "But we were aware that if we could invest and make a difference anywhere, that place would be Karachi."

Fixing Karachi Electric would seal his reputation as an outstanding investor. He hadn't yet proved himself by turning around the fortunes of an ailing company, and there was a sense that he'd got lucky with deals like Aramex and EFG Hermes through good timing—buying when prices were low and selling when they were high. Arif wanted to prove to the world that his team could roll up their sleeves and really improve companies. Karachi Electric was his chance to stand out.

It wasn't a deal for the fainthearted. Karachi was sick like a patient with a failing blood circulatory system. Its nickname—the City of Lights—had become a bad joke since Arif had gone to school there, as blackouts regularly caused air conditioners and hospital equipment to grind to a halt, killing hundreds of people through heat exhaustion. Electricity flowed so faintly through the city's frail network of copper cables that factories were forced to shut and lay off workers. Furious citizens regularly took to the streets in violent protest. Demonstrations intensified in the summer months when temperatures soared to 118 degrees Fahrenheit.

Power theft was rampant. A third of the electricity supply disappeared as thousands of people risked their lives by siphoning off power with homemade metal lines that they hooked onto transmission cables.

The scale of the failure was spectacular. Swathes of Pakistan's textile manufacturing industry—one of the country's largest employers and exporters—were moving to Bangladesh in search of a reliable energy supply.

The problems had started in the 1980s when Karachi's population boomed because of an influx of impoverished farmers and refugees fleeing Afghanistan. The city's streets, slums, and bazaars were crammed with so many people that there wasn't enough electricity to go around. The government didn't have money to build new power plants, so Karachi was frequently smothered in suffocating darkness as blackouts cut lights and air conditioners for days on end.

Violent crime and kidnapping soared. In 2002, terrorists lurking in Karachi's darkened streets thrust the city into a media storm when they murdered the *Wall Street Journal* reporter Daniel Pearl. The American journalist was kidnapped near the Metropole Hotel on the evening of January 23, 2002. Daniel's captors hated America with a passionate intensity. They forced him to appear in a video and call for the U.S. government to release all Muslim prisoners from Guantánamo Bay prison camp. Then they slit his throat and severed his head from his body.

Karachi lurched from one crisis to the next. Terrorist attacks, floods, and earthquakes rocked the city. People struggled to make ends meet as inflation soared, making food and fuel more expensive. The national debt ballooned as the government borrowed to subsidize prices.

Political violence was overwhelming in Pakistan. Prime Minister Benazir Bhutto was assassinated in the streets of the city of Rawalpindi while campaigning in an election in December 2007. Twenty more people died when her attacker blew himself up.

Bhutto was a member of Pakistan's most famous political dynasty and a crucial ally of the West. Her father had been prime minister until a military dictator deposed him and had him hanged in 1979. Western governments relied on her to fill a political vacuum that Islamic extremists were trying to exploit.

Stabilizing Pakistan was critical for the U.S. government. There was already enough trouble in neighboring Afghanistan, where thousands of U.S. troops were battling the Taliban. American diplomats feared that Karachi Electric's failure might tip the city and the rest of the country into total anarchy. Pakistan relied on Karachi because it was the heart of the economy, generating a fifth of output and a third of tax revenue.

Karachi Electric was created during the time of British rule, in 1913. It was nationalized by the newly independent government of Pakistan in 1952 and fell into a state of disrepair during long years of neglect. In a desperate bid to improve the situation the army was put in charge of Karachi Electric at the start of the new millennium but the generals couldn't help. They didn't have weapons to fight the fact that the cost of making electricity in Karachi was greater than the revenue collected.

When the army failed, the government turned to private investors for help. Karachi Electric was offered to Abraaj for $1 in 2005 but Arif declined to buy it. Shirish opposed doing deals in Arif's homeland. Instead, Saudi Arabia's Al-Jomaih Holding and Kuwait's National Industries Group bought 71 percent of the company and the government held on to 26 percent of the shares.

The deal was a disaster. The Saudi and Kuwaiti companies didn't have any experience running a failing utility. They asked Siemens, the German engineering company, to manage Karachi Electric for them but the crisis only got worse. Siemens made turbines for power plants but its managers didn't know how to solve the operational problems, and so Karachi Electric's losses doubled between 2005 and 2007.

No one respected Karachi Electric. Bills were routinely ignored by big companies, and even government agencies such as the city water supplier owed millions of dollars. Karachi Electric, in turn, owed millions of dollars to government-owned gas suppliers.

Electricity demand was growing at nearly 10 percent a year but not a single new megawatt of generating capacity had been added for a decade. Thirteen out of the nineteen power plants were obsolete.

The Saudis and Kuwaitis had made a big mistake. They looked for a buyer, and Arif was approached again. This time things were different. Arif had $2 billion to invest and executives keen to do deals in Pakistan. Shirish was gone.

One of Arif's new employees was Tabish Gauhar. The Karachi native had trained as an electrical engineer and previously worked for AES Corp., an American energy company that owned power plants around the world. Tabish was an accomplished corporate executive, with a shock of slicked-back hair and finely tailored suits. The absence of a tie and open-necked shirts signaled that he worked in the sweltering heat of Karachi rather than the cooler climates of Wall Street or the City of London.

Arif and Tabish both believed that Karachi Electric had plenty of potential if big improvements were made. Arif appointed Tabish to lead a team of thirteen Abraaj executives to draft a transformation plan. Tabish was scrupulously polite and lacked Arif's arrogance. Advisers enjoyed working with him. His straightforward approach made it easy for him to talk to engineers and technicians at the companies he dealt with.

In the summer of 2008 Arif summoned Tabish to his villa on France's Côte d'Azur to present his plan. Tabish carefully made his case with his cool, professional style. He discussed Karachi Electric in terms of financial targets rather than as an entity on which hinged the livelihoods of millions, and geopolitical stability. For both Tabish and Arif, the prospect of transforming a company that was vital to the well-being of their home city was an important but less-discussed motivation.

Buying Karachi Electric was an attractive proposition because it was a monopoly with a number of low-hanging fruit, Tabish said. By low-hanging fruit he meant it was possible to boost profits by slashing a third of the 17,000 employees; eliminating so-called ghost workers who never showed up; ending nepotism; cutting supply to customers who didn't pay; and taking down the illegal power lines. Resolving these issues would soon return the company to health.

Arif and the assembled executives discussed whether to proceed with the deal. Usually a small team of top executives known as the investment committee was responsible for deciding whether to do a deal or not but because Karachi Electric was so risky Arif widened the group of decision makers. This was a tactical move to quell any future dissent or finger-pointing at him if things went wrong. If everyone voted, everyone was responsible. Abraaj's success or failure hinged on this deal, so Arif wanted unanimous approval. But one person at the meeting likened Arif to a judge at a show trial—he had already made the decision to buy Karachi Electric and everyone else knew how he expected them to vote.

. . .

Arif had decided to take on the seemingly impossible task of owning Karachi Electric but there were strings attached. Before closing the deal he wanted the Pakistani government to reduce debts and payments worth millions of dollars that the company owed to state-owned fuel suppliers.

Instead of buying the shares of the Saudi and Kuwaiti sellers, Arif planned to invest $361 million directly into Karachi Electric over three years in return for new shares, leaving the Saudi and Kuwaiti companies with smaller stakes.

The terms of the deal were leaked to Pakistani newspapers. Journalists were critical of Arif and cast him as a multimillionaire who stood to benefit at the expense of the people. The beleaguered Pakistani government, grappling with a failing economy and a fundamentalist insurgency, didn't want to be seen to be in the pocket of a rich financier, so it stalled the takeover talks.

Then, on September 8, 2008, events started moving to Arif's advantage. Asif Ali Zardari, the husband of the assassinated prime minister, Benazir Bhutto, became president of Pakistan. Zardari led a left-wing political party that traditionally opposed the sale of state-owned assets but his rise to power boded well for Abraaj. Farrukh Abbas, who was in charge of Abraaj in Pakistan, had an important connection. His wife was related to Zardari and he was on good terms with the new president.

The week after Zardari became president, events in Karachi forced the politicians to make a move. On September 15, 2008—coincidentally the day that Lehman Brothers filed for bankruptcy in New York— Karachi was plunged into darkness as Karachi Electric's management team walked out and workers downed tools in a strike. Politicians called Arif and begged him to take control of the company. It was a huge risk. Even the army, Pakistan's strongest institution, had failed to turn around Karachi Electric.

Arif agreed within twenty-four hours.

At first he didn't invest a single dollar. Instead, he installed his team at Karachi Electric and they got to work on a provisional basis. They launched a major publicity campaign to explain their strategy, which was to make Karachi a city of lights once more. But a political firestorm immediately engulfed them. Employees who feared the new owner would fire them attacked and looted Karachi Electric's headquarters before the takeover was even signed. They shot at senior executives, forcing Tabish to travel through the city streets with an armed escort. His colleagues carried guns to protect themselves.

Labor unions were infuriated by Abraaj's plans to lay off thousands of workers. Local political parties, which operated like mafia gangs, were enraged by plans to cut electricity to districts where theft was rampant but they had voters.

At Karachi's exclusive Sind Club, rumors circulated about cronyism and corruption at Abraaj. The family connection between Farrukh and President Zardari was discussed. Zardari was a divisive figure at the best of times. He had convictions for corruption and the U.S. Senate had cited him as an example of a politician it would be risky for American bankers to do business with.

Abraaj was in a bind. The whispers about corruption were particularly damaging because Arif had staked his reputation on adhering to the highest standards of corporate conduct. He decided to meet his critics head-on and published a letter in a newspaper refuting the allegations.

"No favors were sought by Abraaj during the course of its negotiations with the government of Pakistan and none were granted," the letter said.

But labor unions and political parties didn't back down. When a delegation from the Islamist political party Jamaat-e-Islami showed up uninvited at Karachi Electric's headquarters, security guards shut them out.

Tabish remained characteristically calm in the face of the unrelenting protests. The disturbances would have scared away foreign investors unused to such hostilities, but Tabish was born and bred in Karachi and he knew that in Pakistan's highly emotive and vocal public life politicians often exaggerated for effect, and he was determined that the violent threats wouldn't stop him. The reputation of Abraaj was at stake, and walking away would have been too humiliating.

Arif agreed to complete the takeover of Karachi Electric in May 2009.

Now Tabish could really get to work. It still seemed like an impossible job. Rolling blackouts pushed people onto the streets once more. From the slums to the business district, rampaging gangs left a trail of carnage in their wake. They threw stones and chanted offensive slogans at the power company that had let them down.

Protesters burned tires and blockaded busy streets. The rioting was worst in poorer areas like Orangi, a former slum, where the unbearable summer heat drove residents crazy. They stormed a Karachi

Electric office, and employees managed to escape just in time. Police officers fired tear gas and charged at crowds with batons. Dozens of Karachi Electric cars were torched.

The plight of the protestors was taken up by the Muttahida Qaumi Movement, or MQM, a powerful political party that represented poor people who had moved to Pakistan from India when the country was founded. MQM had close ties to labor unions. Its leaders accused Abraaj of criminal acts and blamed it for the blackouts.

Tabish did what he could to calm the situation. He quickly installed two small power plants to minimize blackouts in the hot summer. New turbines were added to existing power plants, adding generating capacity for 200,000 homes. He struck a deal to build a new power plant that would add more electricity within three years.

Ambassador Anne Patterson, the senior U.S. diplomat in Pakistan, was worried about the unrest in Karachi. Her officials called Karachi Electric's chief executive, Naveed Ismail, and listened carefully to what he had to say. Naveed said that Karachi Electric was controlled by Abraaj and required billions of dollars of loans and investment to improve its operations and reduce power cuts, which he called "load shedding." After the meeting, Ambassador Patterson sent a cable to State Department colleagues asking for help to encourage Abraaj to raise the required funds for Karachi Electric.

"Black outs and load shedding are a serious impediment to economic productivity. Poor power delivery has also led to large public demonstrations," the American diplomatic cable said. "Embassy Islamabad requests the Department seek Consulate Dubai's assistance."

Days later in Dubai, Arif was summoned to the U.S. consulate, where he was greeted by Consul General Justin Siberell, an Arabic-speaking diplomat who had worked in Iraq. Arif told him that the Karachi Electric takeover had ignited a tinderbox of controversy in Pakistan, where politicians and journalists were demanding the government take back control of the utility. The Pakistani government was fueling the political fire, Arif said, and demands for renationalization were making it harder to attract new investors to the country, so it was really in the interests of the Pakistani and U.S. governments to help Abraaj.

"Pakistan has much riding on the success of this project," Arif said.

He laid out two contrasting scenarios for the American diplomat to consider. If the takeover was successful, investors would look favorably upon future projects in Pakistan. Failure would cause investors to shun Pakistan, and the country would slide further into chaos.

Arif told the American consul general that his quest to transform Karachi Electric was adventure capitalism and his first investment with an overtly political theme. He asked Siberell to help by getting the U.S. government to put pressure on the Pakistani government to tone down its rhetoric on renationalization and gain Abraaj some breathing space.

The consul general warmed to Arif and his commitment to improving Karachi Electric. In a cable to colleagues, Siberell noted Arif's optimism and observed that he was aligned with the U.S. government's objective of bringing greater stability to Pakistan. The veteran diplomat saw Arif as strategically helpful.

Weeks later, U.S. politicians pledged $7.5 billion of aid to Pakistan in an act sponsored by Secretary of State John Kerry.

Back in Karachi, the protests were wearing down Abraaj's team. Farrukh, the Abraaj chief in Pakistan, was clashing daily with Naveed, Karachi Electric's CEO. They couldn't agree who was in charge. Farrukh thought his ties to President Zardari and his close relationship with Arif going back to their school days at Karachi Grammar School made him more important. But Farrukh was being torn between Arif and Zardari by conflicting promises he had made. The Pakistani president wanted Abraaj to deposit the $361 million it had agreed to invest in Karachi Electric in a government bank account so the money could help ease a foreign-exchange crisis engulfing the country. Farrukh had assured the president that Abraaj would make the payment but Arif refused to do so because the money was meant to be paid in installments over three years. The situation became untenable because Farrukh had jeopardized the Karachi Electric deal by promising something Arif never agreed to.

Arif asked Tabish to replace Naveed as chief executive. Tabish agreed, with the condition that Farrukh left the board of Karachi Electric too. Arif consented to Tabish's request and Tabish became chief executive of Karachi Electric in November 2009. He was now completely empowered to lead the turnaround. His objectives were clear. He had to increase power generation, collect more revenue, cut costs, reduce theft, and improve morale.

He wanted to change how residents perceived Karachi Electric and reverse its extreme lack of popular support. While residents of London, Paris, and New York took electricity for granted, people in Karachi knew from bitter experience that electricity was the difference between life and death. Karachi Electric was never going to become a beloved brand like Coca-Cola or Mercedes-Benz but Tabish thought he could do a better job by explaining to people how he was tackling problems. He opened offices across the city staffed with customer service experts and repair specialists. They talked to customers and resolved issues before they escalated into violence. Attacks on Karachi Electric's headquarters lessened.

Tabish went into neighborhoods to meet customers at open gatherings called kucheries. He told them he knew it was hard to save money to pay bills, but if the bills weren't paid it was difficult for him to provide a reliable service. He explained that Karachi Electric subsidized power for hundreds of schools and hospitals, and sponsored literacy programs, football leagues, and the planting of thousands of trees.

Arif's nonprofit Aman Foundation began operating a fleet of state-of-the-art ambulances in Karachi. The foundation also teamed up with Karachi Electric on a project to convert dung from the city's vast urban cattle herd into methane to create electricity.

Tabish started a campaign to end electricity theft. "They steal—we pay" was a slogan he used in advertisements. But he didn't just wait for the stealing to stop. He implemented a novel form of enforce-

ment: customer shaming, with full-page adverts in newspapers listing the names and addresses of people who stole electricity or failed
to pay their bills. Nonpayers were cut off and city districts were divided into three categories based on payment rates—the good, the
bad, and the ugly. It was a very controversial move and it hit hardest
the poorest, "ugly" areas where mafia gangs controlled illegal lines
siphoning electricity. The "good" areas where most customers paid
bills were rewarded with a more reliable service.

The final lever Tabish identified for reviving the company was
arguably the most difficult—reducing the bloated workforce. Employees thought they had jobs for life, and nepotism, bribery, and corruption were rife. Some drivers and meter readers earned more than their
managers.

Tabish drew up plans to lay off thousands. He wanted to fire workers who took bribes and to incentivize reliable employees with training programs and regular performance reviews.

On New Year's Eve in 2010, he made a redundancy offer to 4,500
employees who held mostly low-ranking positions as drivers and security guards. They were offered payouts of about $1,500 each—
more than the average annual income—and Tabish gave them two
weeks to accept the offer. Labor unions rejected the offer on behalf of
the workers, so Tabish sacked 4,500 people in one of the largest mass
firings in Pakistan's history.

Violence flared.

At 10:30 a.m., on a cool day in early 2011, Asir Manzur, Karachi
Electric's human resources chief, was making tea in the headquarters
when a security guard came running toward him.

"Sir, sir, a huge crowd is gathering outside," the guard said.

Two decades of working for multinationals such as Pepsi hadn't
prepared Asir for what came next. A furious crowd of 3,000 employees was assembling.

Minutes later, the workers went on the rampage, pelting the building with stones, looting cars and setting them on fire. Security guards
couldn't stop protesters from entering the building.

The crowd surged in and took hostages.

Managers frantically called for help. Some police officers responded but when they arrived they stood outside and watched. At around 1:00 p.m. labor union officials began making speeches and whipped up the frustration and despair.

"Do not force us to become suicide bomber," read a placard held by a protester.

Union officials brought out rugs for protesters to sit on and vowed not to leave until workers were reinstated. The revolt rumbled on into the weekend. With no sign of a resolution, the government intervened.

Late in the evening on the fourth day of protests, the power minister, Raja Ashraf, announced that the 4,500 fired employees could have their jobs back. They returned to work the next day. A charred reminder of the disturbance greeted returning employees. A burned-out car, torched during the protests, was mounted on a plinth outside the headquarters and draped with a banner reading, "We will never forget." But the dispute wasn't over, as Tabish stayed focused on his goal. In a speech two days later, he said it was vital to reduce the workforce.

"Weeding out black sheep is both our right and responsibility," he said.

Managers told workers that there was no place for them and refused to assign tasks. Employees took to the streets once more and went on a hunger strike outside the Karachi Press Club. Protesters shut down two grid stations, hijacked maintenance vehicles, and stole and vandalized power cables. Tabish's house was shot at while he was inside with his wife and two young children.

He sweetened the offer to workers. This time his proposal gained traction and some workers agreed to leave.

Negative news articles continued to appear in the press. In one titled "Who Wants to Be a Millionaire with KESC?" a journalist wrote that Karachi Electric had hired family members of politicians and retired army officers. According to the article, the majority of the new appointees belonged to the MQM party.

The news reports fueled the perception that instead of sweeping away corruption Abraaj was replacing one set of cronies with its own.

Positive change was coming too. The amount of electricity lost or stolen was tumbling. Half the city stopped having daily power cuts, including in industrial zones. A thousand employees were fired for corruption.

When Karachi Electric reported its financial results in June 2012, the workforce had shrunk to about 11,000 and the company reported its first profit for seventeen years.

The improvements took people by surprise. Abraaj had achieved what many thought impossible. Karachi Electric won grudging respect from citizens, and politicians began to talk about the company as a model for other cities. The steadily improving profits attracted the interest of new potential buyers of the company. Arif's biggest gamble was paying off.

The successful turnaround drew the attention of two Harvard professors. They saw it as a stunning example of what private equity could do to generate profits and positive social change at the same time—contrary to popular criticism of private equity firms as predatory asset strippers.

Professors Josh Lerner and Asim Khwaja wrote a glowing case study about the Karachi Electric deal. Their paper—a joint venture between Harvard's business school and its school of government—started with a typically upbeat statement from Arif.

"If everyone says, 'Heck no!' there should be huge opportunities."

ARAB SPRING

President Barack Obama flew to Egypt in June 2009 on a mission to heal the bloody relationship between America and the Islamic world.

Arif would become an important player in the president's plan.

The United States had been at war in the Middle East for seven and a half years, pouring billions of bullets and trillions of dollars into military campaigns. Thousands of Americans, Iraqis, and Afghans were dead. Obama wanted to try a different approach. He gave a moving speech at Cairo University, in the center of the crowded, chaotic city. An audience of thousands applauded as he greeted them in Arabic: *salaam alaikum*, "peace be with you."

"We meet at a time of tension between the United States and Muslims," the president said. "The attacks of September 11, 2001, and the continued efforts of these extremists to engage in violence against civilians has led some in my country to view Islam as inevitably hostile not only to America and Western countries but also to human rights. All this has bred more fear and more mistrust.

"I have come here to Cairo to seek a new beginning between the United States and Muslims," Obama said, "one based upon mutual interest and mutual respect, and one based upon the truth that America and Islam are not exclusive and need not be in competition."

The West and Islam had fought for centuries in religious wars, colonial wars, the Cold War, the Iraq wars, and in the unending feud between Israelis and Palestinians. The United States traditionally sided with Israel, and Muslim nations supported the Palestinians in a fight that divided the world.

"For decades then, there has been a stalemate," Obama said of the conflict between Israelis and Palestinians. "Two peoples with legitimate aspirations, each with a painful history that makes compromise elusive."

Obama had an answer. Promoting entrepreneurship could solve the conflict between Israelis and Palestinians and across the Middle East. He vowed to invest American money in companies in the region to help entrepreneurs and workers.

"We will launch a new fund to support technological development in Muslim-majority countries, and to help transfer ideas to the marketplace," Obama said.

The audience roared with approval and chanted the president's name in rhythmic unison, "Obama, Obama, Obama."

The theory behind Obama's economic peace plan had deep roots both in American foreign policy and in the president's own family history. Obama drew inspiration from his mother, an anthropologist who had worked in Pakistan and Indonesia to provide small, affordable loans to poor people who wanted to improve their farms and start businesses.

As for the origins of his vision in foreign policy, the United States developed the Marshall Plan after the Second World War to invest billions of dollars to rebuild Europe's crushed economy and infrastructure. The policy evolved during the Cold War. In the 1970s, it created the Overseas Private Investment Corp., known as OPIC, to invest government money in companies around the world to spread prosperity and American influence. America's pro-market, anti-Communist stance made it perfectly natural, imperative in fact, to make investing in companies part of its foreign policy.

After the Cairo speech, OPIC devised a plan to channel U.S. government money into Middle Eastern companies. The objective was to tackle extremism by increasing trade and creating jobs.

Terrorism was wreaking havoc in the region. Days after Obama's speech, a bomb exploded under a vegetable cart in a Baghdad market and killed nearly seventy people. Violent extremists, who went on to form the brutal Islamic State in Iraq and Syria, or ISIS, were amassing followers among Iraq's unemployed youth.

Obama believed that more jobs would give people in war-torn countries a peaceful future. Capitalism was to be the antidote to chaos. But America needed experts on the ground in the Middle East to invest its money, so, in October 2009, OPIC invited investment firms active in the region to pitch to manage its funds.

When Arif heard about the invitation he saw the opportunity to become America's partner. The prospect of getting money from the U.S. government was particularly attractive to Arif at that time because other funding sources, like the coffers of wealthy Middle Eastern investors, had dried up after the financial crisis.

OPIC wanted to give money to private equity firms that specialized in backing small start-up companies, but this wasn't Arif's main area of expertise. To improve his chances of winning American money, Arif acquired a Jordanian venture capital firm called Riyada Ventures, which OPIC had invited to bid.

Riyada's founder, Khaldoon Tabaza, was one of the first Arab investors in internet companies. The enthusiastic young businessman started Riyada, which means "entrepreneurship" in Arabic, from his home in Amman. Khaldoon expected to continue running Riyada after he sold it to Abraaj but he was sidelined by Arif and Tom Speechley, an English lawyer who worked closely with Arif and had big ambitions for himself. Arif and Tom worked on making the pitch to win OPIC's money. They wooed U.S. government officials to convince them to hand over the funds. They finessed their argument with the appealing narrative of making money and solving problems at the same time.

In April 2010, Obama invited Arif along with his old friend Fadi

Ghandour, the founder of Aramex, and 250 other Muslim business leaders to a Presidential Summit on Entrepreneurship in Washington.

Flying from Dubai to Washington, Arif passed over the desert nations where he had become an influential man. The companies Abraaj owned touched the lives of millions of customers, thousands of workers, and hundreds of politicians. In the UAE, children studying in the GEMS chain of private schools and passengers flying with the low-cost Air Arabia were part of the Abraaj network. So were Saudi Arabians who bought medicine at the Tadawi pharmacy chain and who boarded National Air Services planes. In Jordan, Abraaj owned an aircraft maintenance company, and in Lebanon it operated grocery stores.

As the Washington-bound plane flew past Israel and the Mediterranean Sea, Arif could look north toward Turkey, where Abraaj owned the Acibadem chain of private hospitals, and south toward Egypt, where shoppers bought groceries and sugar, farmers purchased fertilizer, and patients received medical tests from companies owned by Abraaj.

Ownership of the sprawling collection of companies—which stretched farther east to energy, finance, and infrastructure providers in Pakistan and India—put Arif in a powerful position. He had a strong claim to be the best person to help Obama deliver American money to Middle Eastern entrepreneurs.

When Arif arrived in Washington, Obama welcomed him and the other guests, along with Secretary of State Hillary Clinton and Commerce Secretary Gary Locke.

Over dinner at the Ronald Reagan Building, Obama complimented his visitors from distant lands and described them as visionaries.

"I know some have asked—given all the security and political and social challenges we face—why a summit on entrepreneurship? The answer is simple," the president said. "Because throughout history, the market has been the most powerful force the world has ever known for creating opportunity and lifting people out of poverty."

Everyone wanted to live with dignity, to get an education, to be healthy, and to start a business without having to pay a bribe. The market provided a chance to dream, to take an idea that starts around a kitchen table or in a garage and turn it into a new business to change the world, Obama said. The president said that his plan to invest in the Middle East was taking shape. He was arranging $2 billion from the U.S. government and other investors.

Obama talked excitedly about Naif al-Mutawa, a Kuwaiti designer of Islamic comic books who had invented ninety-nine heroes embodying the wisdom of Islam.

"In his comic books, Superman and Batman reached out to their Muslim counterparts. And I hear they're making progress, too," Obama said, prompting laughter from the audience.

A sense of optimism spread through the room. The president made a new world of understanding and cooperation seem possible. When Arif's turn to speak came, Raj Shah, head of the U.S. Agency for International Development, introduced him as one of the main movers and shakers in the Middle East.

"Thank you for being here," Shah said.

Arif's speech took a political turn. He was in Washington to win funding from a government that wanted to bring about change. Typically he spoke to investors who wanted profits. Rather than boasting about his ability to make money, he emphasized how he created jobs. Instead of talking about dollars and dirhams he talked about population growth and unemployment: a third of the world's inhabitants lived in the region where Abraaj invested; half of the people there were younger than twenty-five; a billion children would need training and work in the coming decades; 100 million new jobs were needed in the Middle East and North Africa just to stop the already high unemployment rate from rising further.

"That's a rate of job creation that is unprecedented in human history," Arif said. "The only way it's going to happen is not through government intervention. It's not going to happen by large enterprises or by state-owned corporations creating jobs. It can only happen through entrepreneurship."

"This young population is going to want more of everything," Arif said. "It's going to want more consumer products, more of the good things in life."

Arif described a future in which companies—not governments— were going to change the world. National borders that Western colonial powers had imposed on the Middle East were fading as regional trade grew, Arif said. A soap maker from Oman was broadcasting adverts on Arabic satellite television channels and selling its wares from Syria to Egypt, he said. Where Obama sought a partnership between politicians and entrepreneurs, Arif went further. Business leaders could solve the problems alone, without government interference, he said.

"We have an imperative which is not just to serve our shareholders but to serve our stakeholders," Arif said. "Our stakeholders means our communities—we in the Muslim world largely live in communities that don't have access to running water, that don't have access to basic healthcare and sanitation."

As Middle Eastern companies became bigger, better, and richer, Arif envisaged them dedicating more money to philanthropy and replacing Western aid. He said Abraaj was a firm with a beating heart and that he would make each company he bought set aside millions of dollars each year for socially responsible work.

"This may sound a little bit strange coming from a private equity firm which is driven by the profit imperative," he admitted.

The audience loved his message. So did the Obama administration, and OPIC approved a $150 million investment in Abraaj two months after the summit. Arif was becoming a fully funded ally in America's attempt to end Middle Eastern conflicts by promoting business.

"We are pleased to work with Abraaj Capital to make President Obama's pledge a reality," the OPIC chief executive, Elizabeth Littlefield, said at the time.

The U.S. government's due diligence on Abraaj to identify any problems such as fraud found some smoke but no fire. Rumors about Arif's earliest funding coming from questionable sources were widespread but never proven.

Arif mesmerized OPIC executives with his bold vision and enthusiasm. He became a regular visitor to Washington, where government
officials found him to be warm, affable, and sharp. He reassured them
of his sincerity, integrity, and commitment to doing good.

"When looking for a partner that would invest in very difficult
foreign-policy priority places like Pakistan or Afghanistan, on the surface, Abraaj was a logical partner," said Elizabeth Littlefield. "They
were aggressive, they were available, and they were comfortable in
difficult markets. They were certainly among the biggest, the best
known, and the most ambitious investors in these regions."

OPIC pledged more than $500 million of American money to Abraaj
and paid the firm millions of dollars in fees.

Arif set about investing the money in some of the most deprived
neighborhoods in the Middle East. In the Palestinian West Bank town
of Jericho, he invested in an herb farm where poor women grew rose-
mary, thyme, basil, mint, and sage. Arif was extremely proud of this
agricultural project by the Jordan River, believing it to be a small
but important step to develop the impoverished Palestinian economy.

"Arif loved the herb business," said Fayez Husseini, a Palestinian
Abraaj executive who oversaw the investment. "It employed lots of
people. 'A poor lady from Jericho was producing something that was
on a fine dining table in Dubai,' Arif would say. Arif took a lot of the
product and gave it to rich Palestinians in Dubai to show what he was
doing. Arif used to say 'I am the only Palestinian that speaks Urdu.'
He did more, channeled more money into Palestinian projects than
many Palestinians."

Arif also invested in a Palestinian maker of educational online
games.

"We had a brilliant idea," Husseini said. "We thought we could
change things."

Arif also started a new nonprofit organization, the Mustaqbali
Foundation, to channel any profits made through the Palestinian deals
to support poor local children. He was wary of being seen to be making money from a very needy population. For him, the kudos from

helping to improve the tense situation between Palestinians and Israelis was ample reward.

"Arif said we can't make money out of Palestine," Husseini said. "It wasn't all about making money for Arif."

Arif announced the formation of his Palestinian charity in the presence of Queen Rania, a Palestinian, and her husband, King Hussein of Jordan, at a World Economic Forum event. The conflict between Israelis and Palestinians was always a hot topic when the wealthy and the powerful met at such gatherings, and making Palestinian investments gave Arif an edge in these conversations. The forum's founder, Klaus Schwab, wanted to be a broker in the ailing peace process, and he had brought the Palestinian and Israeli leaders Yasser Arafat and Shimon Peres together at meetings in 1994 and in 2001. Arif's efforts to support the Palestinian economy helped him win favor with Schwab.

• • •

White House officials who organized the entrepreneurship summit in Washington urged participants to hold similar events in their countries, and no one took this request more seriously than Arif. He announced Abraaj would host a major event in Dubai in November 2010 called the Celebration of Entrepreneurship.

To promote the conference and its entrepreneurial dream, Arif asked Khaldoon and the other new employees from Riyada, the venture capital firm that Abraaj had acquired, to create a website called Wamda. The goal of Wamda, which means "sparkle" in Arabic, was to pull together a network of start-up founders and showcase the best talent the region had to offer.

With a $6 million budget, Abraaj's events team scoured Dubai for a venue. They wanted somewhere appropriate for what they described as an anti-conference intended to appeal to young entrepreneurs but they didn't have much time. After a frantic search, they picked the Madinat Jumeirah, a five-star hotel. The stuffy ballroom jarred with the trendy vibe they wanted so they attempted to convert the ornate space into something resembling a gritty industrial warehouse. They covered the hotel in imitation corrugated iron walls to create an edgier feel. Boards covered in graffiti were put up. The tagline for the conference was "Empower, Inspire, Connect."

Arif worked closely with Fadi on the guest list. They trawled Khaldoon's contacts and their own address books for high-profile speakers. They invited 2,500 people, including Imran Khan, the future prime minister of Pakistan, the Egyptian billionaire Naguib Sawiris, and Judith McHale, the U.S. State Department's undersecretary for public diplomacy.

Abraaj's dealmaking activities ground to a halt during the conference. It had transformed from an investment firm into an events company, employees joked. They were taken off their day-to-day roles and assigned responsibilities including chaperoning important guests.

Arif turned up on the first day of the conference dressed casually in jeans and a navy jacket. The atmosphere evoked California's Silicon Valley. It was far from the usual Middle Eastern scenes that journalists relayed to Westerners—war, suicide bombings, and religious strife.

Arif announced five new investments at the conference. One was in Teshkeel Media Group, the company of Naif al-Mutawa, the Kuwaiti creator of the ninety-nine Islamic comic book heroes Obama had championed in Washington.

"Entrepreneurship is about success," Arif said.

With hundreds of workshops and talks on offer, it was hard for conference attendees to decide what to do next. Young entrepreneurs from Egypt, Tunisia, Lebanon, Syria, and Iraq finally had an audience for their ideas and aspirations. Surely this was what Obama was dreaming about. But Khaldoon, who had founded Riyada at his kitchen table, walked through the conference with a heavy heart. He realized that Arif had appropriated his vision, contacts, and influence, and he knew that his days at Abraaj were numbered. He'd served his purpose and Arif was casting him aside. The young technology entrepreneur felt like the groom at a wedding that was soon to end in divorce.

The excitement generated at the conference spurred hopes that the entrepreneurial fervor could somehow usher in a new kind of politics in a region dominated by autocratic dictators. Frustration with the political status quo burst to the surface in a speech given by Naguib Sawiris, the Egyptian billionaire for whom Mustafa had once worked. The Sawiris family had also done deals with Arif.

"What does change mean to you in the context of the Arab world?" Fadi asked Naguib in a charged interview during the conference.

"If everybody sitting here will overthrow the governments we have and they will lead, this will be the change," Naguib responded.

The audience gasped, whistled, and clapped with approval.

"What is it that really bothers you, then, Naguib?" Fadi replied, nervously probing for more detail on his revolutionary thoughts. Dubai, after all, was run by a royal dictator.

"All these forces of evil, all these terrorists, the extremists who are taking countries hostages," Naguib said. "I am also bothered by all these dictators ruling the whole region. I am really bothered by that. I mean, we look really silly compared to the whole world. We don't have any free elections anywhere.

"The king lives, the king dies. The president comes, the president goes. Nothing changes. And therefore I am saying change will be if all these young people here take the lead and they come up with all these good ideas and we help move our countries so when we look at Europe we look from up to down, not from down to up."

Naguib was making an extraordinary public challenge to the political status quo. Arif was harnessing the forces of money and business to transform how people lived and worked in the Middle East and now this Egyptian billionaire was answering his call with talk of a political revolution.

Arif closed the conference with an impromptu fundraising session. He asked attendees for $25,000 to create a fund to mentor new business builders. Fadi joined Arif on stage to kick-start proceedings and they raised $500,000 within an hour.

The show impressed the Americans. The *Washington Post* published an enthusiastic article about the conference which depicted Arif and Fadi as visionaries who were sowing the seeds of hope in a troubled region.

In Washington, the State Department official Greg Behrman forwarded the *Washington Post* article to Anne-Marie Slaughter, one of Hillary Clinton's closest aides. He told her that the U.S. government could take credit for inspiring the event in Dubai.

"The organizers said it was '100% a child of the entrepreneurship summit' (they were both participants)," Behrman wrote. He said it was a "great example" of the U.S. government "leading, convening, profiling and catalyzing local leadership to take the baton to lead."

Slaughter forwarded the email to Clinton and added her own message.

"Here is a quite different picture of the Middle East—and an example of our leading in a different way."

Arif had won the U.S. government's approval. A few months later, a State Department official sang his praises in Silicon Valley.

"I was in Dubai for an entrepreneurship conference sponsored by Abraaj Capital, and I sat in on some of the most impressive presentations I've ever seen," Judith McHale said. "I came away convinced that entrepreneurship is a powerful vehicle for dynamic growth in the region."

Arif built on his burgeoning relationship with the U.S. government by making some important new hires. Pradeep Ramamurthy, a former Federal Bureau of Investigation and White House official who played a small role in helping to draft Obama's rousing Cairo speech, joined the firm.

Wahid Hamid, Obama's roommate at Occidental College in California, also joined Abraaj. Arif knew him from Karachi Grammar School. Hamid, a former Pepsi executive, had suffered a bout of ill health and wanted a new job. Arif was more than happy to hire him, securing the services of an experienced executive and potentially strengthening his ties to the president.

. . .

Days after the Celebration of Entrepreneurship conference in Dubai ended, revolutions erupted across the Arab world. The triggers for the tumult were poverty and unemployment—precisely the problems Obama and Arif had identified and wanted to solve. But their efforts proved too little and too late to stop the chaos that was about to unfold.

On the morning of December 17, 2010, a Tunisian street vendor called Mohamed Bouazizi was pushing a small wheelbarrow piled high with fruit and vegetables through his hometown of Sidi Bouzid.

Bouazizi had borrowed about $200 to buy the produce and was going to sell it in the streets that day to earn money for his family. But police officers confiscated his cart and insulted him. Bouazizi was deeply upset by the confrontation with the police so he walked to the governor's office to complain. No one listened, not even when he threatened to set himself on fire.

Bouazizi bought a can of gasoline and stood in the middle of the road.

"How do you expect me to make a living?" he shouted.

He poured the fuel over himself and set it alight.

He died from his injuries three weeks later.

News of Bouazizi's death spread quickly across the Arab internet and caused outrage from Morocco in the west to Iraq in the east. Bouazizi was seen as a martyr. The young street seller inspired protests that built into the intensity and rage of the Arab Spring. Everyday citizens shared his frustration and directed their ire toward their autocratic leaders. As crowds gathered, dictatorial regimes wobbled in Tunisia, Egypt, Yemen, and Syria.

Arif saw the internet as a tool to make business and entrepreneurship forces for good across the Middle East. But the internet was an even more potent force in the hands of young political activists. Thousands of protesters poured onto the streets of Tunis, Cairo, and Damascus, united in the hope that centuries of corruption and oppression could be brought swiftly to an end.

President Hosni Mubarak of Egypt was swept out of office less than four months after the Celebration of Entrepreneurship, ending thirty years of rule.

The revolution that Naguib Sawiris called for had started. The Arab Spring removed old despots from power and sowed hopes that free, economically dynamic societies would replace them. But instead of bringing peace and profit, confusion and violence reigned.

The disarray in Arab towns and cities posed a serious threat to Arif's business interests. Abraaj had hundreds of millions of dollars invested across the region. In Egypt, Abraaj owned clinics, hospitals, a university, and a supermarket. In Tunisia, Abraaj owned a pharmaceutical company and an insurer.

The tragic death of the street seller proved Arif's argument that poverty had to be solved to bring peace to the Middle East but it also underscored just how hard it was to do that. The flow of investment into the Middle East dried up, but Arif kept going. He completed one of Abraaj's biggest deals soon after Bouazizi set himself on fire, buying half of Network International, a payments processing company based in the UAE, for more than $500 million.

As the Arab revolution frightened Western investors away, Arif seized the opportunity to buy their companies as they fled. A French asset manager sold its North African private equity operation to Abraaj.

It seemed that even the Arab Spring couldn't slow Arif down. Thriving in adversity was becoming a characteristic trait. As tensions in the Middle East flared once more, Arif's message of progress through entrepreneurship seemed more appealing than ever.

On April 29, 2011, President Obama authorized a team of U.S. special forces soldiers to fly into northern Pakistan in Black Hawk helicopters and kill Osama bin Laden in his compound in the city of Abbottabad. That same day, a group of American academics and national security advisers met at New York University's Center for Global Affairs to discuss the future of Pakistan.

The academics debated three possible scenarios for the future of the country that harbored the mastermind of the September 11, 2001, terrorist attacks: radicalization, fragmentation, and reform. Two days later, President Obama announced that the American soldiers had seized and killed Bin Laden. Americans danced and celebrated in the streets.

The American academics who had met to discuss the future of Pakistan produced a report inspired by their discussion. At the center of the best-case scenario for Pakistan—reform—they placed Arif. The academics imagined that by 2020 Arif could become the leader of a new, moderate political party that would modernize Pakistan. His credentials for this role were his business success at Abraaj, his unblemished reputation, his philanthropy, and his global network of contacts cultivated at Davos and beyond.

"His pedigree, energy, ideas, and philanthropic work in education and healthcare swiftly lent him credibility throughout society," the academics wrote.

Arif's fame was spreading and expectations of him were growing. He was a trusted adviser to the U.S. government in the Middle East and was being talked about as a potential future leader of Pakistan.

CHAPTER 7

IMPACT INVESTING

The meeting to end poverty started with cocktails before dinner.

It took place over three days in October 2007 at Villa Serbelloni, a Renaissance palace nestled among cypress and olive trees on the shore of Lake Como, a few miles from Italy's border with Switzerland.

Philanthropists and the representatives of billionaires arrived by boat and by car at the villa in the town of Bellagio. The beautiful lakeside residence belonged to the Rockefeller Foundation, which was started by one of the richest men to ever walk the earth. In the early days of the twentieth century, the oil baron John D. Rockefeller was inspired by a fellow American plutocrat, the steelmaker Andrew Carnegie, to create a foundation to use part of his fortune for good deeds.

Carnegie had distilled his philosophy of how to make and spend money in an 1889 article known as "The Gospel of Wealth." Carnegie preached that the capitalist system that had enriched him was the best possible economic arrangement for all mankind but there was one deeply troubling side effect: inequality.

"The problem of our age is the proper administration of wealth, so that the ties of brotherhood may still bind together the rich and poor in harmonious relationship," Carnegie wrote in his Gospel.

Carnegie had a solution to the problem of money dividing society into rich and poor. Once a fortune was accumulated it should be given away, he proclaimed, otherwise "the man who dies thus rich dies disgraced."

A century after Carnegie and Rockefeller made their fortunes, the globalization of the economy had woven humanity into one society with extremes of wealth and poverty unimaginable to America's first oil and steel oligarchs. Carnegie compared industrial society with the Native American Sioux tribe: the wigwam of the chief was, he said, virtually the same as the "poorest of his braves," but there was a huge difference between "the palace of the millionaire and the cottage of the laborer." The contrasting homes reflected "the change which has come with civilization," Carnegie wrote.

In the twenty-first century, the gaping chasm between rich and poor was measured in much greater detail and on a planetary scale. The world's 2,153 billionaires were wealthier than 4.6 billion people in 2019, and the richest twenty-two men in the world owned more wealth than all the women in Africa. The average American annual income of $65,118 was equal to the income of 50 Pakistanis or 129 Afghans.

The stewards of the Rockefeller Foundation feared that philanthropy alone couldn't come close to solving global poverty. Carnegie's Gospel wasn't enough. The problem with charitable donations— and government aid, for that matter—was that once money was given away it couldn't be reused, so there was less available for the future.

Solving poverty by raising taxes for governments to spend on healthcare and education wasn't a popular idea with billionaires or their advisers. They wanted to control where their money was spent and didn't want to hand over taxes or big decisions to elected politicians.

Instead of proposing that governments raise more taxes to end poverty, the Rockefeller Foundation explored how to tap the trillions of dollars flowing daily through financial markets. But in order to use this money it had to flow into projects that would generate profits. If they could figure out how to do this then investment capital could start moving from places where it was abundant, like in the wealthy districts of America's richest cities, to places where it was lacking, such as in Pakistan and Afghanistan.

The big advantage of using investment capital instead of donations or government aid was that it had to be repaid with a profit or interest, which allowed it to be used again and again. The disadvantage of investment capital, from the point of view of poverty alleviation, was that the requirement to generate profit or interest was very difficult in places of extreme poverty. But the Rockefeller Foundation thought it was possible. Their goal was to teach people to fish instead of giving them a fish, according to an analogy that was often used in philanthropic circles.

The purpose of the gathering in Italy was to agree how this could be done. Various groups were exploring how to use investment capital to solve social and environmental challenges. They used different terms to describe their efforts, such as social entrepreneurship, patient capitalism, and ethical investment.

The Rockefeller Foundation sent out invitations to discuss what they called the marketplace for social investments. A handful of well-connected people were invited, including representatives of the billionaires Bill Gates, George Soros, Jeff Skoll, and the Pritzker family.

The organizers believed that more people were warming to the idea of investing in a way that did good and made money, but there was a problem. Most people believed that a choice had to be made between investing for profits or giving money away to do good. It wasn't widely accepted that people could have their cake and eat it too.

As the waves of Lake Como gently lapped the Bellagio waterfront, where prosperous tourists sipped cappuccinos in cafés, the participants of the poverty conference discussed how to really make money and do good at the same time.

The intellectual challenge was formidable because they were taking on the economic consensus of the modern era. Shareholder theory had ruled Western capitalism since the American economist Milton Friedman formulated it in the 1960s. The sole purpose of a company was to make as much money as possible for shareholders, he said.

"There is one and only one social responsibility of business—to use its resources and engage in activities designed to increase its profits," Friedman wrote, "so long as it stays within the rules of the game, which is to say, engages in open and free competition without deception or fraud."

The problem with shareholder theory's exclusive focus on maximizing profits was that it forced investors to ignore vast regions of the world where they thought it wasn't possible to earn a buck.

Africa, in particular, was seen in the finance industry as a continent where money was hard to make outside of the mining industry. Africa deserved aid but not investment, according to consensus views. But there was nowhere near enough aid to solve Africa's economic problems. For poor countries in Africa and elsewhere to break free, they had to find new ways to attract investment capital.

A few days after the meeting in Italy finished, a Rockefeller Foundation official called Antony Bugg-Levine sent a note to participants to memorialize an important decision they had made in the villa by the lake.

"Following our discussions, we are now describing the work as impact investing," he wrote. "The word *impact* implicitly captures the revolutionary spirit that surfaced in Bellagio."

For Ion Yadigaroglu, the term *impact investing* signaled the start of a new way of doing business. He represented the Canadian billionaire Jeff Skoll at the meeting.

"Our selecting this phrase in October of 2007 led directly to the founding of an effort to make a movement out of it," he said.

But there was a crucial absence from the meeting. No poor people attended. This became a constant source of irony at such gatherings. Impact investing was largely a movement made up of rich people talking to other rich people about what they could do for poor people.

The movement caught on at the foundations of rich people and the banks they worked with.

Impact investing gained a major boost from the financial crisis of 2008. The stock market crash provoked profound criticism of capitalism and of Friedman's theory of shareholder capitalism, and not just among the students who gathered at Occupy protests in New York's Zuccotti Park and outside St. Paul's Cathedral in London. Unease with the obsessive focus on profit was building inside the finance industry too. Terrible decisions made by bankers, traders, investors, and regulators had inflicted a catastrophic effect on millions of people who lost their jobs and homes.

The scale of the failure made some capitalists receptive to new ideas. The Wall Street banking giant JPMorgan Chase & Co. teamed up with the Rockefeller Foundation in 2010 to publish a research paper that endorsed impact investing.

"In a world where government resources and charitable donations are insufficient to address the world's social problems, impact investing offers a new alternative," wrote the JPMorgan banker Nick O'Donohoe and his team. Investors were increasingly rejecting the notion that they faced a binary choice between investing for profits or donating to social causes, Nick's team wrote.

Impact investing promised everything to everyone. It was possible to invest for profit and help the poor at the same time. This seductive, inclusive message was widely welcomed. Bankers saw it as an opportunity to develop profitable new products and services. Charities saw it as a way to raise new funds.

Impact investing became such a broad church that it even included *the* church. At Vatican City in Rome, Cardinal Peter Turkson was intrigued by the idea of raising funds from investors in financial markets for poverty projects. He started to discuss how the Catholic Church could jump on the impact-investing bandwagon.

Cardinal Turkson organized conferences on impact investing in the Vatican that brought together Catholics, Protestants, Jews, and Muslims, investors, bankers, priests, nuns, and aid workers. The debates were fascinating. Participants pushed at the ethical, intellectual, and theological boundaries that had defined money and morality for centuries.

"Those who believe that doing good is inimical to doing well financially just have it wrong," Sir Ronald Cohen, a Jewish private equity pioneer from the United Kingdom said during a Vatican impact-investing conference.

Sir Ronald was an adviser to the U.S., U.K., and other governments on impact investing. Born in Egypt, he fled to Britain in 1957 aged eleven. His Jewish family felt compelled to leave after Israel, Britain, and France tried to take control of the Suez Canal from Egypt in 1956. Sir Ronald studied politics, philosophy, and economics at Oxford University, where he became president of the Oxford Union debating society. After a stint at McKinsey, the management consulting firm, he founded Apax Partners, which became one of Europe's largest private equity firms.

Sir Ronald had political ambitions and a keen interest in social issues including poverty reduction and promoting economic relations between Israelis and Palestinians. He was a founder of the impact-investing movement, which he believed could become a trillion-dollar industry within decades. He urged people to rethink their attitudes to money and to recognize that impact investing could be as beneficial to society as charitable giving.

The concept of charity sprang from giving money away, so the idea of investing wisely to do good and earning a return seemed to be completely different from charity, but this wasn't necessarily true, Sir Ronald told the Vatican conference.

Cardinal Turkson listened carefully to Sir Ronald and found himself agreeing with much that the multimillionaire private equity investor said. Turkson saw impact investing as a blend of philanthropy and venture capital which could transform how the church raised and spent money.

"We need a paradigm shift from dependence on donations," Turkson said. "The traditional idea of charity needs to be rethought."

• • •

For Arif, the rise of impact investing was another opportunity to expand his influence. His experience working on deals like Karachi Electric and his knowledge of countries with large, poor populations like Pakistan and Egypt gave him unique credentials that most Western philanthropists lacked.

Arif was relaxed talking to bankers and rich people, and they felt comfortable with him because he spoke the language of money. He was an unusual person—from a poor country but with the education and money to become a member of the Western business elite.

Jacqueline Novogratz was an early champion of Arif and guided him through the impact-investing world. She had strong connections at banks and foundations. Jacqueline began her career on Wall Street as a banker in the 1980s and then moved to jobs at the World Bank and United Nations to explore how to fund businesses for poor people in Africa. She had worked at the Rockefeller Foundation and attended a Vatican impact-investing conference.

Jacqueline was inspired to work on poverty reduction rather than simply enriching herself or her clients during a visit to Rwanda, when she spotted a poor boy wearing a blue sweater that she had donated to charity years earlier in the United States. The sweater still bore her name tag. This discovery shocked her. It impressed on her a profound sense of how everyone in the world was connected, and she felt compelled to act upon this realization.

In 2001 the Rockefeller Foundation provided Jacqueline with funding to start Acumen, a company she described as a venture capital fund for the poor. She would invest in emerging markets businesses and focus on their social impact, rather than on financial returns. Acumen's investments included chicken farms in Ethiopia, cocoa farms in Colombia, and healthcare clinics in India.

Arif and Jacqueline discovered they were kindred spirits. Like Arif, Jacqueline was capable of making speeches to stir an audience, and her husband was an expert in the art too. Chris Anderson was the head of TED, the organization that broadcasts inspirational talks.

Arif learned from them new ways of talking about investing as a way to fight poverty in emerging markets. It was a language that was infused with emotion as well as reason, and it got into Arif's head.

He gave a speech at Acumen's annual meeting in November 2009 in which he called for an "empathetic evolution" in finance. The speech at the Rubin Museum of Art in New York proved he was a fast learner. *Empathy* was a word seldom used in banking and private equity circles, which were often chastised for ruthless profiteering. For Arif, empathy in finance was the pursuit of innovative ways to help the poor. Jacqueline loved the idea.

Mastering the emotive language of impact investing helped open up new funding sources for Arif. The biggest prize was access to money managed by a special group of Western government organizations known as development finance institutions.

Development finance institutions such as OPIC in the United States wanted to hear how investments improved lives and helped people, rather than just making money. Arif wanted to become their partner of choice but many of them were wary of him. Some were put off by rumors about the mysterious sources of money for his early deals. Did Pakistani politicians fund him? The rumors wouldn't go away. Arif's only notable success in raising money from these institutions was OPIC.

The oldest and most respected development finance institution was the British government's CDC Group, and where it led, others followed. CDC was founded by the Labour government of Clement Attlee in 1948 as the Colonial Development Corp. Its mission was to do good without losing money by creating jobs and prosperity in developing countries. CDC managed a widespread group of businesses including rubber plantations in Malaysia, tea farms in Kenya, a cattle ranch in Botswana and a cement factory in Zambia. When Britain's colonies became independent nations CDC got a new name—the Commonwealth Development Corp. In the twenty-first century, CDC continued its mission by investing in private equity funds in emerging markets. It was led by a succession of well-paid former bankers and private equity executives who wanted a really meaningful job before they retired.

Arif had been trying to find a way around the reluctance of CDC executives to invest in Abraaj for years. Jacqueline and other impact investors helped him to refine his message but it wasn't enough.

An unexpected opportunity to win over CDC came through the dealmaking circles of Dubai in 2011. Shakir Merali was attending an African investment conference in a Dubai hotel. Shakir, a Kenyan-born venture capitalist who specialized in investing in Africa, was seated on stage debating with a politician from Uganda when he realized he had a problem. He'd made a rookie error for a seasoned conference speaker by forgetting to go to the toilet before the discussion began.

Feigning the need to make an urgent telephone call, Shakir got up and left the stage with as much dignity as he could muster and headed for the nearest bathroom. Having abandoned the Ugandan politician, he went out onto the hotel terrace for a cigarette. He'd forgotten his lighter so he approached a man smoking nearby to borrow one. They struck up a conversation that would change Abraaj's destiny.

Shakir worked for Aureos Capital, a London-based private equity firm in which CDC was a major investor. Shakir was trying to sell some companies in East Africa that Aureos owned. His new acquaintance said he could help. Yousef Bazian introduced himself and explained that he led the corporate finance team at Pricewaterhouse-Coopers in Dubai and advised companies on mergers and acquisitions. He thought he might know a buyer for Shakir's companies. They stubbed out their cigarettes, exchanged telephone numbers, and returned to the conference.

"I'll give you a call," Yousef said.

A few months later, Shakir's phone rang while he was attending a charity event at a golf club in Dubai.

"I have some people you need to come and meet," Yousef said. He gave him Abraaj's office address.

Shakir traveled into Dubai's financial district to meet Tom Speechley. He offered to sell Aureos's companies in East Africa to Abraaj. Tom thought a deal could make sense. Abraaj had no experience of investing in Ethiopia, Kenya, and Tanzania but purchasing the Aureos companies could give them a foothold in the region. Tom agreed to send an Abraaj executive to check out the companies.

When Tom told Arif about the discussion Arif came up with a bigger idea. Why not buy all of Aureos and not just a few of its companies?

. . .

Aureos was founded in 2001 by CDC and its Norwegian government counterpart with a mandate to reduce poverty by investing in small businesses across Asia, Africa, and Latin America. The firm grew quickly under the leadership of Sev Vettivetpillai, a cheerful, stocky man who colleagues likened to a laughing Buddha. Sev was born in Sri Lanka and went to Britain aged eleven to attend an elite boarding school. He later studied at the prestigious Imperial College in London.

Sev started his investment career at CDC in 1996, working first in Sri Lanka and then in London. He had a friendly, easygoing manner and a keen sense of mischief that sometimes got him into trouble but made him popular with colleagues and investors. He didn't always follow the rules. He enjoyed smoking at his desk when the office emptied at the end of the day and giggled when a strict colleague objected. But beneath his cheery exterior was a driven man. The son of middle-class parents, Sev was married to Menaka, a Sri Lankan from a wealthy family whose father was an important businessman and onetime mayor of the island nation's capital, Colombo. Like Arif, Sev had a strong desire to become very rich.

Aureos employed 150 people in twenty-nine offices in far-flung locations from Papua New Guinea to Peru. The firm had built a good track record under Sev by investing hundreds of millions of dollars in businesses that employed tens of thousands of people. Its investments included banks, chicken farms, breweries, furniture makers, insurers, and dairies, from Zimbabwe to South Africa, Guatemala, India, and Uganda.

Aureos also operated a small healthcare fund that was the first to invest in African hospitals and clinics with the twin goals of generating profit and measurable improvements in the well-being of extremely poor people. The Gates Foundation and the World Bank's International Finance Corp. unit were investors in the fund.

Aureos's success drew Sev into the orbit of Raj Rajaratnam, a Sri Lankan who had made a fortune running the Galleon Group hedge fund in New York. When Sev saw how Raj lived he wanted the same lifestyle too. Colleagues noticed a change in Sev over time as he became more and more preoccupied with personal enrichment.

To make big money Sev needed to own his firm, and the chance to buy Aureos came up in 2008. Sev and his colleagues had to find enough money to buy out CDC and the Norwegian government. Sev received money from Raj to help fund the deal, according to one of Sev's colleagues. The deal was completed in 2008. Raj also invested in one of Aureos's funds.

Less than a year later, photos of Raj in handcuffs appeared in newspapers around the world when FBI agents arrested him. He was later sentenced to eleven years in jail for securities fraud.

Three years after Sev bought control of Aureos things weren't going entirely to plan. Aureos was struggling to raise new funds because investors had pulled back from emerging markets in the wake of the global financial crisis, and operating the global network of offices was expensive.

Sev starting talking to Arif about selling Aureos to him. Sev needed the approval of his investors to do a deal with Arif and he flew to Washington in 2011 to visit the World Bank, one of his main backers. He explained that Abraaj was a strong company which could help Aureos.

The World Bank reluctantly agreed to the takeover, despite having misgivings about Abraaj. The bank had resisted Arif's requests for investment for years because of concerns about the sources of his original funding.

The deal made sense for Abraaj, too, because buying Aureos would transform it from a Middle Eastern firm into a truly global player. Investing around the world could be done properly only by employing people who understood the nuances of doing business in different places and Aureos employees knew how to negotiate with loud, confident Nigerians as well as with subtle, sophisticated Ethiopians. They knew that the smartest investor in New York could well be the dumbest investor in Ouagadougou.

Crucially, Aureos gave Arif access to a gilt-edged list of investors, including CDC and similar government funds in Norway, Germany, France, the Netherlands, and Sweden, as well as the Gates Foundation and the World Bank.

Abraaj urgently needed new sources of funding because Arif's traditional Middle Eastern investors had become reluctant to support him. Some of the Middle Eastern investors were becoming distrustful of Arif and others no longer had money to put in his funds because of the impact of the global financial crisis. An attempt to raise $4 billion for Abraaj's fourth private equity fund had fallen flat. The fund took years to raise $1.6 billion.

Sev and his colleagues discussed combining with Abraaj when they gathered at a Thai beach resort in the summer of 2011 to celebrate Aureos's tenth anniversary. Sev arranged a conference call with Abraaj executives including Tom and Mustafa who were gathered at Arif's country house near Oxford. The conversation went well. Arif invited Sev and his colleagues to continue negotiations in Dubai.

Arif impressed Sev with his ambition and the presence of Deutsche Bank among Abraaj's shareholders reassured him about the firm's professionalism. Together, Sev thought, he and Arif could create an investing powerhouse.

Sev sent more staff to spend time at Abraaj's headquarters. His team mostly liked what they saw and were impressed by Arif's slick marketing and charisma.

Arif agreed to buy Aureos in February 2012 in a transformative deal that added $1.3 billion of assets. Sev received millions of dollars in cash and Abraaj shares as part of the agreement. The takeover made Abraaj a one-stop shop for development finance institutions wishing to invest globally through one firm. It was a game-changing move for Arif.

Tensions between the two firms soon began to emerge. Arif expected absolute loyalty from employees, as he liked to remind them. Aureos, by contrast, was run in a more collaborative fashion. Because of the firm's government roots, its employees had learned to behave as if they were part of a cautious department of the state, rather than a cutthroat private equity firm.

To celebrate the merger, Arif hosted a party at his Emirates Hills mansion, where caterers laid on a banquet in the formal gardens. All employees were invited to speak about how they felt about their new partners. An Aureos employee privately joked that he felt like he was being inducted into a cult.

Most Aureos staff talked about the merger in glowing terms. But Shakir, the Aureos employee who first made contact with Abraaj, took a microphone in Arif's garden and drew on his experience as an amateur stand-up comedian to joke about the contrasting cultures of the two firms.

"We were really nervous about doing this deal," Shakir said. "At Aureos, we always do things by consensus. Is it the same at Abraaj? Arif wakes up and looks in the mirror and asks, 'Is this what I want to do today? If the person looking back at me says yes, then that is what I do.'"

Abraaj employees were stunned. They never dared mock Arif.

. . .

Buying Aureos opened the doors of Western government treasuries to Arif. Just as he had hoped, development finance institutions across Europe and beyond were now interested in doing business with him.

At CDC in London, executives knew that the combination of Abraaj and Aureos was causing something of a culture clash. But the

CDC executives saw Sev as their man and believed that he was strong enough to rein in Arif's excesses and manage their money with the discipline they expected. CDC agreed to start investing in Abraaj funds, and other development finance institutions followed.

In the months and years after the takeover of Aureos, Abraaj raised new funds to buy companies in South Africa, Ghana, Nigeria, Vietnam, Indonesia, Turkey, Colombia, Peru, Mexico and elsewhere. Abraaj gathered hundreds of millions of dollars from the taxpayer-funded development finance institutions of Britain, France, Germany, Switzerland, Sweden, the Netherlands, and the United States. OPIC agreed to lend $250 million to Karachi Electric. And the U.S. Agency for International Development pledged $24 million to an Abraaj fund in Pakistan. The decisions of all these government agencies to invest in Abraaj were significant stamps of approval, and they reinforced Arif's ties to politicians around the Western world.

More powerful people started to believe in Arif. If Western governments trusted him with their money, then why should anyone else doubt him? Just a few months after the Aureos takeover, UN Secretary General Ban Ki-moon appointed Arif to the board of the UN Global Compact, a group of business leaders who advised him. The UN Global Compact's vice chairman was Sir Mark Moody-Stuart, the former chairman of the oil company Royal Dutch Shell. Arif impressed Sir Mark with his emerging markets expertise and charitable efforts.

Arif raised his profile a few notches higher in September 2012 when he paid more than $500,000 to sponsor the Clinton Global Initiative meeting that took place alongside the UN General Assembly in New York. At the Clinton gathering Arif spoke on a panel about how he could make profits and do good at the same time. *Time* magazine's managing editor, Richard Stengel, moderated the panel. A few days later, Bill Clinton returned the favor by speaking to Arif's investors at an Abraaj meeting.

Arif reveled in his expanding sphere of influence. He boasted about how his money was changing the way people treated him in a revealing remark made while speaking to students at the London School of Economics. He noted that when he was enrolled at the school some thirty years earlier he'd been reprimanded for smoking in a common room. Upon returning to make a large donation to the school, he made a point to ask an academic if he could smoke during a dinner.

"Absolutely," he said he was told.

. . .

Arif talked about his passion for impact investing inside and outside his firm. The focus of his speeches was shifting more and more from making money to doing good.

"My vision is to spread a culture of giving among every employee at Abraaj Capital and among the employees of all of the companies in our portfolio," he said.

His charitable giving became more conspicuous. He spent millions of dollars on scholarships for Pakistanis to attend Atlantic College, one of the United World Colleges, a chain of private schools dedicated to promoting multicultural values, and on a professorship in private equity at the American University in Cairo.

The noble mission Arif declared he was leading helped attract more high-profile individuals to his firm. Sarah Alexander, chief executive of the Emerging Markets Private Equity Association, an influential lobbying group based in Washington, joined Abraaj to boost its presence in America. She believed in Arif's vision of doing good and making money and, as a well-known figure in private equity, she bolstered Arif's credibility. Her network of connections was formidable, including her husband, who worked at OPIC.

Abraaj now claimed to be the world's largest emerging markets private equity firm. The combination of the firm's growing size and Arif's ostentatious philanthropy began to win him many plaudits. In May 2013 he flew to Norway to receive a Business for Peace Award. The ceremony was held in Oslo City Hall, the venue in which Nobel Peace Prizes were given out, and the judges were former winners of the Nobel prizes for peace and economics. Arif's introduction could not have been more flattering.

"Arif Naqvi, you are turning the world on its head," a young lady announced. "Arif Naqvi promotes transparency, accountability, and sustainability in a world where business often spends vast resources to achieve their opposites."

For his Norwegian hosts Arif was the perfect example of an impact investor who was triumphing over Milton Friedman's shareholder value theory of profit maximization.

"He has stated that stakeholder value must be on a level with or surpass shareholder value," the presenter said. "This is a powerful idea but one that is not mainstream in a world of business, where too often it is claimed that shareholder interests by definition must trump all others."

Arif stood on the stage, struggling under the weight of a large trophy. The Norwegian television presenter Einar Lunde patronizingly asked him how the hefty prize would influence his behavior and Arif gave a typically sharp response.

"I am going to go to work and do the same thing tomorrow that I did today," he said.

The recognition was coming thick and fast now, and with each new public endorsement the value of Arif's personal brand rose. He was stuck in an apparently virtuous circle of gaining recognition and influence.

In November 2014, Arif flew to New York for a gala awards dinner. His host for the evening was an organization called Endeavor, chaired by Edgar Bronfman, the billionaire media mogul and onetime Warner Music Group chief.

Endeavor was founded by Linda Rottenberg, a charismatic Harvard-educated activist who wanted to promote business in developing countries. Sometimes called "the entrepreneur whisperer," her goal was to connect young businesspeople in emerging markets with the capital and mentors they needed to flourish. Arif had given Endeavor free access to Abraaj's offices so the organization could expand in the

Middle East, Asia, and Africa. He sponsored Endeavor events and made Abraaj staff available as mentors. He also invested more than $1 million in an Endeavor fund.

As a board member of the organization, Arif came into contact with Edgar Bronfman and Reid Hoffman, the billionaire founder of LinkedIn. When Arif talked, the American billionaires tended to listen because he came from one of the developing countries they wanted to learn about.

The awards ceremony was held beneath sparkling chandeliers in Manhattan's old Bowery Savings Bank. Wearing a tuxedo and look-ing every inch the well-groomed scion of one of Canada's richest families, Bronfman introduced Arif to hundreds of New York society members as a visionary. It was a scene that Rockefeller and Carnegie would have recognized.

"Arif is a man who has done very well, but knows that doing well means doing good, and there are very few people increasingly like that," Bronfman said. "Arif is one of those people who harkens back to the days of the great philanthropists, who recognizes that with great wealth comes great responsibility."

Bronfman told the audience how Arif had built Abraaj and the Aman Foundation, and he praised his "astounding" generosity. Arif walked on stage to tumultuous applause. Bronfman embraced him like a dear friend and they posed for a picture together. Then Arif, who appeared perfectly at ease, took the microphone. He began in lighthearted fashion, thanking Bronfman for the generous introduction.

"If I'd known in advance he was going to be saying all these things, I wouldn't have come."

Then he got serious.

"We are living in a world of increasing inequality," Arif said. "There-fore for those of us who have privilege, we actually have a responsi-bility. It is an imperative—not a choice—to act as responsible global citizens."

"We have given close to one hundred million dollars as a business into causes around our regions. Our staff have put in close to ten, twelve thousand hours of their time to mentor people, to participate in community engagement."

Arif echoed Martin Luther King as he spoke about the importance of giving.

"I do have a dream," he said. "My dream is that not only we do it but the giants of the private equity industry that inhabit this city and this world start doing it too," he said. "Then we have had impact."

The crowd applauded. Maybe Arif's investments weren't the biggest in the world, but his message and his example could be huge.

"If you think you are too small to have an impact," Arif concluded, "try going to bed with a mosquito."

He walked off the stage and was greeted by Fadi and other friends. They drank cocktails and champagne as Bronfman's socialite daughter Hannah DJed into the night.

"I guess by now you can see what a special and generous man we honor tonight," Bronfman told his guests. "A gentleman who is a gentle man, who is a caring, concerned, and compassionate man."

CHAPTER 8

THE CULT OF ABRAAJ

The young Indian analyst walked obediently toward Arif, who was grinning and calling to him from the center of a crowd of Abraaj employees in the rooftop bar of Dubai's Capital Club.

"Take off your shirt," Arif barked at him. "Take off your shirt."

The bar wasn't far from Abraaj's headquarters in the Dubai International Finance Centre and a magnificent nocturnal cityscape of illuminated skyscrapers surrounded them. To work at Abraaj was to be at the pulsing center of life in Dubai. People were drinking and having fun on that balmy evening, as Arif bullied his employee with a perverse test of his loyalty.

The employee was painfully shy and thin. He was either unwilling or unable to look Arif in the eye. Arif mistook his humble nature for weakness, and when Arif saw weakness in people, he sought to humiliate or exploit them. The employee removed his shirt and stood in an undershirt in front of Arif and his female and male colleagues. They laughed at him. In most companies, Arif's behavior would be a firing offense but no one was going to stop the man in charge.

"Take off your vest," Arif said.

The employee complied, revealing his thin torso.

Arif took the employee's undershirt, shirt, and tie and tossed them over the edge of the balcony, sending them fluttering to the ground outside the finance center. Arif found this very funny. He showed no empathy, that rare quality he liked to champion.

Half-naked, the employee walked down through the finance center, past staring security guards and art installations Arif had paid for, to retrieve his clothes. He never found his tie. He returned to the bar briefly to show he wasn't upset, and then left. He quit soon after.

Abuses of power like this episode of schoolyard bullying were common. Arif poured a glass of water over the head of a company lawyer in a restaurant. The lawyer was a bodybuilder and would have crushed Arif in a fight but he didn't react to the dousing because the power Arif wielded through his status and connections made retaliation too risky.

Arif constantly talked about being a model of good conduct, but that was a lie most of the billionaires, journalists, and academics he met failed to see through. For although Arif didn't practice what he preached, he poured millions of dollars into ostentatious efforts to convince people that he did. He claimed Abraaj was a guiding light for companies in emerging markets, and to this end he supported the Pearl Initiative, a project backed by the UN to improve corporate governance in the Middle East. It was vital to Arif's strategy that people believed Abraaj was a unique, world-class firm because merely being owned by Abraaj was supposed to increase a company's value by millions, so synonymous was the firm supposed to be with high standards. Belief in the idea of corporate excellence was drilled into employees, who carried handbooks reminding them to stay committed to ethical conduct at all times.

Arif created new systems to monitor the governance standards of companies he invested in and joined performance programs like the United Nations Principles for Responsible Investment, which gave Abraaj its top rating.

To oversee Abraaj, he appointed directors and advisers including Harvard's Josh Lerner, former Prime Minister Shaukat Aziz of Pakistan, the Swiss billionaire Thomas Schmidheiny, the British security expert John Chipman, and Sean Cleary, an adviser to the founder of the World Economic Forum.

Arif paid board members to meet four times a year. Their duties included approving Arif's pay, but they knew little about the firm's finances or inner workings and didn't ask enough questions. So, like fancy ornaments decorating a tree, the directors served mainly to dazzle outsiders. They sent out a message with their mere presence that Abraaj was well connected and, surely, well managed.

But no number of impressive advisers, glossy brochures, or corporate governance codes could hide reality from the people who worked inside Abraaj on a daily basis. For them, Abraaj was a cult, not a company, and Arif was their god.

Arif influenced his followers with a bewildering array of tricks and psychological traits. He combined generosity and charm with aggression and humiliation, secrecy and emotional blackmail. He rewarded employees who complied with his wishes with promotions and bonuses, and he flew into fits of rage with anyone who dared question him. He threatened to throw a female employee out of a skyscraper, and he got upset with a hostess on his private jet after taking off from Paris because the food served was too French—a dispute that vexed Abraaj secretaries.

"I am so sick of Arif," a secretary wrote to a colleague. "He threw some tantrum about the food on his flight being too French or something (duh you're coming from Paris at the last second). He's such a child. I am drafting him an email to tell him to shut the fuck up."

"Oh god . . . Breathe, teamy! Don't be hasty . . . If the only problems he has in the world is the food being too French then he does have serious problems. What the fuck?!" her colleague responded.

"I know right? I'm not actually going to send the email. It just makes me feel better," the secretary wrote.

"Good girl. Send it to me and pretend I'm Arif if it makes you feel any better."

"Lol, can we do a role play?! Practice your f-bombs girl!"

One morning, a junior employee bumped into Arif in the elevator when he was running late after an exhausting weekend of work. Arif was angry that he wasn't already at his desk so to teach the employee a lesson he threatened to humiliate him by making him stand on a chair in the middle of the office.

Arif's dominating and complex personality made Abraaj a workplace full of contradictions. He talked about his love for democracy but his employees experienced a dictatorship. He treasured the notion that Abraaj was a transparent working environment and even installed a whistleblower hotline, but employees joked that if anyone ever bothered to call to report wrongdoing, Waqar, Arif's brother-in-law, would answer and immediately inform Arif. There was no higher authority than Arif. He was by turns charismatic, frightening, inspiring, jealous, and manipulative.

Enthralled employees listened to him talk for hours about their grand purpose in the global economy. A dozen employees described Arif as having narcissistic personality disorder. Some thought Arif displayed the traits of the dark triad—a combination of narcissism, psychopathy, and Machiavellianism.

He crushed the confidence of employees by bullying them, built them up again with praise, and then broke them down again with fresh insults. A military officer who had won medals for bravery in battle was so inspired and charmed by Arif during a job interview that he joined Abraaj to work closely with him. The former soldier was excited about his new adventure but on his first day at work in Dubai Arif behaved strangely and seemed like a different person. Arif ignored him and refused to speak to him for weeks, leaving the new employee confused and disoriented. When Arif finally spoke it was to insult him.

The former soldier prepared a presentation about Abraaj in which he mentioned "partnership capital," a term Arif liked to use in public to describe private equity. Arif rubbished the presentation. He said partnership capital was just a line he used for people outside the firm and it shouldn't be taken seriously. The former soldier was dismayed. Saying one thing and doing another could be fatal in the military, but at Abraaj it was part of the daily routine.

The psychological pressure that Arif exerted on the former soldier made working at Abraaj more traumatic than being shot at or bombed. On the battlefield, soldiers relied on the camaraderie of their fellow troops and on clear orders from trusted leaders to stay alive. At Abraaj, everyone was out for themselves. It was impossible to trust anyone because of all the backstabbing, and the main objectives seemed to be pleasing Arif and getting paid a bonus.

The former soldier wasn't alone in being destabilized by Arif. One year, in front of hundreds of employees, Arif unexpectedly promoted a group of juniors to senior positions, leapfrogging middle managers who were left fuming. To add to the surprise, Arif announced special bonuses for secretaries.

"Arif was a king, doling out little tidbits to begging peasants, like promoting people who weren't on a list for promotion or double promoting them in front of everyone," said a former employee.

The unpredictable psychological games had a purpose. They increased Arif's control. Arif hired the American business consultant Flip Flippen to carry out behavioral tests on executives, and the results provided Arif with insightful, personal analyses of his senior team. Arif never took the test himself.

"Arif mastered people's weaknesses, whether they were financial, sexual, or simply ego," a former colleague said.

The thuggish treatment of staff extended from senior executives to domestic servants. Arif employed an English butler called Terry at his apartment in London. An Abraaj executive witnessed Arif and Terry interact during a visit to the South Kensington home.

"Terry! Terry!" Arif shouted from the book-lined drawing room where the executive was sitting. Terry entered the room wearing a dark suit and striped trousers.

"Bring a cappuccino," Arif said.

"Yes, Mr. Naqvi," Terry replied.

When Terry returned with the coffee, Arif looked into the eyes of the white Abraaj executive and explained what was happening. Terry was a white man who worked for Arif, Arif said. Terry stood beside him awaiting his next order. He didn't react to Arif's description of their relationship.

When Terry left the drawing room, Arif said he could ask Terry to do whatever he wanted, even though he was brown-skinned. Employing Terry really mattered, he said, because when he was growing up in Karachi no one would ever dream of having a white man as a servant.

The white Abraaj executive squirmed in his seat. Arif had certainly been on the receiving end of racism many times in his life but that didn't justify the way he talked about Terry. On the contrary, the executive thought, Arif's experiences of racist bigotry—as a student in Britain and as a resident in Saudi Arabia and the UAE—meant he should know better.

The relative powerlessness of Pakistanis compared with other nationalities was a frustrating reality for Arif. The ingrained unfairness was real and could be measured by the status of the Pakistani passport, which granted visa-free access to 32 countries, fewer than a fifth of the 185 countries U.S. and U.K. passport holders had visa-free access to. Arif was repeatedly held back at airport immigration desks while white colleagues were waved through, especially after the September 11, 2001, terrorist attacks. Maybe the inequality Arif experienced in the world explained why he was so controlling at Abraaj. The company was his domain where he made the rules.

Arif worked relentlessly long hours and was often in the office well after midnight, drinking shots of Kauffman Russian vodka or tumblers of Macallan single malt Scotch whisky and smoking Marlboro cigarettes. Executives were used to being called in for unscheduled meetings in the early hours before sunrise and being made to wait outside his office to talk to him.

Arif closely monitored employees and collected information on them. He sent butlers into the office late in the evenings to see who was working. Those still toiling away were sometimes invited to join Arif at the Capital Club and challenged to drinking matches. He offered $5,000 to a junior staffer if he could drink more shots than him, but the employee declined because he still had work to do.

"Stop being such a pussy," Arif told him.

Arif's capacity for late nights and early starts amazed colleagues. He expected them to work as hard as he did, but even those half his age struggled to keep up.

"This guy could drink half a bottle of whiskey at two a.m. or three a.m. and then be fresh to give a speech at nine a.m.," one of his team said. "He wanted people to work the same rhythm as him but the problem was he was the one getting all the money."

Arif was capable of generous acts, which inspired loyalty.

Matteo Stefanel fell off his bicycle while training for a triathlon in Dubai. The Italian Abraaj executive put out his arm to stop his fall but the impact forced his ulna to pop out of its socket and shattered his radius like a breadstick slammed into a wall. The pain was unbelievable. Matteo dumped his bike and took a taxi to the nearest hospital, where a Syrian surgeon said the arm had to be amputated. Pumped up to his eyeballs with morphine, Matteo desperately called colleagues for help. The head of Abraaj's operations in Turkey told him to get on a plane immediately to Istanbul, where Abraaj owned a hospital which employed an American surgeon who specialized in broken bones.

The last commercial flight bound for Turkey that day had already departed but a private jet pilot agreed to take Matteo for $25,000 in cash. Matteo didn't have the money so he called a senior executive at Abraaj and asked for a loan. He knew large amounts of cash were kept in Abraaj's safe. The executive arranged for a suitcase full of money to meet Matteo at the airport.

Matteo flew to Turkey that night. The surgery was successful. A month later, he returned to Dubai and went to see Arif to ask him to deduct the money he owed for the flight from his salary.

"Ah, that's nothing," Arif said. "We are a big family. We do this stuff for each other."

Like many cult leaders, Arif regularly referred to his followers as family. He told employees he was their older brother and insisted he had their best interests at heart.

Abraaj was literally family in some ways because Arif's two sons, brother-in-law, cousins, nephews, and nieces worked there. The Aman Foundation was overseen by Arif with his wife, sons, daughter-in-law, and sisters. The distinction between the Naqvi family and Abraaj grew fainter as the years rolled by. When Arif's father died, dozens of employees traveled from Dubai to attend the funeral at a cemetery on a green hill in northwest London.

Arif and Fayeeza frequently entertained Abraaj staff at their Emirates Hills mansion. Executives admired their collection of beautiful Islamic miniature paintings before dining on platters of spicy Lahore kebabs washed down with two-thousand-dollar bottles of Petrus red wine. Guests who drank too much sometimes stumbled into the elegant watercourse that trickled around the inner courtyard, causing much laughter.

Favored executives were offered use of Arif's properties in London and in the mountains of northern Pakistan, as well as a yacht, which he kept on the Mediterranean Sea.

In the summer, Arif invited people to his Oxfordshire estate for a cricket match. Arif had a playing field and clubhouse on the grounds. The house was in the quintessentially English village of Wootton, on a wooded lane near a church and pub. Executives mingled with celebrities and the cricket stars Imran Khan and Ian Botham.

Nepotism was normal at Abraaj. Arif recruited the sons and daughters of rich investors and famous politicians to tighten his relationships with them. The son of Prime Minister Najib Razak of Malaysia, the daughter of the jailed Sri Lankan hedge fund supremo Raj Rajaratnam, a nephew of the king of Jordan, and a relative of John Kerry all worked at Abraaj. Najib's son left soon after a massive financial scandal engulfed his father in Malaysia.

Arif cheerily claimed that his young employees were so well plugged in that they learned about important political and economic developments before he did. He called this network of princelings Radio Abraaj. Some of the juniors were already so wealthy, they drove more expensive cars than their bosses, and it wasn't unusual for employees fresh out of university to turn up to work in Ferraris and Porsches. The presence of the privileged young staffers heightened the glamour associated with working at Abraaj.

The firm was notorious for capitalist excess. On Thursday and Friday evenings, the White Dubai club on the roof of the city's horseracing track was filled with Abraaj staff racking up big bills. The Abraaj brand was so strong in the city, it served as a stay-out-of-trouble card. An Abraaj employee who got into a fight during a boozy session in a nightclub ended the dispute when he explained where he worked. His adversary immediately apologized.

• • •

Arif encouraged employees to socialize together to weave tighter bonds between them. He spent millions of dollars on weeklong offsite meetings in luxury hotels on Dubai's palm islands and booked out nightclubs and restaurants to entertain staff. Employees were encouraged to drink excessive amounts of alcohol and share intimate secrets while bouncers removed unconscious colleagues. Some staffers were driven to tears by the pressure to drink. The partying fueled illicit affairs between executives and secretaries. One employee described the offsite meetings as fuckfests. A secretary said she spent the night during one Abraaj event in a threesome in a hotel room with a female colleague and a male executive.

"I am beset by evil perverts," she wrote to a friend after another executive told her he wanted to have sex with her. "Literally. Not a metaphor. He basically just told me he is a very naughty man and he thinks we have a connection and when can we meet. WHAT IS HAPPENING TO MY LIFE."

During one late-night gathering in a hotel, Arif invited a small group of employees for a drink. He broke down in tears in front of them as he talked about his dead father. He encouraged others to open up and share their personal stories. One person spoke about going through a difficult divorce. The atmosphere became emotional and more people started crying.

Sometime later, an employee found Arif's planning notes for the gathering. They included a written reference to the moment when Arif was going to open up and share his feelings. The display of vulnerability had been staged by a master actor.

Emotional manipulation was a favored tactic. Arif was quick to remind people if he thought they owed him. When one employee who worked in Dubai resisted being moved to an office in Africa, Arif turned on him.

"How did you get this job?" Arif asked.

"I applied for it and was accepted," the employee replied.

"I gave you this job because of your family," Arif said. "I know your uncle."

Employees tried hard to please Arif because that was the surest route to promotion and higher pay. The most loyal were chosen to work for Arif's Central Execution Team, known as CXT. The group was led by Anuscha Ahmed, a Karachi Grammar School alum whom Arif treated like a daughter. The zeal with which this small group carried out their work was likened by one employee to that of jihadists. They unquestioningly did Arif's bidding and frequently clashed with other employees.

Of all the tools for control at Arif's disposal, money was the most powerful.

He bought people.

Private equity executives earned hundreds of thousands or even millions of dollars a year in salaries, but their ultimate goal was to make even more money from their share of profits, known as carry, when companies were sold. Arif controlled how the carry was shared at Abraaj. Most employees never saw a single dollar of it, even though some waited for years for a payout. Instead, Arif paid high-enough salaries and annual bonuses to make it hard for people to leave.

For top dealmakers like Mustafa, the expectation of one day receiving a big share of carry compelled them to stay even when they became deeply unhappy. Quitting was so difficult, some executives renamed Abraaj "Hotel California" because, as the lyrics of the Eagles song say, you can check out anytime you like but you can never leave.

Arif pestered favored employees to stay if they asked to leave. He smothered them in compliments, cajoled them, threw money at them. He couldn't accept it when people wanted to quit, because he felt personally offended.

"He couldn't get betrayed," said one executive. "Inevitably when leaving, regardless of whether you say 'it's not you it's me,' there is always an element of disappointment, of unhappiness with the place, of judgment, and Arif always got to the heart of that judgment that you were having and perceived it as a challenge. There was a challenge and that challenge had to be met."

Abraaj became so unbearable for this executive that he decided to leave, but Arif rejected his resignation. A month later, Arif called him to his Dubai mansion and fired him, but the executive refused to be fired. He was fearful of how his departure would be perceived at other firms because he would need to find a new job and didn't want potential new employers to think he had been fired.

The employee asked Arif to relocate him to an Abraaj office outside Dubai instead, and Arif agreed. Weeks later, Arif and the employee were in the same office outside Dubai together.

"I am leaving," the employee said.

"When are you coming back?" Arif responded. He thought he meant he was leaving the office for lunch.

"I am leaving the firm," the employee said.

Weeks of tumultuous discussions followed. Arif moved through rage, insults, pleading, and questioning. After a month, Arif was back in Dubai and called the employee to meet him there again. The employee had definitively made up his mind to quit but went to Dubai anyway.

"You are making the biggest mistake of your life," Arif told him. "I am your elder brother, I care for you, and I cannot allow you to make this mistake. So I have decided that the two most important men in your life need to meet with each other. And so tomorrow I will take the jet and you and I will go to your city and I will sit down with your father. It is very clear to me that you respect his views and I am sure that he will agree with me."

The employee had worked for Arif for years and thought he knew all his tricks but his boss was still capable of surprising him. He had learned that the best way out of tricky situations with Arif was to respond with an overly courteous, obsequious, almost Byzantine diplomatic language to avoid direct confrontation that would trigger his rage.

"Thank you, Arif. I am truly honored by this request," the employee replied. "Allow me to retreat and think about this. I really appreciate you calling me here and making such a thoughtful offer."

The employee left the office. He called his father and they laughed for half an hour.

"Oh, this is really cool, let me call Arif," the employee's father said.

"What are you going to say?" the employee replied.

"I am going to ask how much is my cut if you accept to stay. I mean, I am your agent, right?" the father joked.

The employee turbocharged his diplomacy in an email to Arif.

The words you spoke to me were words of affection and concern for me: they were words of an older brother, as you said.

I am flattered that you would want to meet with my father. I would be delighted by such a meeting, but I would like to make sure that it happened under the right premise, out of respect for you both.

I have a great relationship with my father, and I have discussed with him my decision to leave at every step of the thought process. Having said that I am 38 years old and the decision, in the end, was mine and mine alone.

I was really moved when we spoke. My family and I would love to host you whenever your schedule allows: in the most heartfelt way, our house is your house. After all this is only natural, as you are my older brother!

Thank you again, Arif.

Arif kept imploring the employee to stay. Then, one day, after many more months had passed, he finally relented and agreed to let him go and said the employee could announce his departure during a company meeting. But even after this, Arif continued paying him for two more months. The employee had to beg Arif again to take him off the payroll and company email system.

Whether they were loved or hated, Abraaj employees at some point felt the same emotion working for Arif.

Fear.

"It was never physical fear," said the employee who took so long to leave. "Reputation is everything in the finance industry, and Arif was extremely powerful. He was *the* emerging markets investor. He was super respected."

Arif's power derived from his vast network of contacts. Employees who quit but remained in the finance industry worried that sooner or later they would cross paths with someone who owed Arif a favor, someone who had sympathy for him, someone who would do anything to help or please him. Abraaj employees believed Arif could get people to do things without those people knowing they were acting on his behalf. He had an amazing ability to get what he wanted while maintaining plausible deniability.

Given Arif's masterful manipulation skills, many employees who attempted to distance themselves from him agreed that flattery was the best course of action.

"You are arguably the most talented CEO of any investment firm anywhere," said a partner who quit Abraaj. "Most firms require two to three people to do the job of firm leadership. Only Abraaj relies on one person to do everything. Only Abraaj has found one person who *can* do everything from fundraising to investing, from relationship-building to brand-building and from operations to recruiting," the partner wrote in a note to Arif. "Your timing has been immaculate and your strategic choices have been superb. Some may consider these luck. Those of us who have had a front-row seat to the evolution of the firm know that they are sheer brilliance."

The flattery shielded Arif from any criticism as the globalization zeitgeist fueled his ego further. Outside the firm, Arif's rhetorical skills blinded investors and politicians. They couldn't see the flaws in how he operated. By partnering with Arif, the UN, the World Bank, the Gates Foundation, and the American, British, and French governments were handing control of billions of dollars and important policy decisions to a man who was spiraling out of control.

CHAPTER 9

TURKS WILL ALWAYS DRINK MILK

With the wind at his back after the acquisition of Aureos in 2012, Arif was ready for new risky projects and markets. A decade after starting Abraaj he set off in pursuit of takeovers in countries he had never explored before, from the Philippines to Peru, in industries as varied as milk production, online retailing, and travel agencies.

Most private equity firms focused on a few countries but Arif was confident he had cracked the code for dealmaking and possessed a formula that worked in all developing countries. He was building a global empire. He even attempted, unsuccessfully, to buy Coutts, the London-based bank whose elite clients included Queen Elizabeth II.

Arif's main plan was to raise billions of dollars for a series of funds targeting different regions—North Africa, Sub-Saharan Africa, Asia, Latin America, Turkey, and Mexico. He pushed his team to make high-profile acquisitions with the money remaining in existing funds. These takeovers served as flagship deals to convince investors there were enough profitable targets around the world to justify raising more money.

His focus turned to Turkey, even as the nation's strongman leader Recep Tayyip Erdoğan tightened his grip on power and sparked riots in the streets. Abraaj bought Yörsan, Turkey's fourth-biggest dairy products company, in January 2014. The takeover valued Yörsan at $370 million.

Arif went ahead with the deal despite the worsening political and economic turmoil in Turkey. The warning signs of crisis were clear but for Arif the instability was practically his calling card. He navigated risk in places where fearful outsiders dared not.

Few seemed concerned that as Arif's reach expanded around the world, he himself was increasingly the outsider where he was investing. Turkey was very different from the UAE, and the UAE was not Pakistan. Arif was the beneficiary of an inclination in Western countries—reinforced by his subtle insinuations of ignorance, colonialism, and racism—to let him pass as their expert guide to the vastness of the "emerging" world.

Arif and his team bullishly promoted Turkey's prospects with typical bravado. They told international investors that Turkey's fast-growing economy and population of 80 million made it an attractive target.

Yörsan, Arif said, would prosper as Turkey's rapidly urbanizing population lost its connection to farmers in the countryside and sought out shops full of chilled packages of cheese, milk, and yogurt. Arif also believed that Yörsan and the Turkish food industry in general were poised to become big exporters to the Middle East.

An American television news channel interviewed Arif as Turks protested about President Erdoğan's authoritarian rule behind him in Istanbul's Taksim Square. The reporter asked Arif how the political chaos—which literally surrounded him—was affecting business. Arif nonchalantly brushed off the question.

"Turks are going to drink milk regardless of who governs them," he replied.

It was a cool sound bite, and Arif frequently mentioned this interview in later speeches, but there were plenty of other ways for the Yörsan deal to go sour. And it did.

Şerafettin Yörük founded Yörsan in 1964 near a water well in a sleepy region of olive trees and ancient ruins in northwestern Anatolia. Under his ambitious leadership Yörsan grew rapidly into a modern dairy manufacturer and a household name. It used locally sourced milk and water from the well to make its products.

Şerafettin became a multimillionaire. To further his fortunes, the tough tycoon searched for an investor with international connections. Selling a stake in Yörsan would enable him to convert some of his shares into cash.

An investment banker put Yörsan on the radar of the head of Abraaj's operations in Turkey, a slick former Deutsche Bank dealmaker named Selcuk Yorgancioglu, who had joined Abraaj in 2008. Selcuk gained Arif's favor by working on a successful investment in a Turkish hospital chain called Acibadem, which healed Matteo Stefanel's broken arm after his bicycle accident. Abraaj later sold Acibadem to Malaysian and Singaporean investors for a $355 million profit.

Yörsan seemed like a good deal. Selcuk was looking for a big new takeover to impress Arif and believed he could help Yörsan expand by acquiring other Turkish dairies and selling products in the Arabian Gulf. Selcuk was eager to buy the company and started talks with Yörsan's founder to iron out an agreement. Some Abraaj colleagues weren't so keen because they thought the deal was based on overly optimistic projections for Yörsan's future growth. Selcuk pushed aggressively to proceed and won out.

Abraaj invested $142 million in the Turkish company. The European Bank for Reconstruction and Development, a lender owned by the U.S. and by European governments, agreed to invest alongside Abraaj for the first time. The EBRD had a mandate to promote economic growth and thought that investing in Yörsan would help modernize Turkey's $3.6 billion dairy industry. The Yörük family kept a 20 percent stake in Yörsan.

"We feel privileged to be partnering with EBRD and the Yörük family on the acquisition of this much-loved and iconic Turkish brand," Selcuk, the head of Abraaj in Turkey, said when the deal was announced.

The euphoria soon evaporated. The headstrong Şeraffetin clashed with Abraaj executives and went public with his dispute. Newspapers correctly reported that Abraaj had taken control of Yörsan but this offended Şeraffetin, who was used to being the boss and wanted to remain in charge of Yörsan. He issued a statement saying the deal was a partnership of equals and Abraaj didn't control his company.

Selcuk and his team at Abraaj soon discovered that Yörsan was in worse condition than they anticipated. Yörsan marketed its dairy products as fresh but some items weren't, because the company had been adding preservatives to extend their shelf life. To fix this problem it wasn't enough to simply remove the preservatives. Abraaj also had to improve Yörsan's distribution network so the fresh products could quickly reach supermarket shelves before turning sour. These improvements cost millions of dollars more than Abraaj had expected to spend.

Simmering tensions between Şeraffetin and Abraaj worsened. Sloppy due diligence during the takeover talks was creating major problems for Arif's team in their dispute with the Yörük family.

Abraaj had bought Yörsan's factory in the town of Susurluk but the nearby well it used to create steam to pasteurize milk wasn't included. The well was still owned by the Yörük family. One Abraaj executive thought it was a mistake to have not acquired the well with the factory.

Things went from bad to worse. A year after the takeover, Lactalis, the world's second-largest dairy company, crashed into the Turkish market with the takeover of the nation's leading dairy company, Ak Gida. The French milk giant saw the same opportunities in Turkey that Abraaj saw and was better placed to exploit them. Lactalis generated $18.3 billion in annual revenue and had turned selling milk products into an art form.

Private equity firms can benefit when big multinational companies expand into new markets, by selling them their companies. But Lactalis had decided to buy a much larger company than Yörsan and then proceeded to compete directly. It was a hopeless fight. Yörsan's management team couldn't keep up with Lactalis, let alone increase their market share. When Yörsan discounted prices, Lactalis discounted its prices more. And when Yörsan tried to improve its product range, Lactalis repositioned its products and won that way, too.

"They played a very smart game," a former Yörsan executive said.

The biggest blow to Yörsan came from President Erdoğan. On July 15, 2016, a group of Turkish soldiers attempted to overthrow the president in a coup d'état. The soldiers accused the president of despotic rule and violating human rights. They attempt to seize control of Ankara, the political capital, and Istanbul, the largest city. They failed. More than three hundred people were killed during the attempted coup and thousands more were injured. Erdoğan blamed the violence on Fethullah Gülen, a Turkish cleric who lived in the United States. Erdoğan's rivals claimed the president had staged the uprising as an excuse to consolidate his grip on power.

Erdoğan's reaction to the unrest made the situation worse. He ordered the mass arrest of thousands of soldiers, judges, and teachers. The economy was hit hard. Bombings following the coup scared away tourists who were a big source of income for the country and companies including Yörsan. International investors pulled back and the value of the Turkish lira collapsed.

The currency crash was a serious setback for Abraaj because the firm had borrowed millions of U.S. dollars to buy Yörsan and was counting on income from the dairy company to repay the loan. Yörsan's customers paid for their milk and cheese in Turkish lira, worth fewer and fewer dollars with each month that passed, making the dollar loan more expensive to repay.

With elections fast approaching, Erdoğan desperately needed to hold on to support from an important group of voters, the farmers. The government started buying milk directly from them to prop up prices and buy their votes. This dealt another unexpected blow to Yörsan. The government's milk-buying policy boosted prices and made it harder for Yörsan to buy milk at a price that enabled it to make a profit. Lactalis, a much bigger buyer of milk, was better able to negotiate prices with farmers and navigated the crisis with greater ease.

Turks were still drinking milk, as Arif confidently predicted, but they weren't drinking enough of Yörsan's milk.

Yörsan's dire performance left Arif with a dilemma. Did he tell investors that the company was hemorrhaging money, a move that might deter them from supporting Abraaj in future, or did he throw good money after bad and try to save Yörsan?

He chose to rescue Yörsan. He put tens of millions of dollars more from investors into the dairy company, using money from a different fund than the one he used to originally invest in Yörsan. Using money from a different group of investors to bail out Yörsan was bad practice, and it didn't help anyway. Yörsan's sales and profits kept falling.

. . .

Three thousand miles southwest of Turkey, across the Mediterranean Sea and Sahara Desert, Abraaj dealmakers were working on another dairy company investment in the West African nation of Ghana.

Abraaj's takeover of Ghana's Fan Milk was also a big gamble. Arif believed that any political and economic instability in the country wouldn't adversely affect a food business catering to consumers. The prospects for Fan Milk were promising. Unlike Yörsan, Fan Milk had a loyal customer base for its ice creams and frozen yogurts.

Fan Milk was a unique company. It employed thousands of vendors who pedaled bicycles bearing cool boxes around the busy streets of Accra, the capital of Ghana, and Lagos, the biggest city in neighboring Nigeria. The vendors weaved through traffic and waited for customers outside bus stations, schools, and churches. The sellers were everywhere. Children never had difficulty finding Fan Milk's sweet products, much to the dismay of their parents.

Most days after soccer practice, Kwame Nantwi and his friends flocked to the blue-jacketed ice cream vendors who waited by the school gates with boxes full of frozen treats. Kwame saved up money and ate six or seven ice creams on some days. His grandma tried to curb his sweet-toothed habit without success.

Graham Moriah and his classmates at the Ministry of Basic Health School in Accra eagerly awaited the end of classes, when they streamed out to the waiting sellers. Graham struck up a friendship with one vendor.

"He was our friend," Graham said of the seller, whom he continued to see around Accra as an adult. "He always asked us how we were doing."

Fan Milk's strong customer base made it a compelling takeover target when the company's founder, a Danish merchant called Erik Emborg, decided to sell. Emborg started Fan Milk in 1960, three years after Ghana gained its independence from Britain. Most foreign investors in Ghana were involved in exporting gold, diamonds, and cocoa. But Emborg saw an opportunity to import milk powder since fresh milk was scarce in Ghana. His business was a failure at first because Ghanaians didn't like his milk products, but fortunes improved when a Ghanaian employee who was worried about losing his job came up with a new idea. Fan Milk started manufacturing sweeter products which were more appealing—chocolate milk and ice cream. The company flourished.

Fan Milk survived bloody coups and economic crashes to expand across West Africa. Its presence in fast-growing emerging markets made it a target for Arif, who believed that companies which sold products to urbanizing populations could deliver outsized returns with minimal risks.

Bankers working for Emborg approached Abraaj to gauge its interest in making a bid. Jacob Kohli, who had joined Abraaj from Aureos, knew Fan Milk well and had served on its board. Jacob was well placed to persuade Fan Milk's management that Abraaj was the right firm to partner with.

Abraaj made an offer for Fan Milk and won the auction against fierce competition from bidders including Actis, a private equity firm based in London, and Danone, the world's third-biggest dairy company.

Problems soon emerged. Abraaj didn't have enough cash available to pay for Fan Milk. An adviser to Arif likened the situation to a person who looks around a beautiful house, impulsively buys it, and then realizes they can't afford it. Thinking fast to get around this problem, Arif repeated a trick from years earlier, when he sold pieces of Inchcape before he had bought the company. Danone, the French dairy company that lost to Abraaj in the auction for Fan Milk, was still eager to rapidly expand across Africa. It already had operations in the north and south of the continent.

Arif offered Danone the chance to invest alongside Abraaj and acquire a 49 percent stake in Fan Milk. Danone accepted. Its investment valued Fan Milk at more than $360 million and, crucially, it helped Arif close the deal. Danone provided Fan Milk with deep expertise in how to improve technology and products but the French company didn't have any experience in West Africa.

Soon after the deal completed, Abraaj and Danone discovered that the task of improving Fan Milk was going to be harder than they expected. The new owners thought they were buying a fleet of 20,000 bicycles. But thousands of the Fan Milk bikes were broken and rusting in the streets. A fleet of trucks that moved products from city to city was also in poor condition, battered by potholes in the roads of Ghana and Nigeria. Bribery and corruption were widespread too.

Abraaj and Danone needed to find a chief executive for Fan Milk with local knowledge. At first glance Edouard Spicher seemed like an unlikely candidate. The son of a Swiss oil executive, Spicher spent his youth moving from place to place and had lived in more countries by the end of his teenage years than some people visit in a lifetime. He graduated from the École Polytechnique Fédérale de Lausanne with a degree in engineering and got a job at Nestlé, the world's largest dairy company.

Nestlé sent Spicher to Ghana. He loved the vibrant country with streets full of people selling mangoes and banku, a local dish made out of fermented maize. On the beaches, fishermen pushed brightly painted canoes into the Atlantic Ocean in the morning and returned later in the day with catches to sell in the markets.

Spicher worked on four continents for Nestlé over two decades. He led the Swiss company's ice cream business in the Dominican Republic and served a second stint in Ghana.

Abraaj and Danone appointed Spicher chief executive of Fan Milk in 2014. On his return to Ghana, Spicher found Accra had changed dramatically since his first visit. Apartment blocks, hotels, and shopping malls were rising up next to dilapidated colonial villas and sprawling slums. Fields were being transformed into housing for Ghanaians who wanted to move to the city to grab a slice of the new prosperity. The economy was growing fast, poverty was trending downward, and the politics were stable.

Many Ghanaians worked for the government, and as much as 70 percent of government spending went on salaries for civil servants. But soon after Abraaj bought Fan Milk, the Ghanaian economy was struck by a collapse in the price of gold. Ghana relied heavily on money from exports of the precious metal. The slumping gold price reduced a valuable source of income for the government, which earned taxes from the exports. The loss of revenue made it harder for the government to pay salaries.

The gold crisis also hit Ghana's currency hard. The cedi was the world's worst-performing currency in 2014, falling about 40 percent against the U.S. dollar. The currency free fall was bad news for Abraaj. Fan Milk needed dollars to buy imported milk but its customers paid with cedis. The drop in the value of the local currency made it more expensive to buy the imported milk to make products, so Fan Milk's profits fell.

Wild swings in currency values were one of the biggest risks in emerging markets investing. Currency crashes were a cruel reality that could wipe out good companies as well as bad. Even though Fan Milk was growing fast and performing well in terms of sales, the crumbling cedi was a serious threat.

With costs rising, one possible solution was to raise prices. But Spicher knew that doubling the price of an ice cream would be highly unpopular with the schoolchildren who saved up for their favorite snacks. He needed another solution.

Spicher introduced cheaper packaging to offset the higher production costs and he increased the size of some of the most popular products at the same time as raising their prices. These changes helped maintain customer loyalty and grow sales.

It wasn't long before events in Nigeria plunged Fan Milk's business there into crisis too. Tumbling oil prices hit the Nigerian economy and currency hard. Nigeria's naira lost more than 40 percent of its value against the dollar in one day. The currency collapse caused Fan Milk the same problems in Nigeria as in Ghana. It became more expensive to buy imported milk.

Falling oil prices also reduced income for the Nigerian government, which struggled to pay its civil servants. Nurses and schoolteachers went without salaries, sometimes for months, so they had less money to give to their children to buy Fan Milk ice creams.

. . .

Arif's bet that consumer demand in emerging markets was immune to political crises, economic storms and collapsing currencies wasn't working out in Turkey, Ghana, or Nigeria. Yörsan was sliding toward bankruptcy and the loss of more than $100 million for Abraaj and its investors. Fan Milk was faring better, but the currency collapses in Ghana and Nigeria meant Abraaj investors would be lucky to get the dollars they had invested back, without any profits.

The problems at Yörsan and Fan Milk were largely hidden from public view because of the secrecy that surrounded private equity deals. As private companies, Yörsan and Fan Milk were under no obligation to disclose detailed financial information. Abraaj's slick marketing provided an additional shield. Arif trumpeted Yörsan and Fan Milk as successful examples of his winning strategy. Fan Milk was more famous than Coca-Cola in Ghana, he said. And as for Yörsan, well, Turks are always going to drink milk.

Arif taught his employees how to always put a positive spin on things in public. His methods were institutionalized at Abraaj, and some of the world's leading business experts advised on how to transform Arif's way into Abraaj's way. Prominent among the advisers was Josh Lerner, the Harvard professor of investment banking who authored widely read books and papers on private equity.

Lerner's relationship with Arif was riddled with potential conflicts of interest. As an academic, he wrote supposedly impartial case studies about Abraaj deals, including its transformation of Karachi Electric. He portrayed the firm as a force for good that took capital and expertise into poor countries. The Harvard cheerleader was extremely helpful to Arif in reassuring investors such as the World Bank and as a recruitment tool for young professionals with degrees from America's most prestigious universities. The bullied Indian employee whose shirt and undershirt Arif threw off the top of Dubai's Capital Club had joined Abraaj after reading Lerner's glowing case studies about the professionalism of the firm and its leader.

But Arif was also paying Lerner thousands of dollars as an adviser. Lerner was a member of Abraaj's advisory board between 2008 and 2010 and a consultant to the firm until 2017. He set up an academy to teach Arif's methods to his employees. In one video that he made for the academy he described Abraaj as extraordinary.

"When Arif first broached the idea of the academy he really had a very ambitious vision," Lerner said in one video. "The most important thing behind the vision, and which has really motivated our efforts, has been about language and communication."

Lerner explained in the video that Arif wanted to create a shared language to forge strong ties among Abraaj's many offices and hundreds of employees. Speaking Abraaj's language meant talking about emerging markets as places of opportunity rather than risk and promoting the dual mission to help people and make profit. The shared language was supposed to bind Abraaj together, uniting employees in a common cause. The firm was like a modern-day tower of Babel, with people from different countries and backgrounds speaking the same language.

In reality, Abraaj executives fought one another for resources just like in any other competitive private equity firm. Omar Lodhi and Selcuk Yorgancioglu worked together on the successful Acibadem hospital investment. But after Omar appeared to claim all the credit for the deal in an interview with *Forbes*, the magazine added a note to clarify that he wasn't the only person involved.

Most of the time, Abraaj's public relations team made sure that the firm operated as a smooth-running empire of spin, with internal disputes kept well hidden from public view. Abraaj churned out videos and press releases that gave simplistic explanations about complicated deals in countries far from North America and Europe.

Abraaj executives followed Arif's scripts when they spoke to journalists. When an American reporter asked Tom Speechley whether political instability in Egypt was a problem, Tom gave a response similar to Arif's confident claim that Turks will always drink milk. He said that the replacement of the ousted Egyptian president Mohamed Morsi with General Abdel Fattah el-Sisi wasn't a problem for Abraaj's clinics and food outlets in the country.

"If someone in Egypt's doctor tells them they need a blood test, they're going to get that blood test whether it's Morsi or Sisi in charge," Tom said. "And they're probably still going to get their food from the same restaurant."

As clever as these answers sounded, they were no substitute for making genuinely good investments and often served as smokescreens to hide difficult situations.

CHAPTER 10

CASH CRUNCH

"Ambition. It's the reason we're all here."

The billionaire filmmaker and philanthropist Jeff Skoll welcomed a thousand idealists to his world forum on social entrepreneurship in 2014. The event took place each spring amid the grassy squares and dreaming spires of Oxford University in England. Skoll had made his fortune by helping to start eBay, the online auction and shopping website. He became a billionaire by selling eBay shares and used the cash to fund his dream of inspiring people to help humanity.

Skoll believed that a good story well told could change society, and he founded Participant Media to produce inspiring movies about people who he thought had made the world a better place. His films included an Oscar-winning biopic of President Abraham Lincoln and Al Gore's documentary about climate change, *An Inconvenient Truth*. In *Charlie Wilson's War*, another of his films, Tom Hanks played a congressman who convinced the U.S. government to support Afghans fighting the Soviet invasion in the 1980s.

Skoll's annual Oxford forum brought together a beguiling mix of billionaires and humanitarians. They gathered to discuss how to improve healthcare, provide clean water, and create jobs for the world's poorest citizens.

Ambition was the theme chosen for the 2014 meeting and Skoll invited two superstar speakers who he thought embodied the word. Arif was one. The other was Richard Branson, the billionaire British founder of the Virgin Atlantic airline and Virgin Galactic spaceflight company.

Skoll's forum took months to prepare. Invitations were dispatched to executives and activists on every continent. Dinners were arranged in ancient university halls and a media team prepared a film to show on the opening evening.

When Arif's invitation to the forum reached him, he was working on preparations of an entirely different kind in his Dubai headquarters.

Abraaj was running out of money.

In a decade spent mingling with the world's political and business elite, Arif had taken his eye off the ball. Big projected profits had failed to materialize, his billionaire lifestyle was adding up, and, coupled with a rapid expansion of Abraaj which he couldn't afford, he was struggling to pay bills, salaries, and his own expenses. The cash crunch was so serious Abraaj's finance department didn't know what to do about it.

"We will have a deficit of $100mln by 15th Jan," a finance manager wrote to Arif on January 9, 2014.

Arif had to choose between telling investors and lenders the truth about Abraaj's deteriorating financial situation and pretending everything was going according to plan. He chose the path of deception. The world didn't know about Abraaj's financial crisis and Arif was determined to keep it a secret.

This was the time when Arif embarked on the criminal path that led to the largest collapse of a private equity firm in history, prosecutors at the U.S. Department of Justice later concluded. He directed employees to use all of Abraaj's resources, its international network, and its reputation to steal, bribe, and commit fraud around the world.

Arif had plenty of cash sources from which to take money illegally. Abraaj had many investment funds and bank loans that he could tap to conceal the truth about his financial problems for as long as possible, hopefully forever. Arif stole money that banks and investors provided for the purpose of buying companies and used it to pay huge salaries, bonuses, and for his extravagant lifestyle. He deceived investors by sending them false reports containing inflated valuations for the performance of the funds. The flattering lies in the reports gave the impression Abraaj was performing well and convinced investors to pledge more money to Abraaj.

As Skoll finished his preparations for the 2014 conference, Arif was sending his latest confidential document to investors. The report claimed that Abraaj generated net returns of 17 percent a year, making it one of the world's most successful private equity firms. The calculation of this number was decisive in convincing many investors to hand over their money. The methodology to calculate the number was "independently validated by Prof. Josh Lerner," the document said. The Harvard professor had given his seal of approval, it seemed.

Emails in Arif's inbox told a different story.

Rafique Lakhani, the cash controller in Abraaj's finance department who had worked for Arif since the 1990s, was providing constant updates to his boss about the firm's perilous predicament. Rafique led a small team of mainly Pakistani accountants who maintained spreadsheets of Abraaj's payments due, cash on hand, and anticipated inflows and shortfalls. Their work was kept secret even from some within the finance department, and their loyalty was rewarded with high pay, bonuses, and promotions.

In March 2014, a finance manager told Rafique and Arif that he was struggling to find money to pay $19.6 million owed to investors in an Abraaj fund. According to Rafique, the only way to make the payment to the investors was to raid another fund, called Abraaj Private Equity Fund IV, or APEF IV.

"We cannot pay this until further inflows come in from APEF IV," Rafique wrote in an email to Arif.

To make things worse, Rafique also needed to find $25 million to repay a bank loan. More cash was looted from APEF IV.

There was no public sign that the problems existed at all. Arif continued flying around the world on private jets in a dizzying whirl of self-promotion, conveying a message of unfettered success. He flew to Panama in March 2014 to speak at a World Economic Forum conference with the advertising guru Martin Sorrell. At the conference he lectured Latin American politicians on their dire economic performance, telling them that ten of the fifteen most unequal countries in the world were in their part of the world.

"What you still have is enormous income inequality, and income inequality leads to social issues," Arif said. "And that's just a fact, right?"

From Panama, Arif flew on to England to attend Skoll's forum in Oxford. The university town was conveniently located for Arif as it was just a twenty-five-minute drive from his country house.

On a Wednesday evening in April 2014, Arif settled into a front-row seat at Oxford's New Theatre to watch the opening film of the Skoll conference. Sir Ronald Cohen, the British impact investing pioneer who was inspiring governments and the Vatican to join his movement, sat next to Arif.

Words appeared on the cinema screen.

"It always seems impossible until it's done."

The smiling face of Nelson Mandela, the first Black president of South Africa, flashed up.

Rousing music accompanied images of human progress through history—a stone flour mill, a steam locomotive, an electric light, an astronaut walking in space. Muhammad Yunus, the Nobel Prize laureate who pioneered providing microloans to poor people in Bangladesh, appeared on the screen.

"If we imagine today what kind of world we want, then that's the world we create," he said. "If we do not imagine, it will not be done."

Martin Luther King marches, a man hacks at the Berlin Wall, Mahatma Gandhi prays, an Egyptian girl cheers the Arab Spring, African boys smile on a dusty road.

"It's neither pragmatism nor inspiration that drives me," the Scottish singer Annie Lennox said in the film. "It's more the passion."

A moment of silence. Then a word flashed in red in ten different languages:

AMBITION.

The thousand-strong audience roared. A man walked on stage.

"You are ambitious people and your goal is ambitious," said Stephan Chambers, the head of Oxford University's Skoll Centre for Social Entrepreneurship. "It is nothing less than to improve the state of the world.

"But ambition, of course, has another side. It crawls as well as soars.

"And when ambition crawls it is self-regarding and self-serving and all the opposites of what you wish for.

"And what we wish for here is positive ambition.

"We want Mandela. Not Macbeth.

"We want the sublime unreasonableness of unreasonable goals and intentions.

"We do not want the venality or the triviality of Macbeth.

"I congratulate you on your ambition."

The Oxford academic deferentially welcomed his billionaire benefactor. Jeff Skoll's ambition was colossal, and colossally positive, he said.

Skoll strolled onto the stage. He complemented the audience for their creativity and goodness and started to tell them a story about why he was feeling really inspired by César Chávez. The Hispanic American labor leader who campaigned for poor farmers in California in the 1960s was the subject of Skoll's latest film.

Chavez's rallying cry was *si, se puede*, meaning "yes, we can," Skoll said. He asked the audience to stand up and chant the slogan with him. As the Canadian billionaire cried out and punched the air, Sir Ronald leaped to his feet with the rest of the audience and chanted with his fist jabbing skyward.

"Si, se puede," Sir Ronald cried.

With the audience suitably warmed up, the star attractions entered. Arif and Richard Branson were there to represent the ambition of Mandela. Skoll was anointing them as heirs to a line of civic heroes going back to Martin Luther King and Mahatma Gandhi. Their ambition was not supposed to be like Macbeth's. In William Shakespeare's tragic play, the scheming Scottish lord who plots treachery and deception becomes trapped in a downward spiral of crime and depravity. Macbeth asks the stars in the sky to hide their light to cover his black and deep desires.

On the stage Arif seemed exhausted. Branson gently mocked him for his jet-setting lifestyle.

"He's very, very tired," Branson told the audience. "Someone needs to get him a double espresso."

"It comes from living on an airplane," Arif shot back.

Coffee was fetched.

Joint billing with Branson, a pioneer of space travel, was a big moment for the boy from Karachi.

"One of the most exciting things about sitting on this platform with Richard is I actually remember, when I was a young kid, watching man walk on the moon for the first time, and I remember thinking to myself, wow, how privileged am I to be watching this," Arif said. "If you take me with you I'll sing 'Take Me to the Moon.'"

"Your wife asked me to offer you a one-way ticket," Branson replied. Arif and the audience laughed.

Their interviewer was Mindy Lubber, an American campaigner for social and environmental causes. She praised Branson for starting hundreds of companies and credited Arif for thinking seriously about the social impact of business long before it became popular to do so.

"What drives your ambition to think big and take risks?" she asked.

"Frustration," Branson said.

He described how he started his Virgin airline thirty years before when a commercial flight to the British Virgin Islands was canceled. He impulsively hired a private jet and sold tickets to fellow stranded passengers to get to the Caribbean island.

"Audacity," Arif responded.

He didn't discuss any of his investments. Instead, he lambasted the inequality between Western nations and developing countries and said that he was on a mission to restore balance.

"The part of the world that I live in, which a lot of you mistakenly call emerging markets—it's a bit patronizing—I call them global growth markets," he said. "Most of the world's growth is going to come from those markets."

Abraaj made money and reduced poverty at the same time, Arif told the audience. He criticized other private equity firms for being secretive and selfish.

"For far too long the private equity industry has had a reputation, particularly in the West, of being these alchemists, they stick their hands into this black box, they come out and suddenly base metal is gold, and the longer you keep people in the dark about how we actually go about doing it, the longer we tend to make money," Arif said.

The simple truth, he said, was that he worked very hard.

"Success comes before work only in the dictionary," Arif said. "And what's the biggest premise of being successful? It's to give back."

Branson, casually dressed in a leather jacket, agreed that it was essential for businesses to be transparent and to contribute to social progress.

"Look at corruption in business," Branson said. "Let's make sure we stamp it out."

"If we find a businessman who is corrupt we expose them," Branson said.

Arif looked on approvingly. He stressed that doing good didn't affect profits.

"We are very profitable," Arif said with a confident laugh. "Don't get me wrong, guys, we are very profitable."

If more companies followed Abraaj in considering their impact on society the future was going to be spectacularly good, Arif concluded. The audience burst into applause. There was no doubt in their minds that Arif's ambition was like that of the virtuous Mandela rather than the treacherous Macbeth.

On the last evening of the Skoll forum, Arif strolled into Oxford's centuries-old Oriel College for dinner. With a drink in hand, he laughed and chatted with Branson and his two children. Then he sat down to dine at a long table decked with fine wines and food. Jeff Skoll, one of George W. Bush's daughters, the Oscar-winning film producer Brian Grazer, and other members of the global elite were there too.

There wasn't a poor person in sight.

. . .

The afterglow from the Skoll conference boosted Arif's public profile. But deep within Abraaj the cash crunch was worsening with each day that passed, compelling Arif to find ever more devious ways to raise money. A month after the forum, Arif's team devised a new method, using shares of Air Arabia, a low-cost airline based in the UAE, as collateral to borrow money. The airline shares were rightfully owned by the investors in one of Abraaj's funds but they were pledged to a bank as security for a $90 million loan. Instead of giving the borrowed money to the investors in the fund that owned the stock, Arif's team took the money and used it to pay salaries, bonuses, and expenses.

The pressure on Arif to find cash to plug holes in Abraaj was relentless, and he started searching for buyers for Abraaj's investments in its own funds. When a private equity firm raises a fund, executives usually invest some of their own money in the fund too. Arif liked to boast that he and other Abraaj executives invested hundreds of millions of dollars in their own funds. Now he needed to sell these stakes.

Arif and Sev, the Aureos chief who became a top Abraaj executive after Arif bought his firm, flew to New York in July 2014 to find American buyers for their stakes in Abraaj's funds. They met executives from Hamilton Lane, an asset-management firm that oversaw billions of dollars. Hamilton Lane's clients included pension funds that managed money on behalf of teachers, nurses, police, musicians, and other workers. Arif boasted to the Hamilton Lane executives about Abraaj's high profits and low losses but said nothing about the cash crunch.

Hamilton Lane employed dozens of analysts to determine for its clients whether the claims made by private equity executives like Arif were as good as they said. Arif impressed Chief Investment Officer Erik Hirsch and other senior executives at the firm. They believed his success story and agreed to invest $150 million on behalf of their clients. In return, Hamilton Lane and its clients got stakes in five Abraaj funds, including Abraaj Private Equity Fund IV, which Arif was plundering.

The $150 million cash infusion from Hamilton Lane wasn't enough to solve all Arif's problems but it enabled his spending spree to continue and bought time for Arif and Fayeeza to prepare a fabulous wedding in Rome for their oldest son, Ahsan.

The August 2014 wedding party was a celebration of the Naqvi dynasty in all its power and splendor. Hundreds of invitations were dispatched, and Queen Rania of Jordan accepted. Arif's most important business contacts were invited, including Kito de Boer from McKinsey, the billionaire education entrepreneur Sunny Varkey, the Freshfields lawyer Pervez Akhtar, KPMG's Dubai chief, Vijay Malhotra, and the Standard Chartered banker Viswanathan Shankar.

As guests arrived at Rome's airport a concierge service greeted them and whisked them to hotels. In their rooms, guests found hampers from the bride and groom with a detailed itinerary for the coming days.

On the first night, guests attended a reception at the Cinecittà film studios where Charlton Heston made *Ben-Hur* and Audrey Hepburn and Cary Grant starred in *Roman Holiday*. They dined on an extravagant barbeque as puppeteers and scantily clad female dancers entertained them.

The next day the wedding party lunched in a picturesque Roman piazza. After coffee they boarded a fleet of buses which took them to an estate owned by the Fendi family where the bride had her henna tattoos applied—a Pakistani tradition known as mehndi, popular at weddings.

On the third day the wedding ceremony took place at Villa Medici, a colossal palace perched on a wooded hilltop in the city. The old villa was once owned by Florence's Medici banking dynasty, which gained fame in Renaissance times for their great wealth, patronage of the arts, and brutal intrigues. Arif, a modern-day Medici, remained discreetly in the background, allowing his son and future daughter-in-law to take center stage at their wedding.

John Legend played on a grand piano and sang the romantic ballad "All of Me." Guests from dozens of countries wandered through the ornate rooms and marveled at a wall installation made with hundreds of red roses. They admired the bride and groom's delicately embroidered traditional Pakistani wedding garments and, as the sun went down, they chatted by candlelight in warm evening gardens.

Soon after the wedding, Arif put on another ostentatious display of wealth in London when he announced a scholarship program for the Royal College of Art, a college located near his South Kensington apartment. Sajid Javid, a former Deutsche Bank executive who went on to become U.K. finance minister, attended the launch party. While Florence's Medici family had funded the artistic talents of local Italians like Sandro Botticelli and Leonardo da Vinci, Arif spread his patronage far and wide, to India's Sheroy Katila, Kazakhstan's Ermina Takenova, Mexico's Julieta Cortés Garcia, Thailand's Burachat Ratanasuwan, and Turkey's Derya Adiyaman.

. . .

Attending grand conferences with billionaires, hosting magnificent parties, and bankrolling artists were all elements of a beautiful illusion of success which obscured the cash crunch at Abraaj. In September 2014, Professor Jeffrey Garten of Yale University unwittingly lent a hand when he interviewed Arif in a video posted online. Associating with Western academics like Garten and Harvard's Lerner did wonders to cover up Arif's problems.

"It's a very special thing for us to have someone who is so accomplished," Professor Garten told Arif in the interview.

Garten's career spanned politics, finance, and academia. He had served as dean of Yale's School of Management and worked at Lehman Brothers and Blackstone, and for President Bill Clinton. Arif was in a combative mood for the interview. He bragged about Abraaj's world-class returns and easy access to funding.

"Do I find that we have an issue with capital or raising capital to help finance our businesses?" Arif told Garten. "I have to say no."

"You are operating in emerging markets around the world," Garten said.

"Global growth markets," Arif corrected him. "We don't call them emerging markets."

"Oh yes. OK. Global growth markets," the professor replied.

"China has emerged. India has emerged," Arif said. "These are some very, very large economies that we are talking about, and the future of the global economic system is actually inextricably linked to how these countries develop and progress."

Garten gently pushed back with a question about the risks associated with investing in the markets where Arif was most active.

"If we could just focus for a second on the Middle East, Persian Gulf, North Africa dimension, because this is something that so few American firms really focus on," Garten said. "Give us a sense of what kind of opportunities and also what kind of challenges exist in a region of the world which some people have had great hopes for but where a lot of those hopes seem to be embroiled now in a level of uncertainty and political risk that makes it look extremely risky."

Arif dodged the question by turning the tables on the professor. Surely Western countries were far riskier than people assumed, Arif said. Didn't the global financial crisis of 2008 start in New York, the center of the capitalist West, with the collapse of Lehman Brothers, the investment bank where Garten had worked?

"Guess what?" Arif said. "When risk came into the global financial system, it came at the heart of global capitalism. It came on Wall Street, right?

"That level of risk practically gave us a cataclysmic heart attack to the global financial system. And what did we do to address it and fix it? Nothing. Have we attached risk premiums to investing in the biggest names on Wall Street? No, we haven't.

"And that is why for me it doesn't matter whether you are investing in the West or you are investing in global growth markets. The quality of the investor—the nature of the internal systems and processes—should actually take precedence over the riskiness of an inherent opportunity."

Garten carefully summarized what he had heard.

"You feel too much burden is being put on quantitative models and too little on the judgment that comes with experience and personal values?" Garten asked. "Is that what you are saying?"

"I think you said it far better than me," Arif cheerily responded.

Arif changed the pace of his argument by softening his tone and skillfully changing tack to make a positive case for the Middle East. Perhaps mindful of the professor's Jewish heritage, Arif stressed commonalities among the Middle East's three main religions.

"The region is home to three of the oldest religions and oldest civilizations on the planet, which are Christianity, Islam, and Judaism, and effectively we are cousins," Arif said with a smile.

Garten asked why investors should give their money to Abraaj. What were the reasons to believe the Middle East had a promising economic future when there was such a flow of negative news headlines from the region?

Arif talked enthusiastically about the Middle East's youthful population, its expanding cities, and an emerging middle class of consumers.

"To hear you describe this, you could actually be talking about a country like China," Garten said, seemingly surprising himself with his own analogy.

Everything was to play for, Arif agreed. There were social and education problems in the Middle East but positive change was coming fast. New businesses and entrepreneurs were starting all the time.

"If we can start addressing global inequality, if we can start providing healthcare and education and the sorts of things that we take for granted in one part of the world across the planet, then we are going to see less and less issues that lead to conflict.

"Now how are we going to get there?" Arif asked. "One way could be to pour large amounts of developmental aid into solving the world's problems. Another way is to enable the free market to operate."

But it had to be a free market of companies with hearts big enough to address the root cause of conflict, which was inequality, Arif said. Abraaj had such a heart, he said, and American and European companies should follow his example.

"If businesses in the West and in established financial markets can start embracing the policies that I am talking about, and we start investing into those markets in a more empathetic manner, then I think that business can lead the way towards a future that is far more prosperous," he said.

Arif compared Western attitudes about business being just about profit to old-fashioned ideas about religion.

"Look at the things that don't shift in our world, such as the Bible, such as the Koran, books that are written and we take for granted. The idea is not to continue to interpret them in line with the times in which they were written," Arif said. "The idea is to interpret them in line with modern society."

"Well said," the professor said.

And with that remark, Arif had won the public approval of the professor and masterfully masked the problems at Abraaj.

His job was done.

• • •

Arif seemingly had the reins of destiny firmly in his grasp as more international organizations sought associations with him. His status as a trusted insider of the global elite was sealed in November 2014 when he joined the board of the fundraising foundation of Interpol, the global police agency tasked with protecting society from criminals. He was granted a special Interpol passport.

Interpol plugged Arif into an immensely powerful network. Prince Albert of Monaco, the chairman of the Interpol Foundation, gave Arif responsibility for a special program to protect banks, airlines, and hotels from fraud. Arif sat on the board of the foundation alongside the chief executive of HSBC, one of the world's biggest banks, and Carlos Ghosn, who led Renault-Nissan, one of the biggest car makers. Ghosn was later arrested in Japan for financial crimes. To avoid trial, Ghosn hired a team of private security experts in 2019 who smuggled him out of Japan in a large black box and flew him to Lebanon, where he owned a mansion.

Arif's position at the Interpol Foundation enabled him to hide in plain sight. When Interpol's secretary general, Jürgen Stock, attended one of Arif's investor conferences in Dubai he described the important crime-fighting work that Arif was assisting with.

"I've never seen such a complex situation as of now, today," Stock said at the Abraaj conference. "It's organized crime taking benefit from globalization."

Arif's association with Interpol reassured bankers, politicians, and billionaires about his reliability. When one investor asked Arif how he navigated corruption risks in developing countries, Arif said that with just two telephone calls he could find out anything about anyone anywhere in the world through his Interpol connections.

Arif often told people that he was on the board of Interpol, rather than the Interpol Foundation, and used his position to intimidate others. One day all hell broke loose at Abraaj when a new female employee missed a telephone call from Arif. He summoned the employee to his office that evening. When she showed up, he told her that he was a powerful man to cross because he was on the board of Interpol and that people bowed to him at airports because his Interpol passport could get him anywhere.

"You don't want me as an enemy in this world. You want me as a friend," Arif said, according to the employee, who said, "I went home that night and I was absolutely petrified."

．　．　．

American billionaires invited Arif to their gatherings with greater frequency. When the financial media mogul and former New York mayor Michael Bloomberg hosted a conference in Dubai in 2015 to discuss how to improve the management of cities, Arif attended to sing the praises of the city-state where Abraaj was based.

David Bonderman, founder of the private equity giant TPG, part-nered with Arif on a deal that same year. TPG and Abraaj bought a Saudi restaurant chain called Kudu. The deal proved Arif's growing ability to draw Western capitalists into the Middle East.

But as Arif moved ever closer to the orbit of plutocrats, he found he needed even greater quantities of cash to fuel his lifestyle, and by May 2015 the hole in Abraaj's finances had widened to $219 million. To conceal the deficit, Arif and his team started to systematically sweep all the available cash from Abraaj's funds, companies, and bank loans into a secret set of bank accounts that investigators later named the Abraajery.

By mixing up investor money from different funds in the Abraa-jery, Arif was committing a cardinal sin in the asset-management in-dustry. He was also breaking the law. Abraaj was supposed to buy companies on behalf of the investors in its funds, and when Abraaj sold those companies it was supposed to promptly return the profits to the investors. But that's not what always happened at Abraaj.

Abraaj owned a company called Integrated Diagnostics Hold-ings, or IDH, which operated a chain of medical-testing clinics in Egypt. In May 2015, Abraaj sold its shares in IDH in an initial pub-lic offering on the London Stock Exchange. IDH was a genuine suc-cess story. Under Abraaj's ownership IDH had survived the chaos of the Arab Spring and more than doubled the size of its network of clinics.

Abraaj invested in IDH using money from its $2 billion Infrastructure and Growth Capital Fund, so the profit from the IDH share sale should have been immediately returned to investors in that fund. Instead, Arif kept $154 million of the proceeds of the share sale to spend as he saw fit and deprived his investors of their gain.

Arif could have taken a pay cut to ease the financial pressure on Abraaj but this was never really an option for him, even as the cash crunch worsened. Arif paid himself $53.75 million in 2015, a sum it would take a Pakistani on the country's average wage more than 40,000 years to earn. The pay didn't include the millions of dollars Arif was secretly siphoning from Abraaj into his personal bank accounts.

While the cash crunch worsened, Arif began negotiating to trade in his superyacht, *Raasta*, for a new model costing more than $40 million. Arif had bought *Raasta* secondhand and renamed it with an Urdu word meaning the path, or the way. With its three decks, jacuzzi surrounded by sun pads, a bar, and five bedrooms, *Raasta* transported Arif and his guests in luxury across the Mediterranean Sea, to Corsica, Naples, Capri, and to Monaco for the Grand Prix.

The boatyard Arif approached was reluctant to take old boats as part payment for new ones but started negotiations anyway, and a salesman was dispatched to meet Arif on board *Raasta* in early 2014. Later that year, Arif was still trying to drive down the price of the new luxury yacht when he summoned executives from the boat company to his home in Dubai. The salesman, accompanied by the chief executive and two others, flew thousands of miles to meet Arif but during the meeting Arif declared that a rival boatyard would match their price. The bemused executives had expected to close a deal but left Dubai empty-handed.

Bargaining continued into 2015, when Arif called the yacht salesman to a meeting in a New York apartment. When the salesman arrived, he found Arif with his two sons and daughter-in-law. The salesman was weary of the endless price negotiations but sat down at a table opposite Arif, who promptly demanded a further price cut. The salesman had had enough. He had made it clear that he wouldn't go any lower. He got the impression that Arif was enjoying the negotiation and showing off to his sons. The salesman usually got on well with his super-rich clients because, smart as they were, they considered building a boat for family and friends a pleasant activity, not a locking of horns and a battle to prove who was the best dealmaker. The salesman got up from the table and called his chief executive.

"If it's all right with you I'm afraid I am just going to close my papers and walk out of here because I think we're wasting our time," the salesman said.

His boss agreed, and he returned to the negotiating table.

"I am sorry, Mr. Naqvi, if this is the approach you want to take, we're out," he said. With that he folded his papers, stood up and wished Arif a good morning.

The negotiations for a new yacht ended in June 2015, around the time an Abraaj executive emailed Arif to say the firm was facing a cash shortfall of $168 million. Abraaj was insolvent and lacked the legitimate income it needed to cover the most basic business expenses, such as employee salaries, rent, and electricity bills. But the crisis didn't seem to faze Arif. That same month, Fayeeza traveled to Paris with her sons and daughter-in-law to pick up a prestigious philanthropy award. BNP Paribas, France's biggest bank, announced the prize via Twitter.

Congrats to 2015 BNP Paribas Philanthropy Grand Prize: Fayeeza & Arif Naqvi, founders of @Aman_Foundation #GivingBack #Healthcare #Education.

The bank congratulated the Naqvi family and their Aman Foundation for operating a fleet of ambulances in Karachi and organizing health, education, and job-training projects throughout Pakistan. Fayeeza said the Aman Foundation represented her life's work.

"I feel very, very satisfied and humbled, actually, when I have friends come up and say, 'Well, you know, your ambulance saved my father's live, my mother's life, my child's life,'" she said.

The giving wasn't as generous as the Naqvi family made out, because Arif's personal finances were hopelessly entangled with Abraaj and he was constantly using company money to pay his expenses. Rafique asked Arif for permission to take money from Abraaj investors for the Aman Foundation.

"Can I pay this from Abraaj?" Rafique asked in an email.

"Thank you," Arif replied.

CHAPTER 11

DREAM WEAVERS

"In no other hall, from no other platform, can a world leader speak to all humanity. And for decades, that is precisely what world leaders have done. Kings and queens, presidents, prime ministers, and popes."

United Nations Secretary General Ban Ki-moon welcomed world political leaders to the cavernous General Assembly Hall in New York in September 2015. Heads of government and diplomats from 195 nations were gathered before him.

It was a historic meeting because Ban, after working for years on an ambitious plan to fix humanity's problems, was ready to share his new vision. He had sought the advice of people from all walks of life. Arif, a member of the UN Global Compact, had advised Ban that more private equity investment was needed in developing countries to create jobs and improved services.

Ban announced seventeen sustainable development goals to eradicate poverty in all its forms by 2030. The goals included ending hunger and providing clean water, renewable energy, quality education, and healthcare to every one of the billions of people living on earth.

"The people of the world have asked us to shine a light on a future of promise and opportunity," Ban said. "The new agenda is a promise by leaders to all people everywhere. It is a universal, integrated, and transformative vision for a better world."

UN plans usually involved governments working together but Ban made clear that his seventeen goals required the help of companies, too. The goals needed trillions of dollars of investment, and there was a $2.5 trillion annual shortfall which governments alone couldn't provide. The gap had to be filled with money from companies and investors in global financial markets. Ending poverty was going to be possible only if capitalists like Arif helped.

Ban appealed to spiritual leaders for help too. He had invited Pope Francis to the UN meeting to endorse his sustainable development goals.

"Your Holiness, welcome to the pulpit of the world," Ban said as he introduced the pope to the politicians. "We are here to listen."

It was only the fifth time a pope had visited the UN in seventy years. The UN plan to end poverty chimed perfectly with Pope Francis's own convictions. His cardinals were already exploring how they could make impact investments to do good. The Argentinian pope wanted to renew the Catholic Church by placing the poor at the center of his papacy. His church was scarred from centuries of financial scandals—from relatively recent intrigues such as one that left a dead banker hanging under a bridge in London, to the medieval sale of indulgences, when cardinals forgave sins in exchange for money.

Pope Francis adjusted his spectacles as he stood at a green marble lectern and spoke to the world leaders in his native Spanish. Interpreters provided live translations in Arabic, Chinese, English, French, and Russian. He said that the sustainable-development goals were a sign of hope and that financial institutions had an important role to play in the development of all countries.

The pope also gave a warning.

"A selfish and boundless thirst for power and material prosperity" was damaging the global economy and the environment, he said. If people weren't motivated by genuine concern for the well-being of others, the pursuit of improved living standards was an illusion or, worse, idle chatter which covered up all kinds of abuse and corruption, he said.

"I assure you of my support and my prayers," Pope Francis concluded. "God bless you all."

The hall rose in thunderous applause.

For Arif, the UN's and the pope's embrace of business as a tool to end poverty was the potential mother lode. He had been positioning himself for years as a man on a mission to end poverty through capitalism. Now politicians were proposing to improve humanity with a plan that put companies at the center. And arguably the world's most important spiritual leader had given his blessing. Arif's evangelical quest to bring private equity to the poorest countries was going mainstream. He was doing God's work.

Abraaj was perfectly placed to be the channel for collecting and investing the money needed to achieve the UN goals. The firm owned schools, hospitals, food producers, and energy providers in some of the poorest countries. Arif claimed that his ownership of these companies made him an expert in how to achieve the sustainable-development goals, known as SDGs for short. With backing from governments and institutions like the UN and the Catholic Church, he'd buy and build hundreds more companies to do good and make himself and investors big profits, too.

"Some of you may think I am being completely crazy by suggesting that two hundred and ninety trillion dollars in global assets is going to go and meet these SDG requirements," Arif told politicians and investors. "The fallacy is that people make this mistake continuously— that there is some sort of choice to be made between investing to help the world and investing in a regular way and making profits. That's a complete and utter misconception, because you can do both and you can do them effectively."

"So many of us are failing to receive the most basic needs that we should expect in today's world," Arif said. "Our economic model today around the world is deeply flawed. This goes without question. Inequalities are growing rather than narrowing. And we may have come a long way towards overcoming extreme poverty but we cannot deny that one out of ten people on this planet survive on less than two dollars a day. That's massive."

Arif's network of powerful contacts made him an influential messenger of change. There were few degrees of separation between him and most world leaders. For example, the Abraaj executive Wahid Hamid attended the birthday celebration of his college friend Barack Obama around the time of the UN meeting. The Abraaj executive Tarek Kabil was appointed Egyptian minister of trade and industry soon after.

Adulatory media coverage propelled Arif to greater prominence. *Forbes* published a glowing profile in the fall of 2015 titled "The Story Behind Abraaj Group's Stunning Rise in Global Private Equity." The journalist, Elizabeth MacBride, described Arif as speaking in elegant, Pakistani-accented English in an interview with her at his Madison Avenue office.

"Abraaj is the undisputed private equity king of investing in the seemingly dangerous markets of Asia, Africa and Latin America. There is no shortage of big investors wanting to get into its newest funds," MacBride wrote. She had previously written for CNBC and the *Washington Post* and had interviewed prominent leaders including Tony Blair, the former British prime minister.

Abraaj had a track record to kill for, generating 17 percent annual returns in places where the rule of law often came into question, she wrote.

"We have taken the risk out of investing in what the West mistakenly calls emerging markets," Arif told her. "They're growth markets."

Endorsements of Abraaj from Arif's friends and investors burnished the article.

"I view them as having more depth and breadth [in emerging markets] than the bigger players," said Jin-Yong Cai, head of the World Bank's International Finance Corp. unit. The IFC committed more than $350 million to Abraaj funds and deals including Karachi Electric.

Harvard's Josh Lerner praised his paymaster, hailing Arif as a visionary.

"Arif was a decade-plus ahead in terms of really understanding the potential for investors in private, family-owned companies in fast-growing markets," he said.

Hamilton Lane's Erik Hirsch endorsed Abraaj.

"They've been delivering exactly what we wanted," he said in the article.

Abraaj relied on its wide network of offices and trained staff to avoid corruption, MacBride wrote.

"I have out there a man who runs our Colombia business. I have another colleague who runs our Indonesian business," Arif said in the article. "A guy could come to them and say, 'This is a fantastic deal. You can make $200 million,' or whatever. And they would look at him and say, 'No, thank you,' because they know the guy who runs it is a crook."

The *Forbes* article gave details of Arif's charitable work and explained his motive for signing Bill Gates and Warren Buffett's Giving Pledge, a commitment to give away millions or billions of dollars.

"One of the pillars of what I consider success is when I change the narrative of what people hear about Muslims," Arif said. "Unless people like me stand up and change the narrative, it's not going to change."

Arif's noble rhetoric made him sound like of one of humanity's most enlightened benefactors. What he never said in public was that in return for its efforts, Abraaj charged a 2 percent annual fee on the funds it managed and kept 20 percent of the profits, in accordance with the tried-and-tested rules of the private equity industry. And, of course, there was no mention of looting investor funds.

In public Arif lined up with politicians to inspire people with speeches that wove a dreamlike vision of the future. In private he stole and plotted bribery, even as the pope warned that idle chatter about improving lives could be a cloak for corruption.

Arif's big spending was forcing the firm ever deeper into insolvency. Abraaj was on course to lose $100 million in 2015 alone, so Arif needed to find more money—and fast—to avoid a humiliating bankruptcy. While the UN was meeting in New York, Abraaj sent an email to investors in one of its funds to request that $238.5 million be paid into an Abraaj bank account within two weeks. The firm said the money was needed to finance new deals. Hamilton Lane, Bank of America, and other investors sent the money as requested. But after the millions entered an Abraaj bank account, instead of being used to buy businesses as promised, Arif and Rafique diverted $95 million of it into one of the secret Abraajery bank accounts to spend on other purposes.

Some of the money was used to pay salaries and $50 million was used to replace money missing in other Abraaj funds. Some money was used to pay investors who were still waiting for the proceeds from the sale of shares in IDH, the Egyptian medical company. A $5.4 million slice went to Arif via a mysterious Cayman Islands company he owned called Silverline.

. . .

To raise more, desperately needed cash Arif decided to sell his biggest and most high-profile asset, Karachi Electric. A successful sale of the power company could generate hundreds of millions of dollars.

The *Forbes* article reassured readers that Arif didn't pay bribes, but while the article was being prepared for publication and as the UN meeting to end poverty was taking place in New York, Arif was working on how to bribe the prime minister of Pakistan. The Pakistani government still owned a quarter of Karachi Electric and its approval was required for a sale of the company to go through. Arif needed the support of Pakistan's then prime minister, Nawaz Sharif, and his influential brother Shehbaz. He asked the Pakistani businessman Navaid Malik, who was close to the Sharif brothers, how to gain their favor.

Arif formally hired the American investment bank Citigroup to find a buyer for Karachi Electric. It would take a brave purchaser to acquire the electricity company, for although its performance had improved significantly during Abraaj's ownership, with profits rising and many customers no longer experiencing regular blackouts, there were still enough problems to scare off most companies. In the summer of 2015 a devastating heat wave struck Karachi and a thousand people died as temperatures soared above 104 degrees Fahrenheit. Poor and elderly people were the worst affected. Protests broke out across the port city again and politicians attacked the company in the media. Tehreek-e-Taliban Pakistan, the Pakistani Taliban, accused Karachi Electric of causing the deadly power outages and of profiting at the expense of citizens. Karachi Electric was still owed millions of dollars by the city's government-owned water company. And Karachi Electric in turn owed millions more to government-owned gas companies.

Tabish, the Abraaj executive who transformed Karachi Electric's fortunes, had quit, so Arif appointed Omar Lodhi to oversee the sale of the company. A graduate of the London School of Economics and Harvard Business School, Omar had worked at Abraaj for almost a decade. He was an experienced dealmaker with a fondness for cigars and silk shirts. He was well connected—his brother led Citigroup in Pakistan. Omar could be fiercely confrontational in meetings but one thing no one questioned was his loyalty to Arif. His devotion earned him the nickname "Mini-Arif." "My DNA is Abraaj DNA," he told a journalist.

The task of selling Karachi Electric was inevitably political because business and politics in Pakistan were closely entwined. Prime Minister Nawaz Sharif was from a family of wealthy industrialists based in Lahore, the capital of Punjab, Pakistan's most populous province. The prime minister's brother Shehbaz was chief minister of the Punjab.

To make the politics of the Karachi Electric sale even more sensitive, Arif and Omar realized that the most likely bidders were Chinese state-owned companies. This made it even more important to secure the cooperation of the prime minister. A takeover by a company owned by another country was always a delicate matter because it risked giving away influence in internal affairs.

To gain the support of the Sharif brothers, Arif put Navaid Malik, the middleman, on Abraaj's payroll and backdated his pay to the beginning of 2015. Omar met Navaid to discuss how to proceed. After they met, Omar wrote Arif an email to pass on what Navaid had said about the Sharifs.

"The brothers had given him clearance to work with us but had told him that any appointment with us should not explicitly reference Pakistan (I.e. should be silent on that)," Omar wrote in an October 2015 email.

Omar referred to Nawaz and Shehbaz Sharif by their initials, NS and SS.

> On KE mandate: He has spoken to SS who has given blessings but he now needs to get NS' as well. On the role itself he said that SS was not keen on calling individual CEO's of potential Chinese buyers but was willing to give a strong endorsement if in turn contacted by them. He was also willing to make calls to people like the Chinese ambassador etc. and endorse and recommend KE.
>
> SS was going to China in Jan and NS would be going in Feb. Hence he would like to start preparation from now in terms of reviewing collateral that they could take on the trip as well as receiving names from us on potential buyers.

Omar said he had told Navaid, the middleman, that it was important to sign an agreement about money.

"He said he was aware of the economics and would revert to me as he still needed NS' sign off on this," Omar wrote to Arif. "HE said it was important for him to share every detail with the brothers and get their blessings as well as their instructions as to how this money should be distributed (e.g. A portion to charity OR a portion to the election fund kitty etc etc)."

. . .

Arif was still spending with a compulsive extravagance. He treated hundreds of Abraaj employees to a big town hall gathering in 2015 in the Park Hyatt Dubai, a hotel overlooking Dubai Creek. Egyptian American comedian Ahmed Ahmed gave a private performance in the palatial ballroom and Arif invited friends from the Young Presidents' Organization to give motivational talks. For one new employee who was drawn to Abraaj by the prospect of making investments that would help poor people, the culture was bizarre.

"An annual meeting at Abraaj was minimum three hundred people all flying in to Dubai from all over the world. All day from eight a.m. to eight p.m. we were bombarded with lectures and talks," the employee said. "But in the evening, everybody was getting completely shit-faced and partying hard. It was a finance culture, but a finance culture in overdrive."

Alcohol flowed like water, and many employees felt pressure to stay up late and keep drinking until Arif left the party.

"There was the feeling that if you leave to go to bed, he will see you and hold it against you," the employee said.

Paying for the parties required siphoning more money from funds and investments.

In November 2015, Abraaj agreed to sell Network International, a UAE-based company that provided digital payment services across the Middle East and Africa. Abraaj and its investors stood to earn $330 million from the sale. On the face of it, the profitable sale of Network International to two large American private equity firms was a great success, validating Arif's theory that the center of gravity in the world economy was shifting toward developing countries. But Arif secretly held on to millions of dollars generated by the sale which should have been promptly returned to Abraaj's investors. He had his reasons. One was a looming financial deadline that he had to meet.

The buyers of Network International sent an initial $135 million payment to the bank account of Abraaj Private Equity Fund IV, the fund that had owned Network International, on December 30, 2015. The money should then have been sent on to the investors in the fund. But on the day the money arrived in the Abraaj fund's bank account, Arif and Rafique moved the entire amount into one of their secret bank accounts. Then they moved $92 million from there to fill a hole in the Infrastructure and Growth Capital Fund, which they had plundered to pay salaries, rent, and expenses.

They urgently needed to restore money to the Infrastructure and Growth Capital Fund because KPMG, the global accounting firm, was due to audit the fund's annual accounts for 2015. If KPMG discovered money was missing from the fund, then the theft would be exposed. To pass the audit, Abraaj had to show KPMG that the correct amount of money was in the $2 billion fund by New Year's Eve of 2015. The hole in the fund was filled just in time.

KPMG audited the fund and gave it a clean bill of health on the grounds that the correct amount of money was in the fund at the end of the year. But if KPMG had looked at a single bank statement for the fund or checked the account's balance a few days earlier in December 2015 they could have seen that money was missing from the fund, and the game might have been up.

The ties between KPMG and Abraaj were very close. KPMG had worked for Abraaj for years. Vijay Malhotra, the head of KPMG in Dubai, was a close friend of Arif, and his son had worked at Abraaj.

Having fooled the accountants, Arif sent financial reports bearing KPMG's seal of approval to investors in the Infrastructure and Growth Capital Fund. If one of the world's largest auditors couldn't detect wrongdoing at Abraaj it was unlikely investors could either.

Taking money from one private equity fund to benefit investors in another fund amounted to a crude kind of fraud known as a Ponzi scheme. This kind of fraud was named after Charles Ponzi, an Italian-born swindler active in the United States in the 1920s who used money from new investors to pay off earlier investors. Ponzi schemes like the one operated by the American fund manager Bernard Madoff can go undetected for years and usually come to light during an economic downturn, when investors ask for their money back and the fraudster can't raise funds from new investors to pay them off.

Arif and his team transferred money repeatedly between different Abraaj funds and their investors. In doing so they turned the company's already complex finances into the tangled stuff of an accountant's nightmare.

. . .

Arif was still reluctant to cut back on his own expenses and stayed at London's five-star Ritz hotel on a trip to the city in early 2016. The hotel, down Dover Street from Abraaj's Mayfair office, sent a bill for thousands of pounds to Abraaj's Dubai headquarters. An Abraaj employee thought the hotel might have made a mistake because the amount was so high, but then the employee saw that Arif had booked suites for himself and for Ghizlan, his former secretary.

Soon after, Arif visited Milan, where he stayed at a luxury hotel. Days later, a box containing an elegant pair of ladies' shoes arrived at Abraaj's Dubai headquarters from the hotel. One of Arif's loyal butlers assumed that the shoes belonged to Arif's wife, Fayeeza, and was going to send them to her at the Naqvis' Emirates Hills mansion. But another employee noticed that the shoebox had Ghizlan's name on it and intercepted it before it left the office. This employee placed the shoes in Arif's office, thinking his boss would be grateful, but Arif frowned and was silent when he found them.

. . .

The strain of managing Abraaj was starting to take its toll on Arif and his temper was increasingly out of control. One afternoon in Dubai in early 2016, Arif called Mustafa, Sev, and a few other senior executives for a meeting in Abraaj's boardroom. The discussion was supposed to be an open and frank exchange among professionals. As Arif talked, Mustafa politely interjected to clarify a detail that he thought was important.

Arif exploded with rage.

"How dare you interrupt," he said.

"Sorry," Mustafa replied.

"If it's so important, let's listen," Arif said.

Arif paced up and down the long boardroom table until Mustafa had said what he had to say.

"Have you finished?" Arif asked.

"Yes," Mustafa replied.

"Was it nice to have the courtesy to speak without someone interrupting you?" Arif said.

"Yes," Mustafa replied.

"Don't you ever interrupt me again," Arif said, smoldering with fury.

A witness to the scene was shocked. Mustafa was a popular and respected executive but Arif had cut him down for a trifling reason. The tirade froze the atmosphere in the room, preventing others from talking or asking questions because they feared how Arif would react. The witness had an idea why executives tolerated Arif's behavior: they were handsomely paid.

Perhaps the increasingly frequent flashes of anger were due to the fact that Abraaj's debts were growing faster than Arif's ability to find money to pay them. The constant proximity to the edge of a financial precipice was certainly fueling intense bouts of anxiety in Rafique, Arif's trusted cash manager. Abraaj needed $297 million by the end of March 2016 to pay bills and make investments that had been agreed. The investments included Big Basket, an Indian online grocery delivery company.

"We will not have funds in March to meet various day to day obligations in the absence of any receipts," Rafique wrote to Arif, Waqar, and Mustafa in February 2016.

To Rafique's relief, a few days later a second installment of $195 million from the sale of Network International arrived in an Abraaj bank account. Instead of returning the money to investors in the fund that owned Network International, Rafique transferred cash to another fund to pay for new investments to which they had agreed.

Days later, Abraaj received $185 million from the sale of another company, the Moroccan insurer Saham Finances. Again, instead of returning this profit to investors, half of the money was transferred to a secret bank account and used for other purposes.

Around this time, another payment was made to Silverline, Arif's company in the Cayman Islands.

In total, the sales of Network International and Saham reaped $515 million for Abraaj and its investors. But $219 million was transferred to the secret bank accounts, according to an internal document that Rafique shared with Arif, Mustafa, and Waqar.

As money from the sales of Network International and Saham was being siphoned off, Arif touched down in a plane on the scorching runway of Hamad International Airport in Doha, the capital of Qatar, one of the world's richest countries. He was visiting Her Excellency Sheikha Hanadi bint Nasser Al Thani, a member of Qatar's fabulously wealthy ruling family. She had invited Arif to a board meeting of the Pearl Initiative, the organization created to improve the governance and transparency of Middle Eastern companies.

The Pearl Initiative's board was a who's who of Middle Eastern business executives. Many had links to Arif, including the Abraaj investor and onetime director Hamid Jafar; a partner at KPMG; and the chief executive of the Bank of Sharjah, one of Abraaj's main lenders. Sheikha Hanadi was herself the founder of a finance company in which Abraaj had invested in the early days.

The board members gathered for a morning meeting and lunched with Qatari executives and royals. Sheikha Hanadi told Arif and the other Pearl Initiative members that they were leading by example to ensure that accountability and transparency became top priorities at Middle Eastern companies.

A few days after the meeting, Arif got a nasty surprise that undercut the spirit of the Pearl Initiative. It came in the form of a question. A New York–based investor noticed that it hadn't received any money from the sales of Network International and Saham. The investor sent Arif an email on March 17, 2016, asking when it would be paid.

Arif forwarded the email to Mustafa and Rafique.

"I think we should start paying selectively to ward off noise," Arif said.

On April 1, 2016—a day for elaborate pranks known as April Fools' Day in some countries—Arif hatched a plan to prevent investors discovering money had been stolen. Abraaj would stagger payments to investors over months based on two criteria—first, the likelihood of the investor noticing that it was owed money, and second, whether the investor was likely to invest in Abraaj funds ever again. Arif wasn't joking. He sent a payment schedule to Rafique and Mustafa. "Noise makers and those that will come back" were ranked at the top of the list. "Legacy investors and passive voices" were at the bottom.

"Will need to be managed quietly internally, and will probably have to have a small team comprising those here, [and others,] with everything tightly controlled and nobody outside the loop knowing what is going on.

"As far as the rest of the Firm is concerned, all payments have been made.

"Idea is to get up to date immediately with the first lot, then payments at end of April, May, June. Do I have the allocation correct?" Arif wrote.

Mustafa didn't immediately respond so Arif emailed him again.

"Focus on this," Arif said.

"Been following the trail and will do as it says but very difficult to keep it tight," Mustafa replied. "No choice though. We have to do it."

Arif asked if the payment schedule made sense.

"Seems ok," Mustafa replied. "But the more we narrow the gap between first and last the less the chance of noise."

They agreed to go ahead with the plan. Arif replied to the New

York investor on April 4, 2016, almost three weeks after he received the question from the investor about when it would be paid.

"April 15 latest; hence imminent," Arif wrote. "Cash all pretty much in, doing final tax and corporate sign offs."

Abraaj sent some money to some investors in April 2016. The rest—the legacy investors and passive voices—were left unpaid and in the dark. The bet that some investors wouldn't notice that their money was missing was risky, but it seemed to have paid off. With the problem solved for the time being, Arif continued his global travels and received a rapturous welcome wherever he went.

"He perhaps needs no introduction," Maria Kozloski, a senior executive at the World Bank's International Finance Corp. unit, said at a May 2016 conference in Washington. "He is a strong partner for IFC. Let me introduce now the group executive and CEO of the Abraaj Group, Arif Naqvi."

To applause, Arif strode on stage. He looked confident in his customary navy-blue suit and tie as he paced the stage with his hands stuck jauntily into his pockets. Speaking without notes, he delivered a bullish defense of emerging markets.

"There is going to be a tectonic shift in the way in which we look at business," he said. "A billion people are going to be moving into the consuming middle classes in the next decade, most of them in growth markets.

"The Procter and Gambles, the Unilevers, the Nestlés, the Coca-Colas, and the Kimberly-Clarks of the world have picked this fact up.

"I certainly hope to make the most of it and make the world a better place. I hope all of you do too."

He walked off stage with a new email from Rafique in his inbox. Rafique wanted permission to take $47 million more from an Abraaj fund to pay expenses.

"Could you please approve transfer," Rafique asked.

Arif consented to the plundering but still it wasn't enough because a serious problem was fast approaching. In a few weeks, on June 30, 2016, KPMG was due to audit the $1.6 billion Abraaj Private Equity

Fund IV, which Arif had been continuously raiding. The fund had to be full of money by the end of June but $194 million was missing.

"Don't see any other inflows," Waqar wrote to Arif. "This must be on your mind."

Arif turned to friends in a very unusual place to overcome this predicament. He was a board member at Air Arabia, the low-cost airline, and he asked the company's management team to lend him $195 million. Amazingly, they agreed.

Abraaj received the Air Arabia loan on June 22, 2016, and Arif used it to fill Fund IV with money. This enabled him to give the impression to KPMG and investors that no money was missing from the fund. On July 5, 2016—a few days after the audit took place—the loan was repaid to Air Arabia, emptying the fund once more. Abraaj paid Air Arabia a $4.9 million fee to borrow the money for thirteen days.

Meanwhile, more investors were starting to notice that they were owed money from the sales of Network International and Saham and were becoming disgruntled. Arif and his team drew up a new color-coded payment schedule ranking investors based on the noisiness of their complaints. Mustafa said it would be better to commit to payment dates that they could realistically stick to.

"Better to have a date we can meet even if stretched out than to delay again," Mustafa wrote to Arif.

"Yes, Professor," Arif replied. "While you are at it, it would be nice if you could pitch in and help with the various crises we have been dealing with non-stop."

CHAPTER 12

HEALTHY LIVES

Bill and Melinda Gates went to Africa for the first time in 1993 on an extravagant safari. What startled them most about the continent, according to a story they told, wasn't the wildlife but the poverty.

The tycoon was America's richest man. At thirty-six years old, he was the youngest person ever to hold the title bestowed by *Forbes* magazine. The youthful billionaire had made his fortune co-founding Microsoft, a computer software company that had sparked a revolution in the way humans process information.

Bill and Melinda's African adventure was arranged as a romantic discovery of the origins of man and there was no limit to the budget, according to Joss Kent, the former British army officer who organized the trip. Fine wines were flown in from around the world for the soon-to-be husband and wife to enjoy. A vintage Catalina seaplane was hired and a Canadian firefighting pilot recruited to fly it. The entire party numbered more than a dozen. It included scientists working on the Human Genome Project and Don Johanson, the discoverer of an ancient African skeleton, given the name Lucy, which revealed clues about the origins of human beings. There was also a doctor and, not to forget, a wine expert.

They camped in the Maasai Mara, a vast Kenyan nature reserve famous for the lions, zebras, and elephants roaming its wide savanna plains. They flew to Lake Bukavu in the Democratic Republic of Congo to see the gorillas in Kahuzi Biega National Park.

"It was magical watching Bill coming face-to-face with those gorillas, as he was fascinated by where the brain originated and how to harness computer power to match it," Kent said.

In the evenings they drank and played charades by a campfire. Bill fascinated his entourage with stories about how the internet would change the world.

As they toured Africa, Bill and Melinda met local people who had no access to electricity or running water, let alone computers or the internet.

"The landscape was beautiful, the people were friendly, but the poverty there, which we were seeing for the first time, disturbed us," Bill later explained in a public lecture. "Obviously, we knew parts of Africa were poor, but being on the continent turned what had been an abstraction into an injustice we couldn't ignore."

The African holiday sparked a burning curiosity in Bill and Melinda. Why were there such extremes of inequality in the world? What caused poverty? How big was the problem, and did it really have to be like this? Walking on a beach on the African island of Zanzibar, they resolved to pour billions of dollars into an attempt to end poverty.

It was the beginning of a journey of discovery that led Bill to Arif.

Upon his return to his home city of Seattle, Bill was sucked back into the vortex of managing Microsoft, which was fast becoming the world's most valuable company. Within a few years Microsoft would also become entangled in a massive legal battle with U.S. government investigators who believed it was illegally benefiting from its monopoly status. But Bill's attention kept getting drawn back to Africa and the poverty he was now intimately aware of.

"When we came back, we began reading about what we'd seen. It blew our minds that millions of children in Africa were dying from diarrhea, pneumonia, and malaria," Bill wrote in a letter to his friend and fellow billionaire Warren Buffett. "Kids in rich countries don't die from these things. The children in Africa were dying because they were poor. To us, it was the most unjust thing in the world."

Bill's colossal wealth opened doors to important political leaders around the world. They briefed him and some asked for help in the distant lands where living standards were so different from America. Bill first spoke to Nelson Mandela in 1994, and the South African president and former freedom fighter asked him for funding for his country's first democratic election.

Bill and Melinda's determination to take action to solve poverty was reaffirmed in 1997 when they read an article in the *New York Times*. Under the headline "For Third World, Water Is Still a Deadly Drink," the journalist Nicholas Kristof put health at the center of the global poverty problem. He told the story of Usha Bhagwani, an Indian housemaid who lost a son and a daughter to diarrhea, an easily treatable ailment that was killing three million people each year, almost all of them children. Bill sent the article to one of his most trusted advisers, his father.

"Dad," he wrote. "Maybe we can do something about this."

In 2000, the family started the Bill & Melinda Gates Foundation, the world's largest private charitable organization. A few years later, Warren Buffett, a constant companion to Bill at the top of rich lists, announced he was giving most of his fortune to the Gates Foundation. Bill and Warren also founded the Giving Pledge to encourage other billionaires to give away at least half their wealth.

Healthcare was at the heart of Bill and Melinda's mission.

"Our work is based on the simple idea that every person, no matter where they live, should have the opportunity to lead a healthy and productive life," Bill explained in a lecture in honor of Mandela after the statesman died. "When people aren't healthy, they can't turn their attention to other priorities. But when health improves, life improves by every measure."

In the early days of the foundation, Bill and Melinda pumped billions of dollars into projects to develop vaccines and drugs to eradicate devastating illnesses such as polio, pneumonia, malaria, and

AIDS. But to really get to grips with the problem of poor global health, Bill and Melinda wanted to figure out how to provide basic medical services to billions of poor people living in Africa, Asia, and Latin America.

That's where Arif entered the scene.

• • •

The United Kingdom revolutionized healthcare provision in 1948 when a socialist Labour government founded the National Health Service. Taxpayers funded the NHS so it could provide health services that were free at the point of use to every citizen regardless of their wealth or status. The United States developed a private healthcare system that, supported by many charitable clinics and hospitals, provided services to most citizens.

In poor developing countries, sick or injured people rarely had access to free medicine or functional hospitals. This turned treatable illnesses like pneumonia and diarrhea into killers. For serious accidents or diseases, survival rates were even lower.

Expensive private hospitals were often the only option available in developing countries with vast impoverished populations. These hospitals were usually too costly for people who lived on a few dollars a day to afford and so they focused on serving a small elite of high-ranking government officials, wealthy business executives, and employees of large companies with health insurance.

The experience of a young Indian girl called Jessi illustrated the dangers of growing up in a crowded developing country. She was hit by a bus in the Indian city of Warangal. As Jessi lay on the roadside, her life ebbing away, her parents gathered up her smashed frame into a blanket and took her to the nearest hospital. They were turned away because they were too poor to pay. Desperate, they rushed to the next care provider, where doctors again refused to treat their daughter. The problem was the same: no money, no treatment, they were told.

Eventually the parents arrived at a center run by Care Hospitals, a private healthcare company, which accepted their child. Despite Jessi's complex injuries, which included a shattered pelvis, a team of doctors immediately began treatment. The doctors saved her life, and two months later she was learning to walk.

Jessi was one of the lucky ones.

· · ·

Bill and Melinda Gates weren't alone in trying to find solutions to healthcare provision in developing countries. Dozens of charities and international organizations such as the UN and World Bank were working on how to improve services.

At the World Bank's International Finance Corp. unit in Washington, Scott Featherston and Emmett Moriarty were working on the problem. The mission of the IFC, the private-sector arm of the World Bank, was to provide businesses in poor countries with funding in the belief that this would help reduce poverty and create jobs. Scott, a straight-talking Australian, and his Irish colleague Emmett, were planning the IFC's healthcare strategy. The two had become good friends at work and often socialized together. Over beers in a Washington bar, they debated how they could improve healthcare in Africa. They decided to hire a leading consulting firm to help, but these advisers were expensive. They asked their bosses for permission and were told that they could have some cash if they found another organization prepared to join in. Scott and Emmett asked the Gates Foundation to help. The foundation agreed, and they raised about $2 million to commission McKinsey to carry out two studies.

The first McKinsey report, titled "The Business of Health in Africa," was released publicly. It said that improving healthcare in emerging markets was impossible without the involvement of private companies. Simply improving government hospitals wasn't an option because private-sector healthcare provision was so entrenched in emerging markets.

In a second report that wasn't published, McKinsey told the IFC to start a private equity fund to invest in healthcare companies in emerging markets. McKinsey also advised the World Bank to create a team to lobby governments in emerging markets to encourage them to work with private healthcare companies.

"The rationale for that was because the private healthcare sector was a big chunk of healthcare provision in many of these countries but government basically ignored it," a person involved with the project said.

Encouraging investment in private healthcare companies in emerging markets was controversial. The antipoverty charity Oxfam published a blistering critique of the IFC in a paper titled "Blind Optimism." Oxfam said it was cheaper, fairer, and more effective to help governments develop taxpayer-funded healthcare services like Britain's NHS.

"The private sector provides no escape route for the problems facing public health systems in poor countries," Oxfam said.

The IFC ignored Oxfam and accepted McKinsey's advice to start a private equity fund for healthcare in Africa, and Scott and Emmett started contacting potential investors. The Gates Foundation agreed to invest in the fund—its first private equity investment—joining the IFC, the German government, and the African Development Bank as investors. In total, they committed $57 million to the fund.

Now the IFC needed to find a firm to manage the fund. They put out a tender in 2008. Aureos, the London-based private equity firm led by Sev, responded. Sev claimed Aureos could earn profit "at the bottom of the pyramid" by investing in healthcare companies that provided services to the poorest Africans.

Sev proposed to make the pay of Aureos's healthcare team dependent on their ability to hit targets to serve more poor people. The more extremely poor people they provided services to, the more they would be paid. A member of Sev's team described this approach as "impact with balls."

The IFC and Gates Foundation offered Aureos the management contract for the new healthcare fund and Sev accepted. Sev believed that managing the fund was a great chance to get to know important new investors like the Gates Foundation and Aureos received management fees for taking on the fund plus a share of any profits.

Some of Sev's colleagues at Aureos were uneasy about the African healthcare fund. They thought it was a vanity project financed by Westerners without a clear vision of what they wanted to achieve and an even worse understanding of emerging markets. They were also wary of the newfangled effort to link their pay to so-called impact metrics. Investing profitably in emerging markets was already hard enough.

Aureos executives dodged Sev's offer to manage the fund. They didn't understand how it was possible to make money by providing healthcare to very poor people who couldn't afford it. It didn't take a mathematician to work out that the numbers didn't seem to add up.

Sev took matters into his own hands and ordered Shakir Merali to lead the healthcare fund. Shakir agreed, reluctantly. Wanting to make the best of a bad situation, Shakir tried to figure out a strategy that would keep the investors happy by providing healthcare to poor Africans at the same time as making a profit. And as he thought more about it he started to see a massive opportunity.

Shakir, born and raised in Kenya, knew about the challenges Africans faced trying to access good quality healthcare. There were few options for the continent's emerging middle class. The wealthy few used exclusive private hospitals or flew to Europe or America for treatment but the impoverished many used chronically underfunded clinics operated by governments and charities.

Shakir found one of his first investment opportunities in a scruffy building in Nairobi, the capital of Kenya. The Avenue Hospital was part of a chain of clinics offering something new. It provided basic healthcare to middle-class Kenyans with health insurance or enough money to pay for low-cost treatments. The patient waiting room was a wooden building in a parking lot.

Avenue's formula was so successful, Shakir decided to invest $2.5 million in the company. The money was used to build a new hospital in Kisumu in western Kenya and to open more clinics. Avenue's annual sales increased sharply from about $300,000 when Aureos invested to about $1 million within a few years. Avenue convinced Shakir that it was possible to do good and make money. After helping one African healthcare company to expand, he reasoned it was possible to do the same again on a much larger scale. He sketched out an idea for a pan-African healthcare company, which he named Project Uzima after a Swahili word that means to be full of life.

Shakir's grand plan found a receptive audience when Abraaj took over Aureos in 2012. He explained Project Uzima to Arif, who came up with an even more grandiose plan for a healthcare fund that spanned all emerging markets. Arif tasked Shakir and a trusted longtime Abraaj employee called Abhinav Munshi, known as Abi, with developing a strategy for a new emerging markets healthcare fund.

· · ·

Abraaj's takeover of Aureos and its African healthcare fund meant that Bill Gates was now one of Arif's investors. Arif wanted to get close to Bill, so when Bill traveled to the UAE in October 2012 he invited the American to dinner at his house.

Bill was in the UAE to give a speech at a conference hosted by Crown Prince Sheik Mohammed bin Zayed Al Nahyan of Abu Dhabi. The Microsoft founder explained to an audience of wealthy Middle Easterners why he had dedicated himself to philanthropy and healthcare, and asked for their help.

"Saving the lives of millions of children is not something we can do alone. We don't have enough resources. We don't have enough knowledge. We don't have enough access in many regions of the world," Bill said. "We need partners. That is why I am so happy to be here."

He implored his audience to focus on helping the poor. He appealed to their competitive instincts by challenging them to do a better job than Western countries had done.

"For too long, we in the West worked almost exclusively to develop and apply technology to meet the needs of the rich world, only for those who could pay," he said. "I hope you constantly search for ways to apply technology to help people who can't pay."

After the speech, Bill took the short trip up the Arabian Gulf coast to Dubai, where he was the guest of honor at a dinner party at Arif and Fayeeza's mansion in Emirates Hills. Arif invited prominent locals, too.

Bill and Arif had much to discuss. They had agreed a few weeks earlier that their charitable foundations would work together on a family-planning program in Pakistan. Arif seemed to be precisely who Bill was looking for. He was wealthy and concerned for the poor.

Arif wanted something from Bill, too. Together they could transform the lives of millions of the world's poorest people across Asia and Africa, not by giving money away, but by creating a big new private equity fund to invest in hospitals and clinics in emerging markets. The problem with the existing African healthcare fund which Bill had invested in was that it was simply too small to make a big difference. The idea for the Abraaj Growth Markets Health Fund was born.

In the days after the dinner, news of Bill and Arif's broad commitment to work together appeared in newspapers across the Middle East and Pakistan. A photograph accompanying the news articles showed Bill, dressed in a suit and tie, smiling but looking awkwardly toward the floor. Arif appeared more relaxed in a suit and open shirt, a broad smile across his face.

"This is a significant co-investment partnership," Bill was quoted as saying. "It is also an example of the kind of smart partnerships that hold huge promise for the future."

. . .

Having Bill as an investor and ally was a massive coup for Arif. An endorsement from a man whose $67 billion wealth was larger than the economy of Kenya was a great advertisement to other investors.

Arif was so proud of his relationship with the Microsoft founder that he kept a photo of the two of them in his office. Little did Arif know at the time that his relationship with Bill and the Gates Foundation would lead to his undoing.

Arif told Shakir and Abi to intensify their work on the global health-care fund. If planned correctly, the fund could seal Abraaj's status as a leader of the impact-investing movement and earn vast amounts of money through fees and a share of profits.

Arif took his plans for the new healthcare fund to the World Economic Forum in Davos in January 2013. Two of the most important people in the global medical industry were also in Davos for the conference: Frans Van Houten, the chief executive of Royal Philips Electronics, and Omar Ishrak, the chief executive of Medtronic, led two of the world's largest healthcare companies, with a combined value of almost $100 billion. In May 2013, Arif talked to the Philips CEO about his plan at a World Economic Forum meeting to discuss Africa in Cape Town.

The opportunity for Philips and Medtronic was obvious. By investing alongside the Gates Foundation in the fund, they'd increase their chances of selling their medical devices to the hospitals and clinics that Arif planned to buy and build. The fund would give them a foothold in fast-growing markets outside North America and Europe, where there was huge demand for affordable, good-quality care.

As Abraaj's finances became increasingly strained in late 2013, Arif was ready to unveil more details about his plans for the healthcare fund. He invited a small group of investors including Julie Sunderland from the Gates Foundation to spend a couple of days at his country house near Oxford. Management consultants also attended to help talk through the strategy.

Behind the scenes, Arif was having a meltdown. At midnight on the evening before his guests arrived, he sat down in the living room of his mansion with Sev, Mustafa, Wahid, and other team members and flicked through a presentation on the healthcare fund, on which Shakir and Abi had spent months. They were pleased with their work but Arif hated it and ranted at Abi for almost an hour. The tone of the document was all wrong, he screamed. Sev, Mustafa, and Wahid said nothing. Arif said there was no way he was presenting the document to investors and threatened to cancel the meeting. The outburst upset Shakir and Abi.

"You need to redo this presentation," Arif said.

Abi worked on the document until around 4:00 a.m. and made superficial changes. He shuffled the order of some of the pages and finally went to bed. He presented the document to Arif again at breakfast.

"This is fine," Arif said.

The tantrum was familiar to employees. Arif often caused a scene demanding changes at the last minute. The process allowed Arif to believe that he was crucial to identifying and solving problems, an employee said.

Arif was charming when he welcomed his guests that morning. He talked through how the fund would work. Arif's country mansion impressed the visitors. A butler was constantly on hand to attend to their needs and they enjoyed strolling around the elegant gardens surrounding the old house.

The management consultants peppered conversations with corporate jargon, using words like *synergy* and *rollout*. The business language of the consultants troubled one person present at the meeting. Their concepts seemed out of place in a debate about how to improve healthcare provision in desperately poor countries.

"There were a lot of people there who knew nothing about what they were talking about and who had no experience in healthcare in emerging markets," the person said. "These are very, very challenging places."

Arif made it all sound so simple.

"Rising income, urbanization, and changing lifestyles are driving demand for quality healthcare systems in markets that have historically been typified by systemic underinvestment," he later told investors.

Arif wanted $1 billion from investors for the fund. The money would be used to buy and build a dozen healthcare companies in high-need, low-income cities across Africa and Asia. Arif wanted to invest in his childhood home of Karachi as well as Lagos in Nigeria, Addis Ababa in Ethiopia, Hyderabad in India, Durban in South Africa, and Accra in Ghana. Arif told investors that Abraaj could readily overcome the challenges of operating the fund, such as finding enough hospitals to buy and doctors and nurses to work in them. He talked up Abraaj's track record of investing in healthcare companies, which did include some significant successes. Abraaj had made a fortune from selling the Turkish hospital chain Acibadem.

In return for managing the $1 billion fund, Arif wanted the standard private equity annual fee of 2 percent—amounting to $20 million a year—and a fifth of any profits made.

Arif made his pitch masterfully to investors, but there were differences of opinion at the Oxford meeting. Abraaj executives wanted the fund to invest in companies that were very likely to make profits, but the team from the Gates Foundation was more interested in making investments that were more likely to help the very poorest Africans and were less focused on the prospects for making profits. Shakir clashed with Gates Foundation officials on this issue. He was determined to buy only hospitals and clinics that generated enough profit to pay for themselves and thrive without handouts. He believed a self-financing healthcare system in Africa and Asia would end the need for Western aid.

The clashes presented Arif with a problem. Shakir was an important member of the team but Arif couldn't afford to lose the support of the Gates Foundation. Arif began casting around for a more diplomatic leader for the new healthcare fund.

Khawar Mann, a smooth-talking finance executive, fit the bill. He was born in a poor neighborhood of Birmingham, England's second-largest city, to parents who settled there after immigrating from Pakistan. His father drove a bus and delivered mail to support the family. Khawar was precociously bright and rocketed through the

ranks of the English education system. He won a place to study medicine at Cambridge University but switched to studying law. After
graduating, he followed a well-trodden path to the City, London's
financial district, and spent his twenties working as a highly paid
corporate lawyer at Linklaters. He quit the law firm in 1995 to join
the prestigious MBA program at the University of Pennsylvania's
Wharton School. A job followed at Sir Ronald Cohen's private equity
firm, Apax Partners, where he became a partner and co-head of the
healthcare investment team.

When he wasn't hunting for deals, Khawar helped out at a charity
founded by Prince Charles, the heir to the British throne. The charity ran mentoring programs for young people in poor communities
like the one Khawar grew up in. Khawar's charitable work earned
him membership of the Order of the British Empire, a coveted award
from Queen Elizabeth II.

Khawar's rise to the heights of the British establishment came to a
halt with a poor healthcare investment at Apax that lost millions of
dollars. He left Apax and headed to Moscow, where he got a job at a
private healthcare company owned by a Russian oligarch who later
faced money-laundering charges. The move to Russia didn't work
out. Khawar began talking to Arif, whom he had met in Davos one
year. Arif saw him as a good fit for wooing investors. As one investor
put it, "Khawar could sell sand to the Arabs." He joined Abraaj in
2014 to help lead the healthcare fund. He was excited by the ambitious mission to transform healthcare in the developing world.

Arif hired another big name from the finance industry for the
healthcare fund. Aly Jeddy was a senior partner at McKinsey in New
York, where he led the consulting firm's practice advising American
private equity firms. Aly's curriculum vitae was a checklist of prestigious institutions. He got an economics degree from Dartmouth
College, where he graduated top of his class, and a law degree from
Yale University. He had worked in the prosecutor's office for the UN
War Crimes Tribunal for the former Yugoslavia and designed welfare programs for Egypt while working at the World Bank. He was a

trustee of the Dalton School, an exclusive private preparatory school on New York City's Upper East Side, and sat on the alumni council for Dartmouth. He was also on the board of a charity serving blind people in Pakistan.

Aly had known Arif for about a decade and advised him on Abraaj's strategy. Arif appointed Aly to lead the healthcare fund, with Khawar as his deputy. Investors including the IFC were wary of Aly because despite his elite credentials he didn't have experience investing in healthcare in the poorest countries.

"We had no idea why Aly was appointed," one investor said. "No emerging markets experience, no healthcare experience, no investing experience."

Aly and Khawar worked with Arif and Sev to prepare marketing documents for the healthcare fund. While none of them were true experts in emerging markets healthcare, they were masters of the art of pitching private equity funds to investors.

"The world is now coming to our markets," Aly told *Forbes* magazine.

Aly flew to the United States with Sev to meet investors and delivered a polished pitch to the Gates Foundation and the IFC.

But Aly soon began to doubt the wisdom of his decision to join Abraaj. Having seen how the firm operated on the inside, he was concerned about the ethics of some colleagues and he was troubled by how Arif operated.

"He smelt the coffee," a former colleague said.

He quit Abraaj just a few months after joining and returned to McKinsey.

Aly's exit set some alarm bells ringing among investors, but Arif moved quickly to limit the damage. He told investors that he was personally heading up the healthcare fund and Khawar was responsible for managing day-to-day operations.

Arif wanted bigger-name hires to boost his healthcare credentials and he was prepared to pay what some employees considered ludicrous sums to lure high-profile executives. The search led to Sir

David Nicholson, former chief executive of the National Health Service in England.

He had joined the NHS not long after joining the Communist Party. Starting out as an idealistic graduate trainee, he rose through the ranks and gained a reputation as a strong manager. In 2006 he was appointed to lead the English NHS and took responsibility for a £90 billion budget and a vast bureaucratic machine with more than a million doctors and nurses and thousands of hospitals and clinics.

It was a high-pressure job but he was well paid by government standards. There were other perks, too. In 2010, he was knighted by the queen. His tenure came with controversy. He got caught up in criticism after receiving £41,600 of benefits one year in addition to his £210,000 salary. He was also criticized for overseeing a group of hospitals where death rates rose excessively because managers were too focused on finances. He was forced to apologize as a human being and as a CEO.

After he left the NHS, Khawar asked Sir David to join Abraaj. Khawar was setting up an impact committee to screen investments at the request of the Gates Foundation. Khawar offered Sir David $120,000 a year for just four days' work each month. His annual salary was enough to pay the salaries of six doctors in Kenya but Sir David's responsibilities were limited.

"The consultant shall determine the method, details, and means of performing the services," his contract said. "Abraaj shall have no right to, and shall not, control the manner or method of providing the services."

Sir David accepted. The appointment caused consternation among healthcare fund employees who didn't understand why he was being paid so much money to do so little.

As Arif and Khawar put the finishing touches to the fund's marketing materials, some investors, including the IFC, said that $1 billion was too much to ask for. Arif refused to listen.

"Go big or go home," he said.

The bigger the fund, the bigger the annual fee Abraaj got for managing it.

Another particularly thorny issue kept coming up in discussions with investors. Private equity funds typically have a ten-year life during which companies must be bought and sold. The IFC and Gates Foundation thought the healthcare fund needed a longer life than usual to build durable companies in challenging conditions. Healthcare regulations were complex and finding staff was going to be difficult. To make things even harder, Abraaj was proposing to build some hospitals from scratch. Arif brushed these problems aside because he didn't want to stop the momentum gathering around the project. He decreed that it was best to structure the healthcare fund as a typical private equity fund.

By the summer of 2015, Abraaj was ready for what's known in the private equity industry as a "first close." This was the point at which the fund had collected enough money to start buying companies. The Gates Foundation came good on its promise of investing $100 million. Medtronic and Philips invested too. The IFC wanted to commit but it was proving difficult to get the investment signed off. A committee responsible for deciding how the World Bank's money was spent was reluctant to approve a $100 million investment. The IFC decided $50 million was the most it wanted to invest, Scott Featherston told Arif. Arif wasn't happy. Days later, Scott got a call.

"I just want to congratulate you," Arif told him.

Confused, Scott asked why.

"The IFC is going to be investing one hundred million," Arif gloated. "So congratulations, Scott."

IFC executives wondered how Arif managed to secure $100 million from their organization. They figured that he had used his relationship with the IFC's chief executive, Jin-Yong Cai. Arif told one IFC employee that this was the case.

The IFC money brought the total raised for the first close to $460 million. Arif invited investors to his Mayfair office to celebrate. The meeting was Julie Sunderland's last with Abraaj before she left the

Gates Foundation to start her own healthcare investment firm. As she walked out, she had a final message.

"Don't screw this up," she said.

Flush with new cash, Arif pressured Khawar to find deals.

A big opportunity soon presented itself. Care Hospitals was for sale. The Indian company that saved Jessi's life was renowned for the quality of its doctors. Some patients considered Care's chief doctor to be a guru with almost mystical healing powers. The Indian company was owned by Advent International. The American private equity firm had expanded Care by refurbishing old hospitals and opening new ones throughout India. Advent hired the investment bank Moelis & Co. to manage an auction for Care. The Moelis bankers invited hospital operators, private equity firms, and sovereign wealth funds to make offers, and a fierce bidding war ensued. Abraaj was pitted against the American private equity firm TPG and the Singaporean sovereign wealth fund Temasek. Thomson Medical, a hospital operator in Singapore, also competed.

Khawar was eager to win. He wanted Care's hospitals and doctors to form the backbone of the Abraaj healthcare fund. His plan was to expand Care internationally, across Asia and Africa. Its doctors and nurses could train new staff to work in hospitals from Bangladesh to Nigeria. Some Abraaj executives weren't happy with how Khawar handled the auction. He revealed his hand too early, they thought, making it clear how badly he wanted the deal.

Final offers were due in the fall of 2015 and an announcement was expected by December. Everything went quiet and Abraaj executives assumed they'd lost. The rumor was that TPG's team, led by Bill McGlashan, a leading figure in the impact-investing world and a friend of the Irish rock star Bono, had won.

Then Khawar received some unexpected news. TPG had dropped out and Abraaj was the front-runner. Advent offered Abraaj the chance to do a deal quickly. It gave Abraaj a few weeks to carry out checks on Care to make sure the business was as profitable as Care said it was. Khawar took a big chance by not taking more time to analyze the company's finances, some colleagues thought. The deal was signed in early 2016, with Abraaj investing $130 million.

. . .

Arif returned to Davos in January 2016 eager to tell the world about his new healthcare fund. The World Economic Forum was happy to help broadcast the news. Arif had paid millions of dollars to attend the conference in the Swiss Alps year after year. The forum arranged a press conference on the future of healthcare in developing countries. Arif took to the stage accompanied by top executives from three of the biggest investors in his healthcare fund—the Gates Foundation, Philips, and Medtronic. No doctors or nurses from developing countries were invited to speak. Nor were there any poor patients to tell their stories. The conference moderator, Georg Schmitt, began by asking a question that practically invited Arif to promote his new fund.

"Tell us how private capital can be used to contribute to solving and countering this global health challenge."

"Obviously there is a dual purpose. The first is to make money," Arif replied.

The second purpose was to provide healthcare, he said. "When you take Lagos or you take Karachi or Kolkata, you would be amazed at the fact that even the baseline of proper healthcare does not exist, so our job is actually to put that in place."

The man from the Gates Foundation could barely contain his enthusiasm for Arif's new fund.

"What makes us so excited to be a partner with everyone here on the Abraaj Growth Markets Health Fund is the potential for really— *revolutionizing* may be a little strong but that's certainly our hope in the medium term—how we look at some of the service provision going on in many of these markets," said Mark Suzman. "We are very optimistic about where this is headed."

Care hospitals was the perfect example of the kind of deal the new fund would be doing, Arif said. Abraaj would transfer expertise from Care's Indian doctors to clinics and hospitals in other countries.

"There you have a cadre of doctors and health technicians which actually are world class," Arif said. "If we can use that expertise and training and apply it across Africa, everybody is a winner."

• • •

Back in Dubai, Khawar was facing problems.

After the excitement of sealing the first deal had faded, a closer look at the books of Care hospitals revealed financial challenges. Abraaj had missed some important warning signs in the haste to get the deal done. Members of Care's senior management team began leaving and the hospitals fell behind on their financial targets. Care's problems could be fixed, but Abraaj had paid a high price for the privilege of fixing them. In an internal meeting, Arif put Khawar on the spot by making him explain to other employees what had gone wrong with the Care deal.

Khawar's leadership style unsettled some of his team. He pitched ideas which sounded impossible to people with decades of dealmaking experience in emerging markets. One time, he pulled colleagues into a room and asked them to start work on a project in Nigeria. He gave them six months to build and staff a hospital. It sounded like a crazy request to the team. They knew how difficult it was to recruit and train staff in Nigeria, let alone build a hospital from scratch.

The morale of the healthcare team sank. Abi, an architect of the fund, quit. Shakir wanted to leave too. Arif asked him to stay until the fundraising process was completed, and Shakir agreed.

The extravagance of senior executives jarred with some employees at the healthcare fund. One executive flew business class from Dubai to Nairobi for a single meeting and spent the night in the Norfolk Hotel, a pricey favorite of British aristocrats in colonial times. The cost of the brief business trip far exceeded the annual salary of a Kenyan nurse.

Salaries paid to some of the healthcare team were eye-watering, even by private equity standards. Samir Khleif, a leading cancer specialist and a friend of Arif, was paid hundreds of thousands of dollars a year.

Abraaj finished raising the healthcare fund in July 2016. Commitments totaling $850 million were pledged by banks, wealthy individuals, the pension fund of America's United Church of Christ, the U.K.'s CDC, and its French government counterpart, Proparco. Negotiations with the U.S. government's Overseas Private Investment Corp. for a $150 million investment would soon bring the fund to $1 billion.

By entrusting Arif with $100 million of his money, Bill Gates had helped attract $900 million more to the fund to build hospitals for the poor. Arif and Bill now had the money to transform the lives of millions of people. But Arif had other plans. He requested hundreds of millions of dollars from investors in the healthcare fund within a few months of finishing raising the money. The Gates Foundation, the IFC, and the other investors sent the money to Abraaj as requested. Abraaj told the investors that the money would be invested in companies including Care, the hospital chain that saved Jessi, the young Indian girl hit by a bus. But Arif instead took tens of millions of dollars for himself and his staff.

· · ·

The Abraaj healthcare fund did start work on projects in Pakistan, Kenya, and Nigeria as well as India. It acquired a diagnostics company in Pakistan and hospitals in Kenya, and began building hospitals in Lahore, Karachi, and Lagos.

Even if Abraaj hadn't pilfered millions from the healthcare fund, it's unlikely that this great capitalist experiment in private healthcare for the poorest people in the world would have worked out, at least at first. Abraaj documents show that the fund was allowed to invest in clinics and hospitals for people in the middle of the economic pyramid of humanity—those earning between $3 and $10 a day—as well as for those living at the bottom of the pyramid on less than $3 a day. The fund's strategy was to provide good quality care and diagnostics to those who could afford it first and then reach out to the poorest by securing funding from governments and charities. When Khawar visited Abraaj's hospital in Lahore, he looked out across the surrounding fields and saw very poor farmers toiling with bullocks. He knew that they would never be able to afford to visit the hospital, even though he wanted to provide services to them.

Abraaj couldn't provide free healthcare because its fund, which was announced with so much fanfare at Davos and paid salaries of hundreds of thousands of dollars a year to executives recruited from private equity firms, management consultancies and private hospitals, needed to earn big profits to survive.

CHAPTER 13

BREATHE, SMILE, SAY ALHAMDULLILAH, AND PROCEED

Rafique, a pious man with a white beard, was dedicated to Allah and to Arif. When he wasn't praying five times a day Rafique was busy at work in a corner office deep within Abraaj's Dubai headquarters surrounded by piles of paper receipts. The loyal cash controller scraped Abraaj's bank accounts throughout 2016 in search of dollars to make ends meet. He was finding it harder and harder to cook Abraaj's books, and the stress was damaging his health. One of Arif's secretaries recalled Rafique quaking as he prepared to enter his boss's office. The room was decorated with photographs of the American boxer Muhammad Ali and of Arif with Bill Gates and Warren Buffett. It was scented with a fragrance made by Parisian perfume house Diptyque that one of the butlers liked to spray. Sometimes secretaries overheard Arif playing jazz and 1980s rock ballads like Berlin's "Take my Breath Away."

Rafique moved money around Abraaj's global network of funds, companies, and bank accounts on a daily basis. His actions were guided and approved by Arif, Waqar, and Ashish Dave, who had rejoined Abraaj from KPMG for a second stint as chief financial officer.

Rafique repeatedly told Arif that the strain the financial shenanigans were exerting on Abraaj's health and his own mental and physical well-being was too much to bear but his boss showed little concern.

Arif remained confident in his ability to dodge deadlines for payments and find new sources of money. He was certain that the sale of his biggest asset, Karachi Electric, would solve the cash crisis. Abraaj had made genuine progress with Karachi Electric but it wasn't enough to safeguard its future. The power company still wasn't generating enough electricity to keep all the lights on in Pakistan's largest city and it needed more investment, which Abraaj couldn't provide. The city water company still owed millions of dollars to Karachi Electric, which in turn owed hundreds of millions of dollars to state-owned gas suppliers. The unpaid bills had triggered a flurry of unresolved lawsuits and political wrangling. Arif wanted to find a buyer who could build on the improvements Abraaj had made, but few companies in the world were up to the task.

Arif got lucky at this point. China was rolling out a historic plan to invest $1 trillion in the infrastructure of neighboring countries including Pakistan. China's objective was to create a modern trade and transport network harking back to the ancient Silk Road, which once carried Chinese silk to the West. Shanghai Electric, the giant state-owned utility that powered China's largest city, was interested in making an offer for Karachi Electric, and its executives started negotiating with Abraaj.

As talks between the Chinese and Abraaj intensified in the summer of 2016, Arif and Omar renewed their efforts to gain the support of Prime Minister Nawaz Sharif and his brother Shehbaz. Arif and Omar formalized their agreement with Navaid Malik, the middleman charged with managing their relationship with the Pakistani politicians. Omar prepared a $20 million contract for Navaid in June 2016 and sent it to Arif in an email so he could review it.

"Boss," Omar wrote. "Please see attached for your comments. We have aimed to keep it simple and to the point."

"Keep it generic," Arif replied. "Send it to him from your gmail."

Neither Abraaj nor Karachi Electric should be named in the document, Arif said.

"This document is explosive in the wrong hands," Arif said. "Do not consult any advisors further on it."

"Noted," Omar replied.

Two months later, Shanghai Electric announced publicly that it was preparing a bid for Karachi Electric. Arif was euphoric. The deal angered some U.S. officials, who thought it would give China more influence.

Prime Minister Sharif publicly blessed the takeover talks. He welcomed Arif, Navaid, and Shanghai Electric's chairman, Wang Yundan, to an official meeting in Islamabad, the capital. The prime minister hosted the executives in a ceremonial room dominated by a large portrait of Muhammad Ali Jinnah, the founder of Pakistan, whose gaunt face gazed sternly at the politicians and businessmen. An ornate vase of flowers bloomed in front of the portrait, next to the dark green Pakistani flag. Arif sat between Navaid and the prime minister. When the meeting ended, Arif authorized sending the $20 million contract to Navaid.

· · ·

Most people who met Arif believed what he wanted them to believe about him: he was a rich investor out to make the world a better place. But not everyone kept faith in him, as a chance email exchange days after the Islamabad meeting showed.

Ali Shihabi hadn't spoken to Arif for years. He and Arif had been business partners for an intense few months in 2002 at Rasmala, the precursor firm to Abraaj. Arif and Ali were two of the five men who had vowed to work together in a spirit of one for all and all for one before their partnership quickly fell apart.

After years of silence, Ali sent Arif an email in September 2016. He had found a biography of himself online which mistakenly described him as the CEO of Abraaj.

"Somehow this is on the web somewhere and I am constantly having to correct it," Ali wrote to Arif. "Anyway I corrected it for them but you are getting some free branding."

"Doesn't bother me," Arif replied. "Might get you a job one day."

"Yes sure maybe as a witness to the prosecution," Ali replied.

"Hope you are well old friend," Arif said.

• • •

Shanghai Electric's $1.77 billion offer for Abraaj's controlling stake in Karachi Electric was announced in October 2016. The deal promised to be a huge payday for Abraaj but before Arif could collect the money he had to gather written approval from several Pakistani government departments. This was a complicated process. Some Pakistani government officials were unhappy with the agreement to sell Karachi Electric to the Chinese. Others were jealous of the $570 million Abraaj stood to make. Karachi Electric's unpaid gas bill was another complication. Some officials wanted this resolved before the sale could be agreed.

Omar and Navaid spent days sweating outside government offices as they tried to gather the signatures they needed from bureaucrats. Omar became increasingly impatient and raged at officials, alienating people whose support was crucial. Some of the officials were many rungs below the prime minister in the government hierarchy but they still had the power to obstruct the sale. Arif's elitist strategy of trying to win influence at the top of organizations to sway decisions his way wasn't working with the government in Pakistan.

Completion of the Karachi Electric sale kept getting delayed, making it necessary for Arif and Rafique to pilfer more cash from Abraaj's funds to keep the company afloat. They still owed millions of dollars to investors from the sale of Network International and Saham. More investors had noticed that they were owed money and were pressuring Arif to pay them. To delay making these payments, Abraaj executives made excuses about information technology problems that had scrambled their systems.

In November 2016 Abraaj asked investors in the healthcare fund to send $414 million to pay for deals. Investors promptly sent the money. When the cash arrived in the healthcare fund, Arif and Rafique siphoned $140 million of it into the secret bank accounts. From there, $3.2 million went to Arif.

Arif needed to pay in Abraaj's contribution to the healthcare fund. Since he was running out of money, he decided to return $73 million of the investor money he had taken from the healthcare fund and pretend that this was Abraaj's money. It wasn't. The money belonged to investors.

As money whizzed illicitly from one Abraaj account to another, Arif hit the road for a fresh round of self-promotion.

He entertained investors in London and New York and told them about Abraaj's excellent performance and sound financial health. At a gathering in New York he was joined on stage by executives from companies Abraaj owned, including Hanzade Doğan Boyner, founder of the Turkish online retailer Hepsiburada.

"I love my partners," she said about Abraaj in a promotional video. "We have the same vision, the same culture."

$$\bullet \quad \bullet \quad \bullet$$

By January 2017 the firm's cash crisis was truly alarming. Rafique told Arif that Abraaj needed $85 million by the end of March—even after the recent plundering of the healthcare fund. Making matters worse, Rafique said, the healthcare fund had committed to invest $173 million in deals that it couldn't afford to pay for because there wasn't enough money left in the fund.

The healthcare fund needed money in Nigeria, where Abraaj was in negotiations with dozens of doctors to build a hospital with 350 beds.

Cash was needed in Kenya, where the healthcare fund had agreed to invest in Nairobi Women's Hospital, the operator of a specialist recovery center for women abused by men.

The healthcare fund needed money in Pakistan, where it had committed to building a new hospital with 290 beds in Lahore.

The fact that money for these lifesaving projects was missing made it all the more extraordinary that Arif decided to spare no expense when partying at the World Economic Forum in Davos in January 2017. His display at the annual gathering of billionaires was more splendid than ever. As snow fell on the Swiss resort on the evening of January 18, Arif hosted Pakistan's prime minister and his retinue at a sumptuous dinner in the Morosani Schweizerhof Hotel.

The feast cost Abraaj a grand total of $348,673, the average combined annual income of 271 Pakistanis. The bill to adorn the dining tables with flowers was $7,357.50, the annual income of 5 Pakistanis. The Pakistani singers Akhtar Chanal Zahri and Meesha Shafi were booked for $35,000 to entertain the elite crowd. Another $12,000 was spent on gifts for guests. Navaid Malik organized the evening and charged Abraaj $3,433.50 to stay at the Baur au Lac hotel in Zurich on his way to Davos with the official Pakistani delegation. He added a $981 charge for undisclosed extras.

At the dinner, Arif rose from his seat next to Prime Minister Sharif to introduce his special guest. Flattery was his aim. Arif needed the prime minister's help more than ever because completion of the Karachi Electric sale was still being delayed.

"Bismillah al rahman al rahim," Arif said, starting with a phrase Muslims use to begin a new action. "Your excellency. Friends. Having built a life and a career outside Pakistan, and built a business that is known around the world for what it does, the single point of pride that I have, more than anything else in what I do, is that I am a Pakistani."

There was a burst of applause from the fifty guests, who cost Abraaj 250 Swiss francs each to feed.

"This is a country that over time all of you have seen go through aches, pains, growing troubles, and in my case defeat on the cricket field. Nothing upsets me more than that," Arif said, prompting laughter.

"But the reality is that Pakistan is a country on the move. Pakistan is a country that has fantastic potential.

"There are very few places where you can get as much clarity in terms of government regulations, and I am extremely pleased to say that this government—in my experience more than any other government in the past—has done more to make a business-friendly environment possible."

In other words, the speech could be interpreted as a request to the prime minister to speed up approval of the sale of Karachi Electric. The prime minister thanked Arif for his hospitality but gave no public assurances on Karachi Electric.

After the dinner ended Arif emailed Rafique, who was desperate to talk to him about the financial problems. Arif promised they would talk soon. In the meantime, he told Rafique to use his common sense.

"Just don't shut down the business!" Arif wrote.

• • •

Showing up at a never-ending succession of conferences and media interviews was part of Arif's contribution to keeping Abraaj alive because his public appearances sent out a message to investors and bankers that the firm was in good shape.

A few days after the Davos gathering, Arif flew to New York to speak at the *Economist* magazine's impact investing summit. He was interviewed on stage by Matthew Bishop, the journalist who had written a book about how capitalists could save the world through a blend of investing and giving which he called philanthrocapitalism. Arif was in top form as he described his philanthrocapitalism.

"It is not just about earning the dollar," Arif said. "It is about leaving the world a slightly better place."

Arif gave a bizarre example of how Abraaj made money and did good by forcing Karachi Electric customers to pay their electricity bills. "That is also impact—creating more socially responsible citizens—that's impact," he said.

Arif insisted that Abraaj was a model to follow.

"If you want to build a great company you've got to start with a good company," he explained. "We should be transparent, we should be governance-driven, we should be focused on doing a lot more for society."

A few hours after the *Economist* debate, Arif got more dire news from Rafique. Abraaj needed $4.2 million to pay urgent bills and Rafique said he was going to take another $5 million from the healthcare fund to pay them. Rafique attached a chart to his email which showed that the $140 million taken from the healthcare fund a few weeks earlier hadn't been returned to the fund.

Rafique soon followed up with another email, but this time he had some better news. He had figured out how to get more cash. Rafique told Arif that they could take $110 million more from Abraaj Private Equity Fund IV. But they needed a reason to ask investors in the fund to send the money. Arif told investors he was going to buy Tunisia's main telephone company, Tunisie Telecom, on their behalf. The code name for the deal was Project Dido, inspired by the name of the first queen of Carthage, an ancient city located in modern-day Tunisia. Abraaj sent a request to investors in late February 2017 for $110 million and received the money a month later. But Abraaj never bought Tunisie Telecom. Instead, Arif gave $10 million of the cash to investors who had been waiting more than a year for money owed to them from the sale of Network International and Saham.

And he didn't stop there. He asked investors in the healthcare fund to send $115 million more. Abraaj had by then requested a grand total of $545 million from healthcare fund investors. But only $305 million had been used to buy clinics and hospitals, according to financial reports sent to investors; $240 million remained inexplicably unused, according to the financial reports. So why, one or two investors in the healthcare fund were beginning to wonder, was Abraaj asking for even more money? The answer was that, unbeknown to the investors, Arif was using Abraaj money to finance a bewildering array of expenses and personal projects, including a start-up led by his former secretary Ghizlan.

Ghizlan launched the Modist on International Women's Day in March 2017. The Modist was an online luxury fashion company targeting Muslim women. Like all the business ventures Arif had a hand in, the Modist was dressed up in the language of doing good.

"Our mission is to build a strong sense of purpose to empower a woman's freedom of choice," Ghizlan said in a press release. "We aim to break down pre-conceived notions while building a community and dialogue that invigorates, informs and celebrates the fashionable, modern, modest woman."

• • •

Abraaj's crumbling finances weren't outwardly denting Arif's confidence. He flew to Berlin to attend the world's largest annual gathering of private equity executives in February 2017 and lectured the crowd of mostly European and American dealmakers about how he was on a mission to do good. He even scorned the term *private equity*, saying that he preferred to describe himself as being in the business of partnership capital. Arif told the conference that the private equity industry had lost its sense of partnership. He reminded executives that private equity firms were known in the industry as general partners and their investors were limited partners. But the partners who gave Arif money were being robbed blind.

Days after the Berlin conference, Rafique anxiously informed Arif that one of Abraaj's biggest funds was empty. There was no money left in Abraaj Private Equity Fund IV.

"The cash balance in APEF IV is Nil," Rafique said. "The cash situation is out of control and I don't know how do I manage."

Arif told Rafique to take more money from the healthcare fund. Rafique took $25 million more from the fund and put it in one of the secret bank accounts.

Rafique kept chasing Arif with emails as his boss crisscrossed the world. A truly disturbing missive reached Arif while he was in Jordan in May 2017. Arif was chairing a World Economic Forum meeting in a hotel by the Dead Sea. He read the email after sitting down with the French advertising executive Maurice Lévy and Dominic Barton, the head of the consulting firm McKinsey.

"Please note that we will have no funds available to pay for June salaries of the Group and any other critical payment," Rafique wrote in the email.

Rafique asked Arif if he should continue using Abraaj money to pay his boss's personal expenses. Arif coolly responded.

"Take a deep breath, smile, say Alhamdolilah and proceed."

Arif used the Arabic term *Alhamdolilah*, meaning to praise God, to calm the nerves of his distressed cash controller. He told Rafique to pay $300,000 to his oldest son, Ahsan, and the same amount to Ghizlan's company, the Modist.

"Both are broke, need the cash tomorrow," Arif said.

Arif then reassured Rafique that everything was going to be fine. He told him that Deutsche Bank was approving a $120 million loan. He said that SoftBank, a giant Japanese investment company, was interested in buying a large stake in Abraaj. More money was coming from the sale of properties in Istanbul, Sharm El Sheikh, and Dubai. Inshallah—God willing—Arif said. Pakistan's prime minister was totally focused on ending their nightmare situation, Arif told Rafique.

"Many irons in the fire, but felt you should know," he said.

Rafique finally snapped.

"I have transferred funds as per your instructions to both Ahsan and Modist," he responded. "I am taking the liberty to point out few things."

He listed all the ways Arif was draining cash from Abraaj. Arif owed $25.8 million for his expense account. Another $3 million had gone to Ghizlan's fashion company and $6.6 million to an investment company run by his sons. The Aman Foundation and Arif's private companies in London, Geneva, and the Cayman Islands were taking millions more.

"As you are aware, I am under tremendous pressure re Abraaj cash as well, there is a serious cash crunch and currently I don't have the funds to pay essential payments like salaries for the month of June," Rafique said. "You are fully aware of the situation."

The Abraaj team in Turkey was demanding cash it was owed. There wasn't money to pay for healthcare deals. A Kuwaiti pension fund was owed money for a loan and payments were due to suppliers.

"The list goes on," Rafique said. "I humbly and respectfully request you to please help me in this situation. The tension and stress is unbearable for me and it is affecting my health and my efficiency, and performance at work. I don't know what else to say."

"I will sort it out," Arif replied.

The same day, Rafique transferred $1.6 million to Arif, via Silverline.

Rafique was at his wits' end because an unmissable financial deadline was looming. On June 30, 2017, he had to file annual accounts for both the healthcare fund and Fund IV but there was $225 million missing from the healthcare fund and $201 million missing from Fund IV. Money was needed to fill both holes or else the theft would be exposed.

"We will have to arrange cash to settle this," Rafique said.

Arif had a plan.

He suggested changing the financial year end of Fund IV from June 30 to December 31. This would delay the need to complete the full financial statement for another six months, gaining time to find cash to fill the hole in the fund.

Rafique thought this was a good idea but they needed to find an excuse or, as he phrased it, an "operational rationale" to cover their tracks and convince investors that the change was required. Arif decided they should tell Mustafa straightaway.

"Action it," Arif said.

Mustafa complied, and a letter was sent to investors to inform them that the fund's year end was changing from June 30 to December 31.

Now Arif and Rafique had to fill the hole in the healthcare fund. For this job Arif turned to his old friends at Air Arabia once more. He asked airline executives for a new loan, and they agreed. On June 24, 2017, $196 million borrowed from Air Arabia landed in the healthcare fund. The loan created the impression that money wasn't missing from the fund as of June 30, 2017. A few days later, on July 19, 2017, Arif repaid the loan to Air Arabia. After the repayment the healthcare fund was left with just $28 million to invest in hospitals and clinics in poor countries.

Arif's financial trickery had staved off disaster once more.

"It's a bit like playing poker," he told Rafique.

CHAPTER 14

AMERICA FIRST

Kito de Boer, the management consultant who advised Arif to start a private equity firm in 2001, was watching CNN at a friend's house in Dubai in November 2016 when he saw something that shocked him. Donald Trump was elected president of the USA.

Kito had moved on from McKinsey by then, taking a big pay cut to become the head of mission for the United Nations Quartet for peacemaking between Israelis and Palestinians. The tall Dutchman had spent his career cultivating ties with prominent business leaders and politicians around the world and, like so many members of the Davos elite, including his friend Arif, Kito had been counting on Hillary Clinton to win the presidential election. Trump's unexpected victory turned their world upside down.

Kito's life was one for the globalization textbooks. Born in Venezuela to Dutch parents, he studied management at Loughborough University in England before embarking on a country-hopping career, with stints at the oil company Royal Dutch Shell and the Italian household goods maker Electrolux. He joined McKinsey in London in 1985 and moved to New Delhi in 1993. Six years later, he moved to Dubai to start McKinsey's operations in the Middle East. He had homes in Jerusalem and London. His £4 million white stucco Kensington town house on the west side of Hyde Park was just a brisk walk away from Arif's apartment. The house was finely furnished with Indian art, French furniture, sofas from New York, and a plunge pool in the basement.

Kito was a passionate believer in globalization as a force for good. He thought businesspeople could solve social and political problems—even the intractable Israeli-Palestinian conflict—as well as making profits. During his time at McKinsey his jobs included leading the firm's public sector and social sector practices in Europe, the Middle East, and Africa as well as advising chief executives like Arif.

Kito knew that the Middle East needed more jobs and investment to improve lives in the war-torn region. At McKinsey he had drawn up a plan for Sir Ronald Cohen, the wealthy impact-investing pioneer, on how to improve the Palestinian economy. Kito and Sir Ronald believed they could help the peacemaking process by promoting investment in jobs and companies, even as Israeli and Palestinian politicians stubbornly refused to work together on political issues such as agreeing on the borders and the location of the capital of a future Palestinian state.

Kito and Sir Ronald's plan to develop the Palestinian economy was shared with Tony Blair, who, after stepping down as British prime minister in 2007, had become the representative of the United Nations, the United States, Russia, and the European Union—the Quartet—for peacemaking in the Middle East.

In 2015, Blair and U.S. Secretary of State John Kerry asked Kito to join the Quartet. Kito agreed. At first he took on responsibility for economic policy and then succeeded Blair as head of mission. During his time in Jerusalem with the UN, Kito developed an even grander plan to transform the Middle East based on his work with Israelis and Palestinians. In discussions with John Kerry, Kito sketched out what they called a Marshall Plan for the Middle East. Kerry had been talking about such a plan for the Middle East for years. The goal was to gather billions of dollars from governments and investors to rebuild the infrastructure of the region in the wake of the Iraq War and

Arab Spring revolutions. Kito envisaged Arif playing a leading role in this plan as an adviser on how to invest billions of dollars.

"Countries like Libya, Yemen, Syria, Iraq and Iran will require more than $500 billion in the next two decades," Kito wrote to Arif in an email in May 2016. "The need is for a Marshall Plan 2.0—a plan that recognises the key role that private sector equity has.

"Motivated capital will have to be explored and developed. Governments, Sovereign Wealth Funds, Multilateral Financial Institutions, and Ultra High Net Worth individuals are searching for means to move from aid to sustainable funding of socially valuable initiatives. In addition, there is also faith based funding. Palestine represents an intersection between Christianity and Islam. Islam is seeking to deploy vast sums of Zakat funds in ways that address concerns raised about opacity and impact. Christians—many in Asia want to invest in the Holy Lands and are seeking ways to invest in projects that support peace."

Kito envisaged political heavyweights including the former British prime minister Gordon Brown and the former Nigerian finance minister Ngozi Okonjo-Iweala joining with the likes of Bill Gates, the World Economic Forum founder Klaus Schwab, and BlackRock's chief, Larry Fink, to team up with him and Arif on this project. He believed Abraaj was so important that the world needed ten, twenty, or even a hundred firms like it to channel investment into the Middle East.

"Abraaj is a great example of what is needed," Kito told a journalist. "They have one of the best networks and track records of building and investing in a pipeline of investible projects in markets most view as exotic and risky."

Arif had his own political connections in the United States. He had sponsored the Clinton family's annual meeting and was well known among the Washington elite. Richard Olson, a career diplomat who got to know Arif well while serving as America's ambassador to the U.A.E. and Pakistan, created an opportunity for Arif to meet Kerry in early 2016. Olson later talked to Arif about joining Abraaj after he left government service.

Olson recommended to a former U.S. ambassador to Italy and State Department adviser called David Thorne that Arif should meet Kerry in Davos in January 2016. Thorne agreed. Thorne was particularly close to Kerry, a lifelong friend. His twin sister was Kerry's first wife. Thorne had expertise on Marshall Plans, in part because his father was an administrator on the original effort to assist Europe after World War II. His son also worked at Abraaj for a time.

Arif met Kerry at Davos and talked about his views on the world.

If the globalist Hillary Clinton had won the presidential election in 2016 there was a movement in place that could have led to Arif becoming an even more central partner to America and a manager of billions of dollars more in government funds. But she lost to the outsider candidate Trump, who swept to power on a surge of nationalist sentiment. Clinton, Kerry, and their allies were marginalized as Washington was taken over by the brash New York real estate mogul turned television star.

With Trump in the White House, the prospects for Kito and Kerry's Marshall Plan swiftly faded. Arab governments that had been considering funding the new Marshall Plan lost interest. Kito and Arif, like most of the Davos elite, had backed the losing side in the election. Kerry issued a final plea for a Marshall Plan for the Middle East at a conference at the U.S. Institute of Peace in Washington days before Trump was inaugurated in January 2017. His language was reminiscent of Arif's arguments.

"We need urgently a new Marshall Plan, which is focused on the most critical states in the world, in certain locations, particularly Middle East, North Africa, South Central Asia, where we have got to push back against a huge youth bulge," Kerry said. "In the long run that investment pays off a hundred million different ways and it saves us money and it saves us the treasure of sending our young people to some other country where we have to fight because we didn't do what we could have done early on and preventively."

Journalist Judy Woodruff asked Kerry if he wanted to continue working on these issues after he left office.

"Yeah. I'm trying to find out how—what the best way of doing that is, but yes," Kerry said.

"You going to start your own organization?" Woodruff asked.

"No, I don't want to start my own thing. I—I want to find the right thing to do within the context of something that's there," Kerry said.

But the plea for a new Marshall Plan fell on deaf ears because Trump's victory was a jolt against the forces of globalization that Kerry, Kito, and Arif had successfully surfed for years. The new president condemned globalization for causing carnage in America in his inaugural speech on the steps of the U.S. Capitol, a few days after Kerry spoke. Globalization had taken America's wealth, stolen its companies, and destroyed millions of jobs, Trump said.

"We've made other countries rich while the wealth, strength, and confidence of our country has disappeared over the horizon," Trump said. "The wealth of our middle class has been ripped from their homes and then redistributed across the entire world.

"From this day forward, a new vision will govern our land. From this moment on, it's going to be America First."

Arif made no secret of his dislike for the new American president, whose political vision appeared to be so different to his own.

"Nationalism, populism, isolationism, these are all forces that are beginning to rear their heads again," Arif told investors in early 2017. "We are witnessing a major shift in the United States."

As Trump talked about putting America first, an unexpected new champion of globalization took to the world stage. President Xi Jinping of China traveled to the World Economic Forum in Davos in January 2017 to make his case.

"Globalization was once viewed as the treasure cave found by Ali Baba in *The Arabian Nights*," Xi said in the Swiss town. "Globalization has created new problems, but this is no justification to write economic globalization off completely. Rather, we should adapt to and guide economic globalization, cushion its negative impact, and deliver its benefits to all countries and all nations."

The Chinese president impressed the Davos crowd. He was talking their language. He was talking Arif's language. Arif told people that Xi was filling a political vacuum by becoming the champion of global capitalism. He praised China's international investment strategy—a strategy that had provided him with a buyer for Karachi Electric—and compared its impact to that of many Marshall Plans.

"Imagine what one Marshall Plan did to Europe at the end of the Second World War," Arif said. "These are fifteen Marshall Plans being implemented together across Vietnam, Bangladesh, India, Pakistan, Kenya, and forty other countries."

As much as Arif approved of Xi's enthusiasm for globalization, it wasn't much use to him for fundraising purposes because Arif was trying to raise money from the pension funds and money pots of the Western world, where Trump's isolationism was becoming a real threat to his vision and his marketing pitch.

Arif took every opportunity to preach globalization to America in a bid to drown out the president's words in the ears of the people he needed most. One big global market was the best idea, he told Bloomberg Television in an interview in Davos. Days later, he was promoting globalization in Berlin.

"In India, every thirty days there are close to a million people that turn eighteen," Arif said. "That's not going to change because America becomes more isolationist in the way that it does trade with the rest of the world. These people want jobs. They want to come into the middle classes. They want to consume."

As Trump established himself in power, opportunities diminished for globalists who believed in win-win outcomes to work with the U.S. government. Kito never saw eye to eye with the new administration in Washington and soon stepped down from his role as head of the UN Quartet.

In need of a new job, Kito joined Abraaj on a salary package worth hundreds of thousands of dollars a year. Arif sent out a press release in September 2017 in which he said that Kito would coordinate the firm's impact-investing efforts to help achieve the UN's sustainable development goals to eliminate poverty.

Inside Abraaj, Kito laid out the limits of the firm's impact-investing strategy in an email to Arif and two dozen other colleagues. He referred to the economic pyramid of mankind, which the Indian academic C. K. Prahalad said had a fortune waiting to be made at the very bottom. Kito wasn't so sure.

"Target market will be the lower half of the pyramid," Kito wrote. "Not the Bottom of the Pyramid which is unlikely to be economically sustainable. We will focus on helping those at the bottom of the economic ladder move upwards. We will focus on creating the next generation of consumer."

CHAPTER 15

DOUBLING DOWN

Seen from space, the earth was transformed in the decades after Arif first marveled at men walking on the moon in 1969. New clusters of yellow-white lights sprang up across Africa, Asia, and Latin America. The lights marked the spread of globalization, as sprawling cities emerged to rival London, Paris, and New York in size. Where once there was darkness, now there was light as Dubai, Karachi, Cairo, Riyadh, Kolkata, Jakarta, Lima, and Lagos shone into the night sky and claimed their places in a global constellation that included the electrified urban centers of North America and Europe.

The cities glowed like pots of gold to Arif. They were treasure to exploit, fruits of globalization, beacons of a new prosperity that was emerging as millions of people moved out of the countryside.

"It is cities, not countries, that are going to be driving economic growth," Arif told investors and politicians. "You can invest into the infrastructure of cities and almost anything you touch, whether it's logistics, healthcare, education, financial services, consumer goods, and services—and I could keep going on with that list—there will always be an investible opportunity within urbanization that is going to land up helping you make money."

To seize this opportunity, Arif came up with his grandest, most desperate plan. He decided in 2016 to double down by raising $6 billion for the biggest emerging markets private equity fund the world had ever seen. The fund would buy companies serving the emerging middle classes in the new cities that illuminated the night. Abraaj's internal code name for this fund was Pangea, after the united supercontinent that existed hundreds of millions of years ago.

Raising the $6 billion fund was the only way to keep Abraaj afloat. Many of the firm's investments were struggling and Arif couldn't pay bills without stealing. Convincing investors to hand over $6 billion wasn't going to be easy, and Arif's skill as a storyteller was put to its greatest test yet. He launched a massive marketing campaign to herald the ambitious new fund. Glitzy promotional materials were designed and sent out to investors. Slick new videos were posted on the internet. Abraaj boasted net annual returns of 17.9 percent, ranking the firm among the best private equity houses globally. Abraaj also claimed an unusually low loss ratio for its investments, of less than 2 percent. The numbers were fiction.

The new fund, formally called Abraaj Private Equity Fund VI, was registered in the Cayman Islands, like most of Abraaj's funds and operating units. This helped executives and investors minimize the amount of tax they paid. But Abraaj's excessive reliance on the Cayman Islands as a legal jurisdiction also meant the firm wasn't properly authorized to manage investor money in Dubai, and this legal technicality was making some employees nervous. Arif worked on the fund with his bankers and lawyers in Dubai, London, and New York. The support of hundreds of people in law firms, banks, and accounting firms around the world was vital to Abraaj's fundraising effort. The New York law firm Weil, Gotshal & Manges was Arif's legal adviser for the new fund. The London law firms Freshfields and Allen & Overy worked closely with him too. KPMG did the auditing.

"Thank you so much for all your support," Arif wrote to one adviser in New York. "Let's have a massive success!"

• • •

Deep-pocketed American pension funds were the holy grail of private equity firms trying to raise money, and Arif hired more American employees to help win them over. Vinay Chawla joined Abraaj from the U.S. State department. Arif also brought on board Mark Bourgeois, an evangelical Christian from Tennessee. Short and tanned with slicked-back hair, Mark had an easy southern charm. He dressed like a Wall Street banker from the 1980s, favoring pin-striped suits and brightly colored shirts with collars and cuffs accented in different colors. During his two decades in the finance industry Mark had raised billions of dollars for private equity funds. He became chief executive of Atlantic Pacific Capital, a New York–based advisory firm, after working at the investment banks Credit Suisse and UBS. He had clients around the world and was close to Erik Hirsch at Hamilton Lane, the firm that advised American pension funds on billions of dollars' worth of investments in private equity funds.

Arif first met Mark when he tried to hire Atlantic Pacific to help Abraaj raise funds. Mark's colleagues decided against working with Abraaj but Mark started moonlighting for Arif. When his secret sideline was discovered, Atlantic Pacific executives confronted Mark, who burst into tears. Mark left the firm soon after and joined Abraaj full-time.

Arif put Mark in charge of raising the new $6 billion fund. He was a zealous supporter of Arif's mission to do good. He was heavily involved in his local church and in supporting an orphanage in Africa. Altruism wasn't his only motivation for being at Abraaj, though—he would earn a large bonus if the fundraising was successful.

While Mark opened doors for Arif on Wall Street, another new hire boosted his credibility in Washington. Matt McGuire was a blue-eyed American in his early forties who had served as his country's representative on the board of the World Bank after stints at the Department of Commerce and at a hedge fund. President Obama had nominated Matt for the World Bank role. The two had become friends years earlier in Chicago, where they played basketball together and their daughters attended the same school.

Matt had been keenly interested in the world beyond America's borders since childhood. His parents had both worked for the volunteer Peace Corps—his father in East Pakistan, which later became Bangladesh, and his mother in Ghana. His father died when he was six but left a profound impression on his son, instilling in the youngster a desire to use America's power and influence to make the world a better place.

As Matt's time at the World Bank drew to an end he struck upon the idea of setting up a policy institute to promote investment in emerging markets. He pitched the idea to leading American private equity tycoons including Carlyle's David Rubenstein and discussed it with a senior executive at KKR before contacting Arif. Matt and Arif immediately hit it off. Matt was a perfect foil for Arif, who was supportive of his policy institute idea and offered to hire him. Matt called Obama for advice on his next career move. Obama told him to contact his old college friend Wahid Hamid, who was a partner at Abraaj. Matt contacted Wahid, who didn't deter him from joining but advised him to check it out first.

Matt flew to Dubai in March 2017 to attend Abraaj's annual investor meeting. There were five hundred people in attendance including top bankers, politicians, and journalists. John Kerry, who had recently stepped down as secretary of state, gave a speech after Arif paid $250,500 for him to show up. Matt had heard that Arif was trying to hire Kerry and was offering the former secretary of state millions of dollars a year to join Abraaj. Kerry was considering the opportunity and sounded out friends and colleagues about Abraaj.

As Matt sat down for dinner at an Abraaj event in the towering Burj Khalifa, he surveyed the great and the good clustered around the room. He wasn't easily impressed by such meetings but had to admit to himself that the gathering was significant. There was Vali Nasr, dean of the Johns Hopkins School of Advanced International Studies. And there was Kathy Calvin, the head of the United Nations Foundation. The *Financial Times* journalist Henny Sender moderated some of the discussions. All the signs seemed to show that Arif was a credible person to work for, Matt thought. He decided to join Abraaj.

. . .

Arif launched into a new world tour in 2017 to spread the message that he was raising the new fund. Mark, Matt, and other Abraaj executives often tagged along. In Los Angeles Arif spoke at a conference that President George W. Bush also attended. Other speakers included the chiefs of JPMorgan and Google, and the conference organizer Michael Milken, an American billionaire philanthropist who was trying to rebuild his reputation after spending some time in jail for financial crimes. When Arif's turn to speak about his endeavors came around, he compared himself to Moses, the biblical prophet.

"It is about creating a better world," Arif said. "It won't come up as a directive on a tablet on a burnt-out mountain. It will be us that will figure it out," he said. "We will be the front-runners of changing the way the world thinks."

But creating a better world was way more difficult than Arif let on in his conference speeches. Crises were breaking out across his empire.

In Pakistan, the supreme court removed Prime Minister Nawaz Sharif from office in July 2017. The prime minister was convicted of corruption in a case centering on the ownership of London apartments his family used. The judgment dealt a heavy blow to Arif's hopes of quickly concluding the sale of Karachi Electric. To make matters worse, Bashir Memon, a respected policeman who led Pakistan's Federal Investigation Agency, probed Karachi Electric's unpaid bills and resolved that the company owed hundreds of millions of dollars to a government-owned gas company.

In Saudi Arabia, two Abraaj investments were struggling. The Tadawi pharmacy chain and the Kudu fast-food restaurant group were close to bankruptcy and threatened to wipe out tens of millions of dollars of investor money.

In Turkey, Yörsan was in critical condition. The dairy company had dropped to sixth place among its competitors, with a 27 percent slump in sales in the first half of 2017.

Upon his return to Dubai, Arif called a meeting of his most senior colleagues to discuss the bitter reality. They couldn't possibly raise a $6 billion fund if they told investors the truth about their difficulties. With performance lagging across their investment portfolio, they decided to fraudulently increase the valuation of the companies Abraaj owned, regardless of how they were doing. They increased Yörsan's valuation even though sales and profits were falling at the dairy company. The boost made Yörsan look better on paper than it really was and helped Arif maintain the illusion of strong performance as he raised the new fund. Arif instructed his colleagues to mark up the value of other investments.

"The valuations are not moving in the directions we require," Waqar told Arif.

Arif sat down with a loyal employee who helped coordinate the valuations process. When their discussion finished, the employee contacted Mustafa, Abraaj's top dealmaker.

"We sat with Arif on valuations and have the proposed changes," the employee told Mustafa.

Freshly inflated valuations were soon sent to Arif for him to consider.

"Is this sufficient?" Arif wrote in an email to Rafique and Ashish, Abraaj's chief financial officer. "What more do we need to get into the safe zone."

Ashish forwarded the email to an employee who he told to "plug in" the manipulated valuations to a marketing document for investors.

Sev, the former Aureos chief who was a senior partner at Abraaj, weighed in and suggested that a $5 million uplift could be added to the value of the healthcare fund investments.

The systematic valuation fraud inside Abraaj didn't go entirely unchallenged. Some junior employees knew it was wrong and resisted.

Arif and his team wanted to value Kudu, the Saudi restaurant chain, at 1.4 times the amount Abraaj had invested in the company. But the American private equity firm TPG was also an investor in Kudu and thought the company was only worth half the value Abraaj was proposing, a junior Abraaj employee pointed out in an internal email.

"We need to bring valuation down to cost," another employee responded.

Mustafa forwarded the emails to Arif, who was in no mood for discussion. Arif told Mustafa that no reductions in valuation should be made and said that he needed to do more to keep his team in line.

"Let them understand the big picture and why we are being pushy," Arif said in an email. "Even little things like writing down Kudu should be a no no, and we should reflect our aspirations in the others.

"I need a minimum of $20–25 million profit at Abraaj Holdings in order to keep this effing business afloat and show strength to the banks."

The junior employee who bravely objected to the valuation fraud was brushed aside. Arif ordered Mustafa to silence any other team members who suggested more write-downs. Kudu's inflated value was added to the track record. In total, Abraaj inflated the value of its assets by more than $500 million.

The tense discussions were fraying Arif's relationship with Mustafa, who couldn't deal with Arif's increasing outbursts of fury. They almost came to blows during one tense exchange in the summer of 2017 when Arif was lecturing Mustafa; his brother-in-law, Waqar; and his chief of staff, Anuscha, during a meeting.

"Can you just repeat what you said?" Mustafa asked Arif politely. "I'm not sure I understood."

Arif unleashed a tirade of abuse. Mustafa usually apologized or stayed silent when this happened but this time he decided to respond.

"If you're not willing to explain what you just said then there is no point me being here," Mustafa said.

"If you walk out you probably don't ever want to come in again," Arif said.

"That's actually probably not a bad idea," Mustafa said.

He got up and walked out. Arif followed him into the corridor and confronted him by posturing aggressively and jabbing his finger into Mustafa's chest. Mustafa swore at Arif and walked away. That night when Mustafa was at home his phone rang. It was Arif. Mustafa didn't feel like talking but he picked up anyway.

"I'm feeling really down," Arif said. "Can you come over to my house?"

"Why?" Mustafa asked.

Arif said he regretted the confrontation and wanted to discuss it. He asked Mustafa to apologize. Mustafa refused. Arif said he needed to tell Anuscha, who had seen Mustafa stand up to him, that he had received an apology. Mustafa refused again. Arif later told Anuscha that Mustafa had apologized. He had to maintain his public image.

Arif's erratic behavior was burning through the goodwill of his senior staff. Mustafa resolved to quit. But it wasn't so easy to escape, because Arif kept him at heel through a strange combination of bullying and kindness. Soon after their confrontation, Mustafa's mother passed away from cancer and he returned home to Cairo for her funeral. He put aside the pressures of Abraaj for a few days and mourned his mother with family and friends. When Arif heard what had happened, he flew to Cairo to pay his respects. Arif was the last person Mustafa wanted to see but it was impossible to avoid Arif when he showed up at Mustafa's family home. Mustafa let him in and they sat together for a few hours. The gesture touched Mustafa. He soon returned to work to complete the $6 billion fundraising.

• • •

The decision to lie to investors was paying off and money was rolling in for the new fund. The Washington State Investment Board, one of the world's largest and most experienced investors in private equity funds, was considering making a $250 million investment in Abraaj for the first time. Hamilton Lane, which advised Washington State, recommended Abraaj because of its apparently high returns and low losses.

Arif flew to Olympia, the capital of Washington State, to meet pension fund officials. Wahid and Anuscha accompanied him. When they arrived, the Washington State Investment Board official Fabrizio Natale supported their request for funds.

"Abraaj has a large, institutionalized team with extensive emerging and frontier markets experience and an on the ground presence," Natale told colleagues.

Arif explained to the Washington officials that Abraaj invested in consumer goods, financial services, logistics, healthcare, and education companies in cities across developing markets. He made a positive impression.

"Make sure you take a look at the Abraaj Presentation from the Private Markets meeting today," Stephen Backholm, the pension fund's director of innovation, told the pension fund's chief financial officer. "Great presentation and engaging information. I found the founder (who presented) to be very articulate and insightful."

Washington unanimously approved the $250 million investment in Abraaj. It was a significant endorsement and was soon followed by commitments to invest from the Texas Retirement System, the Teachers' Retirement System of Louisiana, the Hawaii Employees' Retirement System, and the American Federation of Musicians and Employers' Pension Fund.

Arif had finally cracked open the pension pots of America in a big way. But inside Abraaj, rumors were spreading about Arif manipulating investment valuations and the gossip was making some old hands uncomfortable. Sev felt the sting of his conscience even as he conspired with Arif. He knew that his own presence at Abraaj gave Arif cover for his misdeeds.

"It is people like us that give credibility to characters such as Arif because the investors know that Arif is a strong character but at the same time they think we probably will not support those kinds of things," Sev told a colleague. "And since we in front of them confirm what bullshit that Arif says they are ignoring their own instinct."

CHAPTER 16

PEAK ABRAAJ

Arif's scheming might have continued undetected had it not been for an important moment in late 2017 when Andrew Farnum noticed some numbers didn't add up. Andrew managed $2 billion at the Gates Foundation, including a $100 million investment in Abraaj's healthcare fund. He couldn't understand why Abraaj kept asking him to send more money for the fund when the firm didn't appear to be using the cash he'd already sent them.

Andrew was a thoughtful investor who took his job seriously. A slender man with a warm smile and an earnest manner, he fervently believed that the purpose of a career in finance should be about more than making money. He had studied molecular biology at Princeton University, but his childhood dream of becoming a neuroscientist was derailed by an aversion to spending long hours in laboratories dissecting rats. After graduating in 1999, he pursued another passion—finance—and landed a prestigious job at Goldman Sachs in New York. It was the height of the tech bubble when valuations of internet and telecommunications companies soared. Andrew was an investment banker in the communications group and one of his jobs was to win business from WorldCom, a darling of stock market investors at the time. He met the company's domineering founder, Bernie Ebbers, a number of times before the telecommunications company collapsed.

Ebbers was convicted of fraud. Andrew's meetings with Ebbers gave him an insider view of how fraudsters spoke and acted and how a company can rapidly go from being on top of the world to nothing.

Andrew soon became restless at Goldman. In the summer of 2001, he took off with his brother and a friend on a yearlong adventure to explore remote corners of the world. They visited Russia, Ukraine, India, China, and Nepal. In September 2001 they arrived in eastern Turkey, where their trip took an unexpected turn. They watched in horror as television images showed two planes flying into the World Trade Center, not far from Andrew's old office at Goldman. Their shock and rage was softened by friendly locals who treated them with great kindness. The terror attacks thwarted their travel plans though, and they abandoned an attempt to visit Pakistan because it had become too dangerous.

The great beauty of the places Andrew visited was matched only by the poverty of the people he met. When he finally returned to America it didn't seem right to go back to a job in banking. So he started thinking about finance in a new way. Could he make investments that would help poor people in the developing countries he had visited?

First he tried a job at TPG, working for a fund that the private equity firm had started to invest in water projects. The fund operated in developing countries but to Andrew it seemed that the primary objective was still to make rich people richer, and he wanted to accomplish more with his life than that. So he went back to school and studied development economics at Harvard. That led to a job at the U.S government's Millennium Challenge Corp., an agency that provided aid to developing countries. There was a higher sense of purpose in this job but Andrew couldn't stand the slow pace and bureaucracy of working for the government.

He moved to London in 2008 to work for the billionaire British hedge fund manager Chris Hohn, who was setting up an impact-investing program. After a few years in London, an opportunity came up which he couldn't refuse. Bill Gates was starting his own impact-investing program in Seattle, near Andrew's hometown. Andrew joined the Gates Foundation in 2011 and worked for Julie Sunderland, who arranged the foundation's investment in Abraaj's healthcare fund. When Julie left in 2016, Andrew took over her responsibilities, including Abraaj. He had always struggled to see eye to eye with the executives at Abraaj. It was hard to trust them because they rarely gave straight answers to his questions.

Andrew's suspicions were first aroused when Abraaj sold a couple of investments from its African healthcare fund to its $1 billion global healthcare fund. He was concerned that Abraaj executives might be incentivized to pay too much for the assets owned by the African fund in order to generate bonus payments for themselves.

His worries escalated when he saw that Abraaj was asking investors to send hundreds of millions of dollars for the global healthcare fund and not using the money to buy hospitals and clinics. His patience snapped on September 12, 2017.

"I'm concerned about the disconnect between the capital drawn down and the capital actually invested. There seems to be an extraordinary amount of money sitting in the fund for quite an extended period of time," Andrew wrote in an email to Abraaj. "Two questions related to this," he wrote. "First, can you send me details on where those funds are located and how they are currently invested? Second, do you have a schedule you can send of when the actual investments are expected to be made?"

Andrew's tone was polite but the implications of his questions were ominous. He was asking Abraaj to prove it wasn't misusing the money of one of the world's richest men.

"I have asked treasury/accounts to come back with the exact location," the Abraaj executive Raj Morjaria replied. "Will be in touch shortly."

When Andrew sent his email Arif was in the tropical city-state of Singapore, where he was preparing to speak at a conference about dispelling the myths of emerging markets. Arif was on stage with some of the biggest names in global finance. Mark Wiseman, a top executive at BlackRock, the world's largest asset manager, was asking the questions. To Arif's left sat David Bonderman, the billionaire founder of TPG, Andrew's former employer, which had recently started an impact-investing fund with the Irish rock star Bono. The fourth panelist was Binod Chaudhary, a billionaire from the Himalayan nation of Nepal who made his fortune selling noodles.

Arif exuded cool confidence, his silver hair swept neatly back. With the calm authority of a veteran professor, he launched into his speech and lectured the audience about why emerging markets should be called global growth markets.

"Call it part laziness, call it part patronizing, to call them emerging markets," Arif said.

BlackRock's Wiseman nodded in agreement. Wasn't there just one problem, he asked? In a word: corruption.

Chaudhary, the Nepali noodle king, agreed. Corruption was a constant problem. Sticking too closely to the law didn't work in developing countries, he admitted.

"We are talking about a completely different rule of the game," Chaudhary said. "If you position yourself as a credible, transparent organization and maintain that kind of identity and image, and yet you have your own mechanism to deal with some of the necessary evils, so to speak, in terms of dealing with the expectations, you can do it."

This admission triggered a strong reaction from Arif.

"I am sorry, Binod, but I am going to have to emphatically disagree with you," he said. "Corruption exists in every market around the world.

"The key is, as a disciplined investor, you've got to be able to say there are things that you will do and there are things that you will not do. And if you are very focused on what you will not do, I'd call that, in very loose terms, a corporate foreign policy.

"Private equity is actually a great unwrapper of the identity of businesses. So you can actually unwrap the business during due diligence and figure out whether you want to do it or you walk away,"

Arif said. "We know what we stand for and we know what we won't do. And as a result of that what we are actually doing—without saying it—is we are also bringing good practice into our markets. And that, I think, is one of the most important things we do."

It was a good speech but Chaudhary wasn't convinced.

"If anybody tells me that in emerging markets—whether you are the world's biggest multinational or private equity firm—you do not indulge in favor taking and favor giving, I disagree," he said.

"Now this is getting fun," Arif replied.

To win the argument, Arif deployed his finest example: himself.

"We invested in a utility company in Karachi in Pakistan eight years ago. It is a country not known for transparency. It is a country where in government you are often asked for either favors or money or whatever.

"We went into that organization knowing that if you could have employed all the consultants in the world to design a broken company you wouldn't have done a better job.

"We did everything by the book to the extent that business school case studies around the world have been written about it. We avoided every single point where you would have had to come into contact with government—even though you were a utility—and have to pay someone something. And because we stood for doing the right thing civil society rallied around us.

"You can do these things. It just is a matter of how you want to position yourself."

The Nepali noodle billionaire conceded victory.

"It happened because it is Arif Naqvi," Chaudhary said. "The government, the people he was dealing with, they don't have to make a deal on a deal specific basis. They know that Arif is there."

"That's too simplistic," Arif said.

"So what is it?" Chaudhary asked, exasperated.

"It's called bloody-mindedness," Arif said. "It's about doing the thing the right way."

As Arif preached doing the right thing in Singapore, his colleagues were doing the wrong thing in Dubai. They were debating how to throw Andrew Farnum and the Gates Foundation off their tracks and cover up one of the most audacious frauds in history. First, they decided to fob Andrew off with a vague answer to his question.

"The funds are currently held in the top Cayman Holdco which sits below the Fund vehicle," Abraaj's Raj Morjaria told Andrew on September 15, 2017.

That wasn't good enough.

"Hundreds of millions of dollars are sitting in this account," Andrew replied. "Do you have bank account or investment information you can share?"

His persistence worried Ashish, Abraaj's chief financial officer. Sending real bank statements for the healthcare fund to the Gates Foundation wasn't an option because it would reveal that the money wasn't where it should have been.

Ashish had a better plan. Abraaj could send Andrew a months-old bank statement which showed that $224 million was in the healthcare fund on June 30, 2017—when the fund was full of money borrowed from Air Arabia. Ashish and senior colleagues also agreed to try to intimidate Andrew and isolate him from the other investors so he didn't share his concerns with them.

A few days later they sent Andrew an old Commercial Bank of Dubai statement which showed $224 million was in the fund on June 30, 2017. An employee stressed that they were making an exception by sharing the bank statement.

"It was finally agreed to send this information based on this one time request and the relationship between Abraaj/Gates," the employee wrote. "This is for your internal use only and to be kept confidential."

• • •

Sending Andrew the bogus bank statement bought Arif time to continue his global fundraising tour. He gave his most important speech in New York on the morning of September 18, 2017. His goal that day was to convince more investors to pledge billions of dollars to his new fund. As Arif spoke at the Mandarin Oriental hotel by Central Park, world leaders were arriving a few blocks away at the United Nations headquarters for the annual meeting of the General Assembly.

To most observers Arif was at the peak of his power. He was bolstered by an enamored press and the reflected glow from financiers who oversaw the world's riches. Abraaj was sponsoring this impact investing conference alongside Bank of America and Arif was the keynote speaker. On stage he claimed that the era of the impact investor had arrived. The only criminal act which he was prepared to admit to was the risk of missing the chance to do good.

"We are at the beginning of a rare inflection point, opportunity, that is in front of us, and for us not to grasp it right now and to focus on its energy would be a criminal waste of an opportunity," Arif said.

He reminded the mainly American audience that it was arrogant to think emerging markets were riskier places than their country.

"We have a perception of risk that is not commensurate with where risk is actually coming from. Dare I say it, cheekily, that when risk came into the global financial system and into all our lives it came from right here in New York City in 2008 with the Lehman Brothers crash."

Arif talked about problems—not his problems, of course, but the problems of the global economy and all humanity.

"Let's start with the plumbing of our financial system," Arif said. "It is broken. The system of global finance that we have always depended on to finance growth is just not functioning well at all. And what I mean by that is that it is not allocating capital to places where the demands are greatest and therefore the returns are potentially highest."

Abraaj was the solution to these problems, according to Arif, because his firm had proven that it was possible to make big profits and improve society at the same time.

"Our organization is evidence of that fact," Arif said. "That is how we do our investments."

It was an ambitious pitch. It was also a necessary one, because Abraaj was well and truly broke. Rafique had emailed Arif to ask him to delay three hospital projects because Abraaj didn't have enough money to pay for them. So much for healing the sick. Arif had already spent the money on himself and his firm.

Arif spent the rest of that September week mixing with the most powerful politicians and billionaires on earth. He was a featured speaker at Michael Bloomberg's inaugural Global Business Forum, where he rubbed shoulders with Bill Gates, Bill Clinton, BlackRock's CEO Larry Fink, Goldman Sachs's CEO Lloyd Blankfein, and UN Secretary General Antonio Guterres.

"Is there a tradeoff between doing good and making money?" Arif rhetorically asked the audience at the Bloomberg forum. "There's no tradeoff. You can do both."

He told Unilever's CEO Paul Polman and John Elkann, heir of the family that founded the Italian carmaker Fiat, that the global financial system was broken. There wasn't enough trust in the markets where Abraaj invested, markets Westerners mistakenly believed were too risky, he said.

No one who saw Arif in New York that week would have believed he was in trouble. But details of Abraaj's problems were about to leak out of the firm. An Abraaj employee had discovered that Arif was committing fraud and didn't want to be party to it. While Arif was in New York, the employee broke ranks and sent an anonymous email to investors in the new $6 billion fund. The email warned about years of wrongdoing at Abraaj.

> Do your due diligence properly and ask the right questions. You will be amazed what you discover. The areas you should focus in are like unrealized gains valuations—these are manipulated beyond anything you have seen in any fund and easy to uncover. Don't believe what the partners send you.
> Abraaj fund 4 is the biggest sufferer and has funded the Abraaj Holdings balance sheet for years. Audit the managing directors who

really still works for Abraaj and who resigned many months ago but are waiting for the fund 6 first closing to announce.

Ask for the financials of Abraaj. Audit related transactions and don't trust the partners. The directors and below know the truth. Get to the bottom of the Karachi electric story, presented as a success of Abraaj.

Don't believe the slides and presentations or any information which comes, diligence it yourself with primary data and you will find the truth.

Don't believe what they tell you and check the fact.

Protect yourself.

Arif's viselike grip on Abraaj was slipping, but he still held considerable sway over crucial investors. When Tarang Katira, a Hamilton Lane employee who managed his firm's relationship with Abraaj, received the anonymous email from a more senior colleague he forwarded it to Arif to alert him about the whistleblower. Katira's allegiances were torn between Hamilton Lane and Arif, with whom he'd built a strong relationship. Arif had offered him the chance to join Abraaj on a big salary when the firm completed raising the new $6 billion fund, so it wasn't entirely in Katira's interests to kick up a big fuss about the anonymous email.

Nevertheless, Hamilton Lane executives did ask Arif about the allegations in the email, and he gave them an outraged response.

"It is bizarre and frankly unintelligible for anyone to insinuate that the group would be using LP money for working capital," Arif told Hamilton Lane. He didn't offer any proof that the accusations in the email were untrue.

Arif's priority was to find and silence the whistleblower. He told senior colleagues to make a $500,000 payment to a disgruntled former employee who he suspected of sending the email and hired Nardello & Co., a New York–based investigations firm founded by a former federal prosecutor, to find evidence of who the whistleblower was. Daniel Nardello had spent years catching criminals. Now he found himself unwittingly working for someone heading toward a major showdown with law enforcement. Nardello's team searched for the leaker but the trail went cold. The whistleblower had used a Russian email account and couldn't be tracked down.

The web of lies that Arif had spun was unraveling fast. Officials at the Overseas Private Investment Corp. were becoming suspicious too. The U.S. government fund sent Abraaj $68 million for the healthcare fund in late September 2017, but instead of using the money to build clinics and hospitals in poor countries Arif immediately spent more than half of it on other purposes.

Inside Abraaj, Arif projected confidence as best he could. At the firm's annual town hall meeting at the Dubai Hilton in late 2017, he told 350 employees who had flown in from across the world that everything was going to plan: $3 billion had already been raised for the new fund. Employees were glad to hear about the billions that were rolling in. They had been waiting almost six months for their bonuses. Perhaps now they would be paid.

On stage, Arif randomly pulled out of a goldfish bowl questions that employees had written on pieces of paper. One question was particularly challenging. The note asked whether Ahmed Badreldin, the head of Abraaj in North Africa, was leaving the firm. Arif turned the question over to Ahmed in the audience.

"Are you leaving?" Arif asked.

Ahmed was surprised by the question because Arif already knew the answer. He had been negotiating his exit from the firm for months.

"I am leaving," he replied.

Arif, taken aback by the direct public response, paced up and down the stage like an angry bear. It didn't help that there were more questions from the audience about when bonuses would be paid. Some employees lowered their gaze to avoid eye contact with Arif. The atmosphere was so awkward, one employee thought he would rather leave the room by crawling over broken glass than watch Arif's performance.

More executives were discreetly planning to head for the exit. Tom

Speechley, one of Arif's most trusted advisers since the early days of Abraaj, wanted to leave the firm. Hushed conversations were taking place across the hotel as executives discussed rumors about problems at the healthcare fund.

It was becoming impossible to juggle all Abraaj's problems at once. Payment deadlines were looming thick and fast, and telling brazen lies was the only way to palm off creditors. A $5 million interest payment on a loan from a Kuwaiti government pension fund was due. Arif asked colleagues what to do.

"What obfuscation ideas can you come up with to delay this by a few weeks?" Arif asked.

Tell the Kuwaitis that there was a delay in receiving money from the sale of a company, Ashish suggested. Arif agreed.

• • •

Arif's tactics weren't working with the Gates Foundation. Andrew wasn't satisfied with the answers he was getting and he had talked about his concerns with a few other healthcare fund investors. The investors didn't pull their punches during a healthcare fund meeting in Nairobi on October 12, 2017.

Clarisa de Franco, an executive at the British government's CDC, asked why Abraaj had drawn down more than 50 percent of the healthcare fund but not deployed all of the money.

The money was unused because of unexpected delays on hospital construction projects, an Abraaj executive replied. Andrew dialed in to the Nairobi meeting from his office in Seattle and asked Abraaj to confirm which bank account the fund money was in.

It was in an account at Standard Bank in the Cayman Islands, said Badruddin Hilal, the chief financial officer for the healthcare fund. The recent recruit was passing on information he got from Rafique. Andrew was astonished. Abraaj had previously sent him a bank statement from Commercial Bank of Dubai, not Standard Bank. Andrew asked Badruddin to explain.

There was an awkward silence. Badruddin, a former Microsoft executive, said he needed to check where the money was. He'd get back to investors as soon as he had an answer.

The alarm bells ringing in Andrew's head turned into sirens. Fund managers don't forget where they put $200 million, he thought. Misplacing hundreds of millions of dollars destined to build hospitals in poor countries was a terrible admission for a fund management firm, particularly for one that boasted about its professionalism and good corporate governance.

When the meeting ended, Andrew sent a message to a group email account used by all the healthcare fund investors but his email bounced back. Abraaj, which managed the account, had disabled it to stop the investors from communicating with one another.

Andrew forwarded the Commercial Bank of Dubai statement Abraaj had sent him to CDC, the World Bank's International Finance Corp. unit, and Proparco, the French government fund. "Given that we are being told two different things I thought it was important to share it with you," Andrew told them. "We should now absolutely confirm where the cash is invested."

Abraaj's Raj Morjaria emailed the investors to say they would soon be told where their money was.

"We need to see as soon as possible (can't be that hard to remember where the $200m+ is sitting)," Andrew replied.

After another two days had passed, Badruddin informed the investors that he'd been mistaken. Their money was indeed safely deposited at Commercial Bank of Dubai and not Standard Bank as he had said in the meeting.

"A total amount of $544.8mn was drawn from LPs and against this, $318.9mn was deployed," Badruddin said in an email. "This leaves cash available of $225.9mn."

The investors no longer trusted Abraaj and wanted their money back. The trouble was, Abraaj didn't have it. Tom Rostand, an official at the French government's Proparco, got on the case. He emailed Abraaj on behalf of Proparco, the Gates Foundation, and the IFC. He demanded an up-to-date bank statement for the fund and said that unused money should be returned. Sev swatted down the Frenchman in a reply to him, his boss, and other investors.

"Your email below is not appropriate," Sev wrote. "Abraaj has already spoken to the IFC, CDC and Gates directly on this matter."

Rostand apologized.

"I had not been informed about this," he replied. "Therefore apologies for the setback and confusion if all the information requested was about to be provided."

Arif forwarded the email chain including the Frenchman's apology to the IFC. This prompted a further apology.

"We apologize for this form of communications on behalf of the IFC," wrote Mouayad Makhlouf, the head of the IFC in the Middle East. "We are terribly sorry for this."

Andrew replied to everyone on the email chain—including Abraaj executives and investors.

"I would like to reiterate the questions below in Tom's email and the request to return the overdrawn funds," he wrote.

Arif forwarded this email, which he described as tetchy and offensive, to Andrew's boss at the Gates Foundation, Christopher Elias. Arif pointed out that Proparco and the IFC had apologized to him but Andrew had not.

"I am quite upset," Arif wrote. "We were asked once by Mr. Farnum a month or two ago for proof of funds in that we had the funds unused in a bank account; despite being embarrassed at the request (one that we had not experienced before), we provided a bank audit certificate, as part of our audit procedures. To ask for it again one or two months later when there has been no change is frankly demeaning.

"I, and we, are not, with respect, an average fund manager running an average fund. I Hope you don't mind if I put down my perspective in plain English so you have a clearly expressed view from me."

Christopher Elias called in Andrew to discuss what was going on. Andrew explained that it was Arif who was being offensive, not him.

Andrew was certain Arif was committing fraud. Why else would he react in such an extreme way to a few reasonable questions?

At the IFC, Chief Executive Philippe Le Houérou received a call from Arif, who demanded that the questions from his subordinates cease. After the conversation, Philippe called Maria Kozloski, who was in charge of investing IFC money in private equity funds, and asked her what was going on. Maria explained that Arif's irate response to straightforward questions raised her suspicions that something was seriously wrong. Philippe told her to investigate and not to be deterred by Arif's complaints.

Back at the Gates Foundation more executives gathered to discuss how to respond. Arif was a self-proclaimed philanthropist, a signatory of the Giving Pledge, and an important partner in Bill Gates's quest to build a better world. Was he really a fraudster and a thief? Andrew's bosses agreed he should amp up the pressure on Arif and get to the bottom of the problem. Andrew asked Abraaj for more information.

"Please provide the actual bank statements from all banks in which all of the contributed funds have been held from November 24, 2016, to November 30, 2017, showing all transactions," he wrote. "To be clear, we are requesting actual bank statements, not a summary in another format."

Arif told Sev to keep Andrew's latest demand a secret.

"Let's not forward to ANYONE internally yet please," Arif told him.

Sev replied to Andrew with a ruse to buy time.

"I have just landed in London from Nairobi and I know Dubai is closed for religious festivities until next Tuesday and hence most people tend to take this opportunity to take the week off," Sev said. "As soon as people are back will deal with this request."

Then Arif proposed a solution to Ashish, Waqar, and Rafique.

"Air Arabia is easy to give us 100 on Monday into a designated account for a week," he said. "Can we make it work?"

They did make it work.

Arif borrowed $140 million more from the airline and the money entered the healthcare fund's bank account on December 5, 2017. The loan stayed in the account for fewer than ten days—long enough for a December 7 bank statement to show $170 million in the fund. Arif ordered staff to send a new bank statement to Andrew and the other investors to prove everything was fine. But the statement for December 7 made the investors even more concerned. Andrew had asked for statements for an entire year, not for one December day.

Andrew and the other investors appointed Ankura, a U.S. forensic accounting firm, to find out what was really going on. Sev tried to reassure Andrew. He explained that the healthcare fund was being operated like a company, rather than a fund, and that under such circumstances it was normal for cash balances to be kept for long periods.

Arif's only option now was to return all the missing money to the healthcare fund investors and hope they stopped asking questions. He needed to find $200 million to make the payment. Arif turned to the wealthy UAE investor Hamid Jafar for money in December 2017. Hamid was an early investor in Abraaj, and his Eton-educated son Badr was a member of Abraaj's board of directors.

Hamid agreed to lend $350 million, repayable within two months. Hamid insisted on a hefty $18 million upfront fee for the loan but he was confident Arif would repay the money. He trusted Arif so much that the agreement was sealed orally and without documentation.

Arif also sold $100 million of Abraaj shares in December 2017 to the Swiss billionaire Thomas Schmidheiny and to the Indian billionaire Prakash Lohia. Schmidheiny was a member of Abraaj's board, and Arif had invested in one of Lohia's companies.

Arif used some of the money he had collected to pay the healthcare fund investors back, but the investors still wanted answers. It was too late to simply pay them off. U.S., U.K., and French government money had gone missing and officials wanted to know what it had been used for.

Arif changed his tactics with Andrew. He called him repeatedly and tried to win him over with flattery. He said that he had closely followed Andrew's career for a decade and told him he wasn't surprised when the Gates Foundation promoted him to lead its impact-investing program. He wanted Andrew to call off the investigation by the forensic accountants at Ankura and urged him to appoint KPMG or another of the big accounting firms to do the audit instead.

The handful of Abraaj employees who knew about the precarious situation were extremely nervous.

"It's fraud. Simple," an executive told Mustafa in December 2017.

"Even beyond that," Mustafa replied.

Arif still pressed on with meetings to raise the $6 billion fund. He flew to New York to meet more prospective investors and told the usual lies. Abraaj investments always outperformed; Abraaj rarely lost money on a deal; Abraaj had impeccable corporate governance.

To maintain the illusion of outstanding performance, Arif insisted that the fraudulently inflated valuations for Abraaj's investments should be kept until the fundraising was complete. Mark Bourgeois said lowering valuations would affect fundraising.

"To be brief/blunt, if we take these write downs and announce them on our usual end of year schedule, I do believe it will have a negative influence on later stage investors and could derail some of them," Mark said.

Sev concurred. Keeping the valuations up gave them a better chance to collect more money for the fund, he said.

CHAPTER 17

DON'T MAKE NICE WITH A FRAUDSTER

Billionaires and politicians embarked on the annual capitalist pilgrimage to the Swiss mountain town of Davos at the end of January 2018. President Trump attended the meeting for the first time that year. Arif was there, as he had been almost every January for more than a decade, mingling with three thousand participants.

Each evening as snow fell, the Canadian entertainer Barry Colson played the piano and sang hit songs in the warm intimacy of the Piano Bar at Hotel Europa. Colson was a late-night legend in Davos. He had an enthusiastic fan base of politicians and executives who sang along and danced on tables on the understanding that any journalists in the bar wouldn't write about their antics. Arif always went to see Colson play. He would sit on the window ledge behind the singer, drinking whiskey and listening to him. This year, Colson noticed that Arif paused as he made his way up the staircase leading to the Piano Bar. Arif didn't seem to be his usual confident self. Colson thought Arif was wonderful—he was by far the best tipper in Davos. But this time Arif didn't come into the bar. He waited outside. Colson had heard a rumor—a rumor that something was going on at Abraaj.

· · ·

The Thursday before the Davos meeting began, Will Louch woke up at 7:00 on a cold morning in London. He might have gone back to sleep if he hadn't glanced at the emails on his phone. A message caught his eye. It had arrived at 4:51 a.m. from an unknown sender using the email address wbabraaj@mail.com.

"Sev Vettivetpillai Managing Partner at The Abraaj Group and founder of Aureos Capital has resigned," the email said.

A quick Google search on Abraaj yielded an article about the private equity firm seeking $6 billion from investors for a new fund. There were flattering *New York Times* and *Fortune* articles about its founder, Arif Naqvi. He seemed to be a very important person. The news about Abraaj's fundraising effort made Sev's alleged departure more significant because senior executives don't usually leave private equity firms during a fundraising. Their departures can spook investors who have a close working relationship with them.

Will emailed Sev to ask if he was leaving.

"I have not left Abraaj," Sev replied promptly. "I have been hearing this quite a bit and have informed everyone I am not leaving."

Will emailed the mystery source, who replied a few hours later.

> I am an employee at Abraaj who cannot accept that Abraaj is raising money currently from investors for the new $6bn fund pretending that the managing partner of the firm is still working there. Also there is a potential fraud investigation for the $1bn Abraaj global healthcare fund which IFC, gates foundation, CDC, and Proparco are investigating.

This was big news if it was true, but at this point there were more questions than answers. Was the information accurate? Did the sender really work at Abraaj? What was the motive for getting in touch?

The internet was flooded with positive news articles about Abraaj, and Arif was all over YouTube. He showed up in news clips from Bloomberg, CNN, and CNBC and in debates with Richard Branson, David Bonderman, and other billionaires. It seemed crazy to think that such a man was involved in fraud. Big private equity firms sometimes lost money in unsuccessful deals but they were rarely accused of outright theft.

The source sent another email later that day. This message contained details that seemed so specific it would be too strange to make them up.

$200m was drawn down from investors to be used in fund investments in late 2016 but the money was actually used to finance Abraaj working capital and balance sheet leverage and commitments.

It didn't make sense that a private equity firm would take money from a fund like this, because the firms charged investors exorbitant fees to cover wage bills. Will fired off another email to the mystery source and waited in a state of nervous anticipation. Early the next morning, a thousand-word email arrived riddled with grammatical errors and granular detail. It was a reporter's dream.

"As the problem got bigger and bigger Arif needed to find larger sums of money to plug the hole and he had to resort to borrowing from the funds larger and larger sums short term. This is now leaking everywhere so many partners started resigning," the source said in the email.

"Good luck with your story. Bottom line is there is no governance in Abraaj and this led to the spiral of events as Arif Naqvi controls everything and no one has a full picture of the problem.

"Now they are trying to find a way out of the hole but it is too late," the source said. "Key question is will the cover up manage to conceal this from the new apef6 investors until the final closing of the fund."

Will asked the person to speak on the phone. This time the source replied less helpfully. The person didn't want to talk and said they had emailed a reporter at the *New York Times* as well. Now a race was on to break the news first. We needed to verify the information provided by the anonymous source with other people because the source refused to give their name.

It was Friday, the day of rest in Islamic countries, but Mitali Atal,

Abraaj's spokesperson in Dubai, was answering emails. Mitali, an Indian, was the first point of contact at Abraaj for journalists. She was fiercely loyal to Arif and a true believer in his mission to improve the world. She carefully controlled which journalists talked to executives and usually imposed strict terms to grant access. But upon receiving Will's email, Mitali immediately arranged a call for him with Matt McGuire, the American who joined Abraaj after working at the World Bank, for the next day.

The Abraaj executive was friendly enough on the phone. He name-dropped a *Wall Street Journal* reporter he'd known during his time at the World Bank and another he'd once taught. Will didn't know either of the reporters because he was a recent recruit to the newspaper. A question about whether Abraaj was under investigation for misusing money in its healthcare fund triggered a firm response.

"Categorically there is no money that disappeared anywhere at Abraaj," Matt said. "We wouldn't have gotten to be the size and reputation that we are now if we did operate that way," he said. "I didn't leave a Senate-confirmed job back in the U.S. to fly halfway around the world without doing a lot of due diligence myself. That's not the kind of place this is."

There was no way Abraaj could get away with theft, because it was regulated in seven jurisdictions, Matt said. It simply wasn't possible.

The question was offensive, Mitali said.

The conversation was over.

Mitali and Matt weren't the only people working in Dubai the weekend before Davos started. Arif was plotting fraud in a meeting with Mustafa and Sev. They were still intent on propping up the falsely inflated valuations for Abraaj's investment portfolio. Arif told them that the valuations were frankly erroneous. He laughed quietly as he explained what he wanted to happen next. When the $6 billion fundraising was complete, the valuations would be gradually lowered.

"We just could not have done it before now," he said, chuckling. "Because to do it before now is to chop your own legs off while you're involved in running the race. Right? And that's stupid, right?

"So, every time I get an email from you or someone, saying 'this valuation is indefensible,' I just do like this," he said, making a gesture. "Because you know what? At the end of the day there are just some things that we have to carry forward until the time is right."

. . .

Simon had met Arif and other Abraaj executives over the years and had recently caught up with Kito to talk about his new job at the firm. When Will told Simon about the anonymous source, he emailed Kito to ask whether $200 million from the healthcare fund was misused in some way. Kito was preparing to make his way to Davos when Simon's email reached him. He said that he had been traveling across Asia and the United States for the last two weeks to meet Abraaj investors. Kito said he wasn't aware of any wrongdoing.

"Not a single one raised a concern of the nature you suggest," Kito said. "I believe that the information you have been given is off the mark. Let me try to understand what is going on and why."

Kito arranged a telephone call for the following day. He wanted Matt and Khawar, the head of the healthcare fund, to be on the call too. They were also preparing to travel to Davos. In an email sent before the call took place, Kito said that lawyers at Freshfields Bruckhaus Deringer were advising Abraaj.

"It goes without saying that in the opinion of Freshfields, Abraaj is fully compliant," Kito said.

Freshfields lawyers had written notes based on documents from their clients and talks with them that Abraaj executives were telling people confirmed that the firm had done nothing wrong. Kito believed Freshfields was an impartial and credible guarantor of Abraaj's reputation.

There were close links between Abraaj and Freshfields. Pervez Akhtar, the managing partner of Freshfields in the Middle East, had previously worked at Abraaj, and he forwarded the notes that cleared Abraaj's management of its funds to Abraaj's general counsel, Andrew Chvatal, in an email. Pervez also sat on the board of the Aman

Foundation—Arif's charity—in Britain, and he was a guest at the wedding of Arif's son in Rome.

Kito emphasized his own personal commitment to doing good for the poor and for Abraaj's investors, whom he referred to as LPs—shorthand for limited partners.

"We are truly making millions of lives better in difficult markets," he wrote. "The LPs we have been meeting are equally excited about being part of a pioneering initiative. It is not easy—we are building hospitals in tough places like Lagos, Karachi, and Lahore.

"The life of an impact fund operating at the outer edge of the possible is not always smooth. Our LPs are mature and understand that we are creating something out of very little. What they want from us is clarity, transparency, and engagement.

"I know that we returned funds that had not been deployed when requested to do so."

This last sentence from Kito was revealing. It was an admission from an Abraaj executive that money had been returned to healthcare fund investors. It was the first corroboration of the story being told by the anonymous source.

Kito gave more details in the telephone call on Sunday afternoon. Abraaj had kept millions of dollars unused in the healthcare fund because there were delays to hospital projects in Pakistan and Nigeria, he said. Khawar said that the delays were minor setbacks to initiatives that would save thousands of lives. The call ended.

• • •

In Davos, Arif prioritized talking to his most important contacts. He met in private with Christian Sewing, who was soon to be appointed chief executive of Deutsche Bank, one of Abraaj's biggest shareholders. Arif's usual entourage was banished from the room.

He sat down with William Lewis, the chief executive of Dow Jones, publisher of the *Wall Street Journal*, and Thorold Barker, the *Journal's*

European editor. Arif pitched the meeting as a chance to discuss advertising and how Abraaj could partner with the *Journal* in emerging markets, but another motivation became clear as they talked. Arif wanted our investigation to stop. One of the people in the meeting said, "He was really like get Simon and Will to back off and he was pretty explicit. He was working very hard to get the senior folks at the *Journal* to kill what you were up to." Lewis listened to Arif but didn't bite, the person said.

Around lunchtime on Thursday, Arif took center stage at Davos in a televised debate about global healthcare. He shared the platform with Bill Gates and three others. Arif was nervous. Before the discussion started he milled around the greenroom and exchanged pleasantries with the other speakers, including Bill, who seemed inclined to keep his distance.

They walked out into the Davos spotlight and Arif sat at the center. Bill was seated on the far left. Arif was charming on stage. He credited Bill with inspiring Abraaj's efforts to bring affordable healthcare to Pakistan, Nigeria, Kenya, and India with the $1 billion fund.

"Bill was instrumental in that vision," Arif said.

Bill shifted uncomfortably in his seat and pursed his lips. Whenever Arif attempted to make eye contact or engage him in conversation Bill looked the other way.

"It all started with a discussion with him," Arif continued.

Arif claimed that Abraaj's hospitals were already earning profits. It was a typically bullish performance from Arif. He didn't let on that Abraaj was in big trouble with the billionaire seated near him, and Bill, wearing a poker face, didn't give anything away either. His team had fully briefed him on the situation at Abraaj.

Bill almost succeeded in dodging Arif's attempts to interact with him. But as the hour-long debate drew to a close, Bill praised the American and European medical regulators—the Food and Drug Administration and the European Medicines Agency.

"Even the developing world expects their medicines to be approved by the gold-standard regulators," Bill said. "Unless it's FDA or EMA approved, which are the two gold-standard regulators, it doesn't get in."

Arif stared quizzically at Bill when he heard this. Bill had triggered Arif's finely tuned sense for patronizing Western attitudes.

"Can I just add something slightly provocative there, Bill?" Arif said. "Maybe I am being a bit simplistic but, you know, these gold-standard regulators and the drugs that are approved in the United States and Europe, essentially also there is one big flaw in it."

The American and European regulators were biased because they mainly tested medicines on white people who weren't genetically representative of all of humanity, Arif said. It was a classic Arif Naqvi move which drew on his long experience as a debater going back to his school days—a good point made well to put his intellectual adversary on the defensive. Arif's observation made Bill seem presumptuous and, perhaps, even a bit colonial.

"What is a fact is that we are all different," Arif said. The healthcare industry needed more data on people of African and Asian origin to make medicines that were more suitable for them. That was where Arif and his healthcare fund came in. They were going to make a big contribution by collecting this data, Arif said.

Bill was compelled to agree with Arif.

"Yes, these regulators, they are starting to pay attention to that," Bill said. It shouldn't be the case that once the American or European regulators approved a medicine it was ready to be used by the world's seven billion people, he said.

When the discussion ended Arif moved across the stage toward Bill but the American billionaire still didn't want to talk to him. The Microsoft founder's team whisked him away through a backstage corridor.

• • •

As Arif jousted with Bill in Davos, the mystery source sent more information to Will in London.

"Please find attached the Abraaj healthcare fund reports," the source wrote in an email.

The reports showed that most of Abraaj's hospitals were losing money, rather than making profits as Arif had claimed in Davos. They also proved one of the source's main allegations that Abraaj had been sitting on more than $200 million of investor cash in the healthcare fund for a long time.

We still needed more proof because the source refused to reveal their identity. After another week of telephone calls, people confirmed that investors were investigating Abraaj for mismanaging their money but no one was prepared to speak publicly about this. Healthcare fund investors including the Gates Foundation had appointed Ankura, a forensic accounting firm, to investigate what had happened to their money, we were told. Now we had enough information to write an article.

When the Davos meeting ended, Arif flew to London. He told his top team to drop whatever they were doing and join him in Abraaj's Mayfair office in a final effort to kill our news story. There were frequent visits from advisers at Finsbury, a public relations firm run by Roland Rudd, brother of the U.K.'s home secretary at that time, Amber Rudd.

We repeatedly fact-checked the article to make sure it was accurate and company lawyers vetted the article. We gave Abraaj another opportunity to comment. In a fraught conversation, Matt admitted that there were issues between Abraaj and some investors. He said the firm had asked KPMG to audit the healthcare fund's accounts.

Abraaj's carefully cultivated public image finally cracked at 7:10 p.m. London time on February 2, 2018, when we published an article about the Gates Foundation and other investors hiring an auditor to trace their money. The *New York Times* published an article soon after. The news articles spread worldwide online, on laptops and on mobile phones. They unleashed the floodgates on Abraaj as hundreds of investors and lenders called Arif and demanded an explanation.

Arif dismissed the reports as fake news but it was hard to believe that both the *Wall Street Journal* and the *New York Times* had gotten it wrong. Banks called in loans and canceled plans to lend Abraaj more money. Arif was running out of options.

The day after the *Wall Street Journal* article was published was a Saturday and Arif was still in London. In a meeting with CDC executives at his office, Arif was stressed and emotional as he tried to assure his investors that he had done nothing wrong. CDC executives were deeply troubled by the turn of events because they had so much at stake, with investments in many Abraaj funds, whereas the Gates Foundation had only invested in two funds. If the House of Abraaj collapsed it was going to be an even bigger problem for CDC than for the Gates Foundation.

The news soon reached the Washington State Investment Board in Olympia, 7,400 miles to the west of Dubai. David Nierenberg, a director of the Washington State pension fund, was profoundly disturbed by what he read. The fund managed more than $130 billion on behalf of teachers, police officers, judges, and firefighters. Nierenberg fired off an urgent email to colleagues.

In the presence of fraud investors must move fast to engage expert legal counsel and investigators and must be maximum tough to cause the bad guys maximum reputational harm, maximum damage to their net worth, and take away their liberty by sending them to jail.

Just like you don't negotiate with a terrorist, you don't make nice with a fraudster. The only language they understand is force. We don't even know how to think the way they do; they are wired differently.

If there's bad stuff going on here, or we think there may be, let's get to the bottom of it immediately and take all appropriate protective action.

Mark Bourgeois wrote to the Washington State Investment Board and other investors to reassure them that there was no cause for alarm. "You may have seen media reports," Mark wrote. "They contain a number of erroneous allegations which have been categorically rejected by us. All capital drawn from investors was approved for fund investments. Some of this capital was not deployed as quickly as anticipated primarily due to unforeseen regulatory delays in building new hospitals."

. . .

Arif reassured his employees that no crime had been committed. He sat down in London with Kito, Matt, Khawar, Sev, and others and debated what to do. Kito was completely bewildered by what was happening.

"We were saying what the hell is going on?" Kito said.

KPMG provided a fleeting moment of hope for Arif with a report that, Abraaj claimed, absolved Abraaj from wrongdoing in how it used healthcare fund money. But the report wasn't released publicly. Instead, Abraaj sent out a press release saying that KPMG had found that Abraaj behaved "in line with the agreed upon procedures."

KPMG was hardly an impartial judge, because its ties to Abraaj ran so deep. It audited the firm and most of its funds as well as companies Abraaj invested in, including Air Arabia. KPMG's Dubai chief was a close friend of Arif's. Ashish Dave, Abraaj's chief financial officer, had worked at KPMG.

Kito stepped out of Abraaj's London office one February morning for a walk with Khawar. They wanted to discuss what was happening. They strolled past Mayfair's luxurious shops and cafés. They didn't want anyone to hear their conversation. Khawar had news to share. Arif had told him about how he used loans from Air Arabia to plug holes in the healthcare fund. Arif didn't see any problem with the loans but Kito did. What were loans from an airline doing in a fund to build hospitals? It was madness. To make things worse, the KPMG report hadn't even mentioned that Air Arabia had lent money to the fund. The information about Air Arabia was so explosive, Kito and Khawar used a code word to refer to the airline: *pigeon*.

"The Air Arabia loans were a big shock," Kito said. "That was a big blow."

Ankura proceeded with its investigation on behalf of the investors in the healthcare fund and dispatched two of its experts, who flew from the U.S. to Dubai in February 2018 to conduct a forensic audit. Jean-Michel Ferat had previously helped trace money in Switzerland belonging to Jewish victims of the Holocaust and uncovered massive bribes and kickbacks in the United Nations oil-for-food program in Iraq. Collin Anderson was an expert in data-driven forensic accounting.

Abraaj didn't permit Jean-Michel and Collin to work in its headquarters—a refusal that wasn't customary for the auditors—and instead handed them a box of documents and set them up in the Habtoor Palace hotel with a minder. Their job was to follow the money flowing in and out of the healthcare fund's bank account but the documents in the box were incomplete. Jean-Michel and Collin made repeated demands for all the bank statements and wouldn't take no for an answer. After days of tense conversations with Abraaj officials, they finally received bank statements that showed something highly unusual had taken place. Huge sums of money had entered the healthcare fund from Air Arabia, an airline with no obvious reason to be involved. The game was up.

Arif's world was crumbling. Checks he'd given Hamid Jafar as surety for the $350 million of loans bounced in the UAE in February 2018. Bouncing a check was a criminal offense in the country, so this crisis had to be resolved fast or Arif could go straight to jail. In a bid to raise some cash, Arif sold six pieces of Abraaj art at Christie's auction house in Hong Kong.

Arif put *Raasta*, his luxury yacht, up for sale for $20 million through a broker in the south of France.

The Dubai Financial Services Authority began asking Abraaj difficult questions. Hamilton Lane had told the Dubai regulator that money may have been taken from Abraaj Private Equity Fund IV as well as from the healthcare fund.

Arif tried to limit the damage. He announced a plan on February 23, 2018, that he hoped would help him regain the trust of investors. He split Abraaj into two different companies: Abraaj Investment Management and Abraaj Holdings.

Abraaj Investment Management would run the private equity funds with Omar Lodhi and Selcuk Yorgancioglu in charge as joint chief executives. Arif promised to play no further part in running this business. Abraaj Holdings would continue to be an investor in the funds and Arif would lead this company. But the separation didn't reassure anyone. Washington State Investment Board's CIO Gary Bruebaker ordered his team to stop working with Abraaj.

Abraaj was dropped from an invitation list that Catholic officials were preparing for the Vatican's impact-investing summit in the summer of 2018.

In Dubai, executives in the newly separated fund management business started probing the company's books and records for information. Rafique warned Arif that a new auditor was coming to the headquarters at 3:00 p.m. on March 1, 2018. Rafique fretted about boxes of documents that contained sensitive information about cash transfers to Arif.

"I will send my driver to pick up the boxes," Arif told Rafique. "How many boxes are there?"

"Nine," Rafique replied.

"OK pls make sure the driver takes the boxes out from the door near accounts and not the main reception," Arif said. "There is a trolly in which he can load quite a few at one time so have the trolly loaded."

The day after the boxes were removed, Omar and Selcuk told investors that the $6 billion fundraising was canceled.

Chaos ensued.

Arif had ruled Abraaj with unassailable authority for its entire existence but now his control was shot. Abraaj couldn't survive without the $90 million of annual management fees that the new fund was going to earn. Abraaj had even borrowed $150 million from the

French bank Société Générale based on the expectation of receiving those fees.

Arif's closest colleagues attempted to cover their tracks. Ashish told Reuters in March 2018 that he had quit Abraaj six months earlier. Sev also told journalists and lawyers that he had resigned months ago in a bid to distance himself from the firm's impending collapse.

A few conscientious staff members opted to stick around and try to stabilize the company. Bisher Barazi, Abraaj's Syrian chief operating officer, rolled up his sleeves and coordinated discussions between the firm and the Dubai Financial Services Authority.

Bisher was a fiery character. He was respected by many employees as perhaps the only senior executive who was prepared to stand up to Arif. The Abraaj founder had assured Bisher that the firm's problems were no worse than some commingling of money in the healthcare fund, and based on this assurance Bisher was prepared to stay but was in no mood to become embroiled in a major financial scandal. He had previously served as the chief financial officer of a government investment fund in Dubai that got into financial difficulties, and he didn't want to repeat that experience. Arif had convinced him to join Abraaj by insisting that he and his firm adhered to the most rigorous governance standards.

Bisher was experienced at negotiating difficult situations. Born in Damascus in 1972, he registered to attend the American University in Beirut in 1991 but the institution was bombed by terrorists, forcing his parents to insist that he switch to Damascus University instead. Disappointed at not being able to leave Syria, Bisher put more energy into partying and playing football than studying.

His parents were frustrated by his attitude so they introduced him to their accountants at Arthur Anderson to get him a summer job. Bisher turned up to the interview with long hair and wearing jeans, a Led Zeppelin T-shirt, and the gold chain he'd worn since birth, bearing a medallion inscribed with a verse of the Koran—a gift from his aunt—and a charm gifted by his Ukrainian grandmother.

Bisher learned to love accounting at Arthur Anderson in Damascus.

He worked there while he studied, and each year he made sure to deliberately fail his math exam to delay graduation so he could avoid military service. In 2000, after nine years, he still hadn't graduated, but he wanted to progress with his career at Arthur Anderson. To do so he needed to pass a special exam to become a certified public accountant. The trouble was, in most places the exam could be taken only after graduation. But not in Montana. So Bisher flew to the remote northern U.S. state to take the exam.

With the Syrian Army breathing down his neck in 2000, Bisher finally graduated from university and got Arthur Anderson to transfer him to Saudi Arabia. Syrians living abroad could avoid military service by paying a fee instead. Bisher's career flourished outside Syria and he moved on from Arthur Anderson to work for a number of investment firms in the Arabian Gulf. He joined the board of Abraaj as a director for a time, representing the Dubai investment company where he worked.

After Bisher joined Abraaj full-time in 2016, Arif reminded him of how years earlier when he was a board member he had questioned Arif's excessive control of Abraaj. Bisher thought that Arif had the memory of a camel, a Middle Eastern expression for someone who never forgets a slight.

"Is there any truth to this?" Bisher said he asked to Waqar about the controversy that the *Wall Street Journal* article exposed in February 2018.

Waqar responded that the journalists who wrote the article hated Abraaj because of their success, according to Bisher. Waqar denied that he said this.

Soon after, Bisher learned that money had been taken from Fund IV as well as the healthcare fund. He was really upset by this because Arif had assured him that there weren't any more problems at Abraaj outside the healthcare fund.

When Arif split Abraaj in two, Bisher was appointed chief financial officer of the fund management business. To enforce the separation of the two new companies, Bisher locked a passageway between

Abraaj's offices on levels three and four of the Dubai International Financial Centre. Level three was to be the headquarters of the fund management business and level four was for Abraaj Holdings, where Arif was still in charge. Bisher's decision to shut access to the stairs deeply angered Arif.

When mismanagement of a third Abraaj fund emerged Arif blamed the problem on Waqar, Rafique, and Ashish in a meeting that Bisher and other executives also attended. The problem was that shares which the Infrastructure and Growth Capital Fund owned in Air Arabia had been pledged as security for a loan that Abraaj used instead of giving the proceeds to fund investors who were the rightful beneficiaries. Now the money was missing. Arif humiliated Waqar in the meeting and claimed that he himself didn't have anything to do with the new problem.

The day after the meeting, Bisher said that he and Waqar went for a drink together at the Luna Sky Bar on the roof of the Four Seasons Hotel in Dubai and Waqar burst into tears as they talked.

"How the heck do you accept that?" Bisher asked.

"He's a bully," Waqar replied, according to Bisher. Waqar said he often went to the Luna Sky Bar with Bisher but disputed this conversation occurred.

Bisher had by now lost all faith in Arif. When Arif came to his office days later to ask for help with his legal problems Bisher refused because, he said, what Arif was asking him to do wasn't right. Arif told Bisher that he had changed, that he wasn't respectful anymore, and that he hadn't stood up a few days earlier when Arif entered a room.

"I didn't realize you are a black-and-white person," Arif said as he started to cry.

"I need to walk away from this with three things," he said. "Wealth, dignity, and reputation."

"If someone told you that you could walk away from this mess with all of those three things you are delusional," Bisher said.

"We come from the same background," Arif answered, imploring Bisher to see things his way.

Bisher said he had to leave for a meeting. He got up and went to the bathroom. Arif followed him out and stood alongside him at the urinals.

"I'm not going to fall down alone," Arif said. "I'm going to take everyone with me and there will be nothing left for anyone."

"Good luck," Bisher replied.

"I'm having to fight this on my own," Arif complained. "Where is Mustafa? Where is Sev?"

Bisher pushed on with his investigation of Abraaj's finances. He asked Rafique for access to financial reports and bank statements. Rafique warned Arif about the requests for information from Bisher and other accountants. The documents would reveal how Arif extracted money from the company, so Rafique tried to doctor them to hide the transfers.

"Your balance is appearing under your name," Rafique told Arif about one financial statement. "I will move this receivable amount to Abraaj Holdings and therefore you will have zero balance."

But the transfers to Arif and his companies were still visible in bank statements.

· · ·

In London, Kito was facing a financial challenge of his own as Abraaj stopped paying his salary, which was part of a compensation package worth hundreds of thousands of dollars a year. On a rainy London afternoon, Kito rushed into the Connaught Hotel in Mayfair. He was late for a meeting that he had arranged in the hotel lobby with Simon because he had been delayed at Christie's auction house, where he was in talks to sell his Indian art collection to raise cash.

Over coffee, Kito said that there was no transparency at Abraaj and governance was a problem too. The firm didn't even have a chairman who might try to hold Arif to account because the last chairman wasn't replaced when he died three years earlier, Kito said.

After the meeting Simon accompanied Kito as he walked briskly through Berkeley Square to a jeweler on New Bond Street, where he picked up a watch he was having repaired. Then they walked to a gated parking lot beneath Hyde Park, where Kito's car had been cleaned. The Dutchman drove home to Kensington.

Simon walked to the nearest subway station. He liked and respected Kito for making genuine efforts to address the economic inequality in the world. But never had the gaping chasm between Abraaj and the poor people it claimed to help seemed so great. The gilded Mayfair world that Abraaj executives like Kito operated in was so far removed from the impoverished reality of most people living in Kenya, Pakistan, and other developing countries. Most Pakistanis would never enter a place like Mayfair's Connaught Hotel, where Kito and Simon had just met—the $4,455 cost of a one-night stay in the hotel would take most Pakistanis three years to earn.

· · ·

In Dubai, the party was almost over for Abraaj. Its last investor conference—a jamboree once graced by Tina Turner, John Kerry, and ice bars melting into the hot sand—was canceled in March 2018. But Abraaj's annual art prize went ahead one last time. The Jordanian-born artist Lawrence Abu Hamdan won the final $100,000 prize with a political work about tortured prisoners in Syria.

Davos's favorite musician, Barry Colson, flew in to Dubai to perform at the art event. Arif had told him that he was guaranteed a gig at the annual show.

As Colson sang into the warm Arabian night guests gossiped about whether Abraaj could survive and whether Arif would show up. Arif unexpectedly appeared and the elegant Dubai crowd froze. The moment was like in the Wild West when the bandit comes in and everything stops, Colson thought. People put down champagne glasses and canapés. Art catalogues were tucked away. Colson kept playing.

Upon his return to Canada, Colson discovered he wasn't going to get paid for playing one last song for Arif. Abraaj had run out of money, an executive told him when he called to ask about his unpaid bill. He received a long creditor list on which his name appeared near the bottom. Creditors were ranked by the amounts they were owed. Hamid Jafar, who was owed hundreds of millions of dollars, was at the top. The writing was on the wall for Arif, Colson thought when he saw the list.

Arif remained defiant and was confident no one would hold him accountable for Abraaj's demise. His conviction was based on conversations he said he'd had with regulators at the Dubai Financial Services Authority.

"No one will start an inquiry," Arif told Mark Bourgeois in a telephone call. "They said, 'Look, we're under pressure so we're asking process-driven questions.'"

"Wow, wow," Mark replied in astonishment.

"None of which involves anybody getting fucked, none of which involves anybody getting damaged," Arif said. "And it's what I've been saying all along."

"Wow," Mark repeated.

CHAPTER 18

KEYS TO THE KINGDOM

Paul Morris slept with a knife by his bed. Giles Montgomery-Swan checked for bombs under his car. The two Abraaj employees were determined to discover what was happening in their firm. They no longer believed in the firm's leadership after reading the *Wall Street Journal* article in February 2018. Explanations and denials from senior executives were not convincing.

Paul was an accountant at Abraaj, and Giles was in charge of information technology. They both considered quitting when Abraaj was split into two companies and the $6 billion fundraising was canceled but decided to stay on because there was still a job to do and billions of dollars of investor money was at stake.

"I can't walk away from this," Paul resolved.

Investigating Abraaj was risky. The two British men had to tread carefully and there were moments when they feared for their lives. Arif remained a powerful man. He was still on the board of the Interpol Foundation and the UN Global Compact and there were no signs that the Dubai authorities wanted to prosecute him. Local newspapers, which were closely monitored by the government, were still publishing supportive articles about Arif.

Paul and Giles worked to clean up Abraaj with Bisher and Matt, who was appointed chief operating officer of the fund management business after Abraaj was split into two.

The guardians of the Abraajery, the firm's hidden financial heart, were still a major obstacle to any investigation. Rafique and his loyal subordinates still controlled the finance department and were reluctant to share information—least of all bank statements and financial reports—with anyone. Arif wasn't supposed to have anything more to do with running Abraaj's fund management business but in reality he still pulled the strings in the finance department, guiding Rafique and other faithful employees.

Bisher emailed Rafique on April 4, 2018, to ask him to provide urgently needed information. Rafique forwarded Bisher's email to Arif.

"FYI—Pls see email below from Bisher. He will ask for Oracle access and will be able to see mcmhl entries," Rafique wrote to Arif. "I will speak to Bisher and understand why he has sent this email."

The reference to mcmhl was an abbreviation for Menasa Capital Management Holdings Ltd., one of the Cayman Islands companies controlled by Arif that was receiving millions of dollars from Abraaj. Oracle was the database system that would enable Bisher to see what had been going on all along with the illicit payments to Arif.

"Remove MCMHL from Oracle," Arif replied to Rafique. "Give access going forward, not looking back."

When Bisher asked Arif for access to information in the finance department, Arif refused. Stop worrying about the past, Arif told him on a conference call. A new bank account would be opened, Arif said. This would prevent Bisher from being able to see the history of payments in the old account. Abraaj's problems weren't caused by its accounts, Arif told him, but rather by leaks to journalists.

On the conference call Arif compared himself to the submarine commander in *Crimson Tide*, a Hollywood film. The commander, played by Gene Hackman, is challenged by his crew during a dangerous mission that goes badly wrong. After a mutiny, the commander makes peace with his crew and retires with honor.

For Paul, who was listening on the call, the drama unfolding at

Abraaj had a very different plot. "This is a crime scene and the crime is ongoing," he thought. "The finance department is full of information they want to hide."

The priorities of Omar and Selcuk, the new joint CEOs of Abraaj's fund management business, weren't clear to Bisher and Matt. Did they want to search exhaustively for evidence of wrongdoing and immediately report any problems to regulators?

Omar's approach soon became clearer.

Paul was investigating how Arif had valued Abraaj's assets. Paul prepared a report after Ahmed Badreldin, the head of Abraaj in North Africa, showed him emails in which he was pressured by executives to inflate valuations in a way he didn't agree with. Paul emailed a note about Ahmed's evidence to Peter Brady, Abraaj's chief compliance officer. Peter emailed Omar, Selcuk, Bisher, and Matt to notify them that he was going to send the information to the Dubai Financial Services Authority. Matt told Peter it was fine to send the information to the regulators.

Omar responded soon after. Under no circumstances should the information go to the regulator, he said. But it was too late because Peter had already sent it, Peter told Omar in an email. A few hours later, Omar called Peter and yelled at him for the best part of an hour. Omar had made his position clear.

There was a way around Rafique, who was guarding the Abraajery. The secrets of Abraaj were also stored on the firm's information technology system. It contained all the employee emails, financial reports, and bank statements, but neither Paul nor Giles had full access to the IT system. While Giles was in charge of the system he wasn't authorized to view all of its contents. Instead, one of Giles's team members, a man called Charles Jonathan, had authority to enter the system. The access code for the IT system was kept by Bisher and Charles Jonathan. Giles asked Bisher for permission to monitor Abraaj's email system as part of a data collection exercise.

"I approve your request," Bisher wrote in an email to Giles on April 8, 2018. "I have copied Matt."

The following day, Giles was visited by an Abraaj employee who said Arif was desperate to contact Charles Jonathan, who was on leave in India at the time. Another employee asked Giles whether the firm's computers were owned by Abraaj Holdings, the unit Arif still controlled.

Two weeks later, Giles got back in touch with Bisher and Matt with important news. Computer usage records showed that Charles Jonathan had accessed Matt's emails at 11:05 p.m. on February 5, 2018, and deleted emails to which were attached KPMG's report about the healthcare fund. Giles and Paul questioned Jonathan about why he had removed the emails, and he said that Rafique had asked him to do it. Jonathan's admission that he was acting on behalf of Rafique, Arif's right-hand man, made it vital for Bisher to grant Giles full access to the IT system.

Giles and Paul now had the keys to the kingdom. The IT system was a treasure trove of information. Bank statements showed money had illicitly moved around Abraaj and into Arif's private accounts for years. Arif and Omar discussed bribing the prime minister of Pakistan and his brother in perfectly preserved emails. With every thread they pulled and every stone they turned, the problems just got more shocking. The financial hole got bigger and bigger.

When Arif found out that Giles and Paul had full access to the IT system he called Omar and threatened to kill all the staff. Rattled, Omar called Bisher and relayed Arif's anger to him.

• • •

Arif desperately defended the remnants of his empire. As lenders demanded loan repayments, he bought time with excuses. He appointed the New York–based advisory firm Houlihan Lokey to find a buyer for Abraaj Investment Management. Many firms expressed an interest in buying all or part of the business.

The Aman Foundation, the private family charity Arif and Fayeeza started in 2008, ground to a halt. There was no more money. Scholarships for Pakistani teenagers to attend Atlantic College, an elite private boarding school in Wales, were unceremoniously canceled. Students at the school launched a successful emergency fundraising campaign to pay for the Pakistani students. Arif and Fayeeza's names remained written in gold paint on a board listing benefactors in an Atlantic College hall. Above their names was Andrea Vella, a former Goldman Sachs executive whom the Federal Reserve banned from banking for his involvement in the Malaysian financial scandal which unseated the country's prime minister, Najib Razak.

In Karachi, Aman ambulances that saved lives on the sweltering streets were offered to other charities.

Abraaj investors were still demanding daily explanations about where their money was. Investors in the healthcare fund wanted Abraaj to give up control and allow another private equity firm to manage their money.

Employees likened the atmosphere at Abraaj's Dubai headquarters to the last days of Rome. Staff who were used to working exhaustingly long hours under Arif's all-seeing gaze had nothing to do. They chatted on a terrace, watched Netflix films on work computers, and drank in nearby bars, joking that each day could be their last. Then one day it was. Dozens were fired at once on a day remembered by staff as the Red Wedding after a brutal scene of mass slaughter in the *Game of Thrones* television drama.

Some wept. Others were glad to leave a sinking ship. For most of them, losing their jobs meant they had to depart Dubai. Executives from around the world had flocked to work at the firm, attracted by high salaries and the social mission. Their work visas were tied to Abraaj, so now they had to leave or risk deportation.

Abraaj was in turmoil but only a small fraction of the fraud was public. Arif insisted he had done nothing wrong and continued to dodge questions from journalists. He stonewalled us with the utmost charm during a long telephone interview in March 2018. He deflected questions about whether money was missing from more funds and played down the notion that there was a dispute with the Gates

Foundation. There was, he said, merely a difference of opinion about whether Abraaj's agreement with investors permitted him to temporarily move money out of the healthcare fund.

"They are well within their rights to interpret it in a certain way and we felt we were within our rights to interpret it the way we wanted," Arif said. "And if you ask me in hindsight would we have done things differently? Possibly."

The worst thing Arif was prepared to admit to on the call with us was being "a little bit verbose" in his lengthy answers. He assured us of his humility.

"I am very fond of constantly telling people that today's peacock is tomorrow's feather duster."

It was frustratingly hard for us to prove the allegations that the anonymous source was making about Arif. The source had sent us financial statements for the $1.6 billion Abraaj Private Equity Fund IV and said money had been misused from it, as well as the healthcare fund. Arif categorically denied this. We had to find more evidence.

An investor tipped us off about a meeting Arif had called to discuss the $1.6 billion fund. It was to take place in the ballroom of London's five-star Langham Hotel in late May 2018. Early on a sunny Wednesday morning we walked up Regent Street to the grand hotel opposite the BBC's headquarters.

The cavernous ballroom of the Langham cost £20,000 to rent for a day, a sum that would take most Kenyans fourteen years to earn. We politely asked hotel staff if we could enter the ballroom, and they politely refused. A peek through the doors revealed a room that was absurdly large for the few people who were invited. We bought coffee, sat down in the lobby outside the ballroom, and waited.

A procession of Abraaj executives and investors arrived for the meeting. Mark Bourgeois walked past wearing one of his signature pin-striped suits. He paused to chat briefly with us. He was doing his utmost to help investors, he said. He talked about his continued faith in Abraaj's social mission and the orphanage in Uganda he supported. We asked to talk to Arif, and Mark said he'd see what he could do.

He said he was available to talk on the phone anytime. He never re-turned a call ever again. Selcuk glided swiftly past at lunchtime, his eyes looking straight ahead without a glance to the left or the right.

An investor we knew left the ballroom and headed for the ho-tel exit. He silently gestured that we should follow him. He had a streaming head cold and was looking for a pharmacy to buy medicine. He walked across Regent Street and entered a branch of the Boots pharmacy. We entered with him and paused to talk amid the aisles of toothpaste, soap, and shampoo. He seemed a bit dazed, partly be-cause of his cold, but also because of what Arif had just told him and the other investors in the ballroom.

"Abraaj used our money to fund its business," he said, sniffling through a blocked nose. "Money is still owed to the fund."

Arif had told investors including Bank of America and Hamilton Lane that he had spent more than $200 million of their money on expenses instead of buying companies as he was supposed to do. The information was strictly confidential; anyone who leaked details was breaching a nondisclosure agreement and Abraaj would sue them, Arif told them. The investor exited the pharmacy and headed back to the hotel. We waited so we weren't seen with him and made some calls. A senior Abraaj executive confirmed what the investor had said.

As the meeting continued into the afternoon, we published an arti-cle about Abraaj misusing investor money in a second fund.

The meeting finished around 5:00 p.m. This was our opportunity to talk to Arif face-to-face but he took evasive action by departing through a courtyard at the back of the hotel. We tried to talk to more investors. Tarang Katira, the man from Hamilton Lane, exited the front of the hotel and jogged down the street as we shouted ques-tions after him. A lady from Bank of America haughtily declined to comment. She said the meeting was confidential as she jumped into a black cab that took her away into the evening traffic. Their re-luctance to talk didn't matter. The news that Abraaj had plundered a second fund was already published. At 10:48 that evening, Simon sent Arif thirteen questions in an email under the subject line "How to understand Abraaj?" It began:

Dear Arif,

I was sitting in the lobby of the Langham Hotel all day today, hoping we might meet. Unfortunately we didn't.

I would very much like to see you and to talk to you again. Will you be in London for the rest of this week?

There is such a lack of transparency around the Abraaj Group. You have been such a great outspoken champion for the need for transparency in business.

However the general public—and it seems also investors—don't really understand how Abraaj works.

How much debt does it have? Who are its shareholders? Who are its lenders? What is its full relationship with the Abraaj private equity funds which investors help create with their money and their trust?

Arif responded twelve hours later:

I wish you had just emailed me, I would have had no issue meeting you yesterday! I will be back very soon, but in order to spend meaningful time, I need to say the following.

Most of what you write below is contextually and factually inaccurate but any attempt to take you thru a briefing is unhelpful Simon.

There is no attempt to not show you details you seek but if the mindset is pre-disposed, what is the point?

You ran an article yesterday, again out of context. Someone has an agenda and you are feeding it. Numbers, alleged facts and context were erroneous.

There is no lack of transparency about the Abraaj Group or Abraaj Holdings, but it is a private company and we do comply with all information and reporting needs of all investors. With the number and quality of investors and stakeholders involved, do you honestly think that we could run a business without that?

If I thought you were keen to be dispassionate and unbiased, of course I would engage with you! Face to face meetings achieve a lot especially with your positive mindset about emerging markets and impact. There is much good that is happening but you don't talk about it.

Best regards.

Simon responded two hours later:

Dear Arif,

Thank you for your reply and for explaining your perspective.

I sent you 13 questions in my last email. You haven't responded with a single answer.

Please don't think there is no point answering my questions. I really want to understand what is happening and I have an open mind.

I look forward to hearing from you and hopefully seeing you soon.

Best wishes.

Arif replied from Islamabad four days later. He said he was in Pakistan working on the long-delayed sale of Karachi Electric:

I do feel you are pre-disposed; and you have "data" being thrown at you from numerous directions, some of whom may not have intentions that are as dispassionate as yours!

I am unable to speak to you from Islamabad through this final working week of the present government until Thursday (and much needs to be done by them to resolve and give clarity on prior issues and permissions needed to consummate this transaction), given the centrality of this transaction in solving many of Abraaj's issues.

It clearly needs us to spend a full day together.

Friday or Saturday? Where?

Best regards,
Arif

Simon responded early the next day.

Dear Arif,
Thank you for your response. Yes, I'd be glad to meet you on Friday or Saturday. Anywhere in the U.K. that's convenient for you would be best for me. Is that possible?
     Best wishes.

The next day, the *Wall Street Journal* reporter Nicolas Parasie published an article about a Kuwaiti pension fund trying to force Abraaj into bankruptcy proceedings in the Grand Court of the Cayman Islands. Abraaj owed the Public Institution for Social Security $100 million. The article drew an exasperated response from Arif, who emailed again the day after it was published.

Simon, apologies for the delay in responding, but as you can guess, I have been relentlessly embroiled in discussions.
     You keep reporting on 'work-in-progress' which creates uncertainty for us, but I guess you have to do your job, and I have to do mine! Problem is what I am doing here involves creating value but needs full time focus, whereas the news reported slows stuff down.
     Can you either give me a few days reprieve from reporting, or add 10 hours a day to the 24 that God gave?!!
     I am sorry for having suggested that it might be possible to meet Fri/Sat.
     More later.

It was the last email we got from Arif. He hired Simkins to do his talking for him. The London law firm specialized in representing celebrities from the media and entertainment industry. Simkins said it was concerned that we were going to write about Arif behaving in an improper or unlawful way and that such a false narrative could cause him serious harm. Hiring lawyers to deter or delay journalists was a tactic straight out of the billionaire's playbook. The lawyers slowed us down and bought Arif more time.

. . .

Abraaj was on the brink of bankruptcy. A firm that had taken years to build had imploded in a matter of months. Having tapped just about every financial institution and wealthy connection he had for cash, Arif started looking farther afield for help. Desperate, he considered the unlikeliest sources for assistance.

Two of America's most powerful and politically connected private equity firms were considering bids for Abraaj. Thomas Barrack's Colony Capital and Stephen Feinberg's Cerberus Capital Management were assessing the firm. Buying Abraaj's operations could give them footholds in new markets across Africa, Asia, and Latin America. Ironically, their interest in buying Abraaj confirmed Arif's argument that emerging markets represented the future.

Barrack was a close ally of Donald Trump and had organized his presidential inauguration ceremony. He also had strong connections in the Middle East. Born into a family with Lebanese roots, Barrack had worked for the Saudi royal family. His firm specialized in real estate investments worldwide.

Cerberus was a New York private equity firm named after the three-headed dog that guards the gates of hell in Greek mythology. It had established a reputation for buying and turning around struggling businesses. Like Colony, Cerberus's billionaire founder had close ties to Trump. Feinberg chaired the president's intelligence advisory board, which oversaw the work of American spies.

Cerberus offered $125 million to buy Abraaj. Most of this was intended to repay money taken from investors in Abraaj Private Equity Fund IV. But before the deal could be completed a creditor tried to force Abraaj into bankruptcy. Hamid Jafar, the rich UAE investor who lent Abraaj $350 million just months before it collapsed, was furious that he hadn't been repaid as promised. He transferred his loan to a fund management company, which filed a petition to liquidate Abraaj in the Cayman Islands.

This move forced Arif to ask the Cayman Islands court to oversee a restructuring of Abraaj. A judge appointed liquidators from Deloitte and PricewaterhouseCoopers to investigate what had happened at Abraaj and to sell its assets to raise money to repay more than $1 billion of debts. The appointment of the liquidators triggered an emotional farewell email from Arif to employees and advisers.

> Dear Friend of Abraaj,
> I never thought this business would end up spanning the globe.
> We have created jobs, built soft and hard infrastructure and expanded life sustaining services to reach a multitude of individuals and families.

He said he was proud of all the people they had helped through mentoring and charitable acts, including a recent fundraising for Afghan children in need of heart surgery.

> These actions did not meet unanimous support internally in Abraaj— yet this was an element of our culture that I was most proud of and never compromised on. We have touched the lives of hundreds of thousands of less fortunate people along our journey.

He alluded to the failure that broke Abraaj in the most delicate terms.

> Earlier this year gaps in our internal governance and operating procedures were discovered and as a result we continue to navigate the business through very challenging circumstances. As you can imagine, the negative reports on Abraaj, many of which are out of context, have significantly damaged our Firm's value and undermined the business at different points over the course of the last four months.

Moreover, the way in which these factors (many of which were private) have all emerged as a matter of public record, has only aided to our loss of value.

He insisted that no laws were broken in his quest to make a better world.

Despite all the rumors and briefings against us, and me personally, to my knowledge there was no intentional wrongdoing.
It has been a privilege for my colleagues and I to work with you and your organizations in trying to make this world a better place.

Cerberus canceled its offer and Arif's closest allies deserted him. Abraaj's recently installed chairman, Sean Cleary, Badr Jafar, and Thomas Schmidheiny resigned from the board of Abraaj Holdings. Omar and Selcuk resigned from Abraaj Investment Management, joining Bisher and Matt, who had already stepped down.

The liquidators from Deloitte and PricewaterhouseCoopers restarted talks to sell Abraaj with a host of private equity firms. Colony, Cerberus, TPG, and Actis were interested. Arif still wanted to play a role in these discussions.

Colony and Cerberus submitted new, lower bids. The liquidators accepted an offer from Colony. But investors in Abraaj's funds objected to it. The World Bank was particularly unhappy. As talks dragged on, Colony pulled out.

Cerberus made a second bid for Abraaj in July 2018. This time, Cerberus wanted to be paid to take over the Abraaj funds but offered $25 million to keep the business afloat in the short term.

A new bidder entered the fray. It was Barack Obama's former commerce secretary. Penny Pritzker was a scion of the fabulously wealthy American family that founded the Hilton hotel chain. A Chicago native, Pritzker had known Obama for years and had run the finance team for his 2008 presidential campaign. She joined up with Obama's old friend Wahid Hamid to make a bid for Abraaj. They worked closely with other financiers with ties to Obama including Marty Nesbitt, a close personal friend of the former president, and Michael Sacks, a donor to Obama's foundation. The group planned to combine Wahid's emerging markets experience and knowledge of Abraaj with their political connections and financial expertise.

They needed support from Abraaj investors to succeed. Pritzker reached out to a senior Washington State Investment Board executive named Theresa Whitmarsh, who she had met in Davos earlier that year. She asked for an introduction to Abraaj investors.

"Theresa, I hope your summer is going well," Pritzker wrote in an August 2018 email. "Thank you again for the time together in Davos."

Pritzker said she had formed a bidding group that had "significant relationships at the highest levels of government and the private sector which, as you know, can be critical to unlocking opportunities for growth in emerging markets."

More wrangling with Abraaj investors followed but an agreement couldn't be reached.

All of the bids to buy Abraaj as a firm fell through, so the liquidators decided to break it up and sell off the pieces. Arif made a last desperate offer to buy back the business he had founded but his proposal was rejected.

• • •

As people fled Dubai's unbearable August heat in 2018, a few Abraaj employees were still turning up at the office each day to assist the liquidators with their investigations. Extraordinary discoveries were being made about years of fraud and theft.

Simon was talking to some of the investigators. They were extremely wary of talking and didn't want to be identified or found out. During one telephone call, the line became scrambled. Simon could hear people talking on the line. In horror, he realized he was listening to the beginning of the conversation he had just been having with the person on the line. The call was being recorded and now it was being played back to him. Simon hung up and called the source again. The source was surprisingly relaxed. Telephone calls into and out of the UAE were recorded by the government, and this playback problem had happened before, the source said.

The source agreed to show some of the Abraaj emails and bank statements. After months of telephone calls, the source agreed to meet in a café a few steps from the Tower of London. Finally this was the chance to prove what had really been going on inside Abraaj.

The source had said on the phone that they would hand over a trove of information. During a two-hour meeting, the source showed a few dozen emails and bank statements on their laptop computer. Simon asked permission to photograph some of the documents as they appeared on the computer screen. The source agreed and said they would find a way to transfer more information electronically. That never happened because the source was worried it would leave an electronic trail that could be tracked. After the meeting, Simon walked quickly back across London Bridge to the newsroom, firmly clutching the evidence.

The photographs of the emails and bank statements proved to be enough. The emails showed Arif and Omar discussing a bribe for Nawaz Sharif and money moving out of Abraaj to Arif's sons and to Ghizlan. They also showed Rafique's desperation as Arif ordered him to transfer cash out of the firm.

Over the phone, another investigator explained the significance of the emails and bank statements. The finance department, or Abraajery, as the investigators called it, managed all Abraaj's money as if it was one big pile of cash. There wasn't any real distinction about where money came from. Cash from the Gates Foundation, the U.S. government, the U.K. government, and Bank of America was mixed up with bank loans and other funds. Then it was paid out to Arif, his family, friends, and employees and to pay for investments and other expenses as and when it was needed. This meant that, for example, money provided by the U.S. government to fund hospitals in poor countries might have been used to fund Arif's charities or to pay bribes to politicians.

The finance department sent Arif a spreadsheet each month showing all the money coming into and going out of Abraaj. He treated Abraaj's funds as if they were his own. This system enabled Arif to live like a billionaire even though he wasn't one.

• • •

Peter, Paul, and Giles thought more needed to be done to protect Abraaj's investors and wanted to contact other financial regulators around the world. Peter emailed the Dubai Financial Services Authority in September 2018 to inform the regulator about his plan to share information with other regulators. The DFSA told Peter it wasn't their place to tell him whether to contact other regulators and that it was for him to decide how to proceed. Peter sent information about Abraaj's fraudulent finances to regulators in New York, London, and Singapore.

Around this time, Peter didn't show up at Abraaj's office for a day or so, as Paul had expected him to do. Paul couldn't contact Peter for a period of time and began to worry about him. Paul prepared to go to Dubai's Al Barsha police station to report Peter as a missing person. Before he got to the police station, Peter got back in touch. Peter said that he had never felt threatened and that there was no need for Paul to be so worried.

• • •

In London we prepared to publish our investigation in the *Wall Street Journal* after scouring the emails and bank statements and pulling apart the Abraaj creditor lists, which revealed the army of consultants Arif had enlisted, including management guru Flip Flippen and Daniel Nardello, the New York investigator. The firm even owed money to

Shred It, a company that provided equipment to destroy documents. A lawyer for the Sharif brothers said they didn't have any financial dealings with Arif or Abraaj. Our investigation was published on October 16, 2018. It showed that at least $660 million of investors' money was moved without their knowledge into Abraaj's hidden bank accounts. Then more than $200 million had flowed from those accounts to Arif and people close to him. Arif denied wrongdoing.

It seemed that no authority on earth had the will or the power to hold Arif accountable. Arif ranted about the incompetence of the Abraaj liquidators during a conference call with creditors in November 2018. He criticized their fire sale of artworks, which made just $4.7 million, a quarter of the estimated value. He described the failure of the liquidators to sell Abraaj's fund management business as value destruction and took no responsibility for what had happened.

A new anonymous source contacted us via email with news of Arif's latest antics in November 2018. Arif was in Pakistan advising Imran Khan, the new prime minister. Khan, a former international cricket star and playboy, had been elected four months earlier after pledging to stamp out rampant corruption but instead of investigating Arif for wrongdoing at Abraaj, Khan turned to him for advice on how to run the national economy. Arif was a funder of Khan's political ambitions. Khan's former wife Reham wrote in her autobiography that Arif paid for two-thirds of Khan's unsuccessful attempt to become prime minister in 2013.

According to Bashir Memon, the head of Pakistan's Federal Investigation Agency, Khan told him that Arif was a good friend who had funded his political campaigns. Memon told us that Khan also complained to him about his investigation of Karachi Electric, which had found that the power company owed hundreds of millions of dollars to a state-owned gas company. Memon said that he had shared the findings of his investigation with Pakistan's privatization commission and financial regulator. Khan told Memon that his investigation had ruined Karachi Electric because it had delayed the sale of the company to Shanghai Electric, according to Memon.

"Why am I responsible?" the policeman said he told the prime minister. "How can I ruin it?"

Weeks before Memon was due to retire, after serving his country for more than thirty years, he was unceremoniously transferred from his prestigious position as chief of the Federal Investigation Agency. He resigned in protest. A spokesman for Prime Minister Khan declined to comment on Memon.

The new source who had contacted us by email said that Arif was working with the prime minister and his finance minister, Asad Umar, to create a sovereign wealth fund. The fund, called Sarmaya, would control Pakistan's state-owned companies, and Arif and other former Abraaj employees were being considered as executives for the fund—positions that would give them great influence in Pakistan.

A spokesman for the government gave a curt response when we called to ask what Arif and the politicians were working on.

"Prime Minister Imran Khan and Finance Minister Asad Umar are public leaders and are accessible to business leaders from within and abroad."

Arif appeared more and more regularly in public with Khan.

"He is in Islamabad frequently to attend meetings with senior government officials," the source said. "He is trying to escape scrutiny or implication in the fraud by getting some sort of government immunity.

"Imran Khan is not corrupt but gullible. Arif has made him believe that this is a Western witch hunt against a successful brown boy who has done nothing wrong.

"The truth needs to come out before a lot more damage is done. Again."

CHAPTER 19

FLIGHT RISK

Sixteen years after Arif founded one of Dubai's most iconic companies he was no longer welcome in the Arabian city-state that had made him rich. His palatial Emirates Hills mansion gathered dust and fell into disrepair.

Arif had to stay out of Dubai from mid-2018 onward because he risked being arrested after Hamid Jafar, his former ally, filed criminal charges against him for bouncing checks worth millions of dollars. One lawsuit was settled out of court in late 2018, and rumors spread around Dubai that Arif had signed over his Emirates Hills house to Hamid. The threat of jail still loomed over Arif in early 2019 because Air Arabia began legal proceedings against him due to losses the airline had incurred from investing hundreds of millions of dollars in Abraaj.

Arif shuttled between the United Kingdom and Pakistan while Fayeeza and their sons lived in the London apartment. His phone no longer rang all the time. Arif sat and stared at it, waiting for bankers and politicians to call, but they rarely did now because he was a liability. The master chess player had become a pawn in a game he no longer controlled.

Arif was still attempting to complete the sale of Karachi Electric in his native country. Shanghai Electric was still keen to do the deal if the unpaid bills and regulatory questions could be resolved, and Arif believed that its successful conclusion could restore some of his wealth and reputation. Abraaj's liquidators didn't object to Arif continuing to work on the sale of Karachi Electric.

Chinese officials including President Xi questioned why the Karachi Electric sale kept getting delayed. Arif and some Pakistani politicians suspected the U.S. was somehow obstructing the deal to limit China's growing influence in the country.

Arif insisted that he had broken no laws. Yet he took precautions when traveling. He flew directly between London and Pakistan or went via Qatar to avoid stopping in Dubai, where he might be arrested. Before flying, he checked for his name on Interpol's Red Notice list of international criminal suspects. To his relief, his name never appeared.

· · ·

Detective Constable Matthew Benedict stood in London's Heathrow Airport on Wednesday, April 10, 2019, waiting for a commercial flight from Islamabad to arrive. As the plane touched down and taxied along the runway to the passenger gate, the detective from the extradition unit of London's Metropolitan Police prepared to make his move.

When Arif stepped off the plane Benedict arrested him and read him his rights. Arif was surprised that he was being arrested. He told the detective that he had made inquiries about whether Interpol had issued a Red Notice for him and he had taken comfort from the fact that it had not. Benedict didn't need a Red Notice to arrest Arif. The court for the Southern District of New York had issued an arrest warrant charging him with fraud, and U.S. law enforcement officials had asked the British to arrest him and extradite him to stand trial in New York.

Arif handed Benedict a travel bag containing four passports. Two were from Pakistan, the third was from the Caribbean nation of St. Kitts and Nevis, and the fourth was an Interpol travel document. Arif wrote down seven telephone numbers for the police officer. One was for Imran Khan, the prime minister of Pakistan, and another belonged to an Interpol Foundation board member.

The police drove Arif to Wandsworth Prison, an austere Victorian fortress in south London whose 1,600 inmates had only recently been granted electricity connections in their cells.

The following morning, police officers in New York swooped on another Abraaj executive. Mustafa was in America visiting colleges with his son. The Egyptian was arrested at the Four Seasons Hotel and led away from his family. He was taken to the Metropolitan Correctional Center, the jail that held the Mexican drug lord Joaquin "El Chapo" Guzman and would soon hold the convicted sex offender Jeffrey Epstein. Mustafa wanted to die when he realized where he was going.

In London, Arif made his first visit to Westminster Magistrates' Court from jail and offered £250,000 for bail. He wanted to live at home in South Kensington while he waited for an extradition trial in which a judge would decide whether to send him to the United States. British lawyers representing the U.S. government in the case against Arif told the judge that the defendant would likely flee the country if granted bail because Arif was immensely wealthy and had powerful friends around the world. If he escaped to Pakistan it would be very difficult for U.S. law enforcement to catch him again, they said. The judge denied bail and sent Arif back to his cell in Wandsworth Prison.

News of the arrests of Arif and Mustafa unleashed a wave of panic among former Abraaj executives scattered across continents.

"Everyone is shitting bricks," said one former executive in Dubai. "I have to go back to the family. They want to see me before I get arrested."

Wild rumors circulated. Former employees talked about Rafique fleeing to the Tora Bora caves in Afghanistan where Osama bin Laden hid after the September 11, 2001, attacks.

A few days after Arif and Mustafa were arrested, Simon was traveling into central London to meet Sev for breakfast at Brown's Hotel in

Mayfair. The hotel was still the favored meeting place for Abraaj executives, even though their office nearby had been closed. Sev abruptly canceled the meeting in a 7:35 a.m. message.

"I am not going to be in London today as I need to take my wife to another appointment. Sorry for the late notice and I will get back to you with new times."

He never did.

A police officer had just knocked at the front door of Sev's mansion on a leafy street in northwest London. Sev had already left home, and his wife, Menaka, answered the policeman's knock. She called her husband and told him he was a wanted man. Shortly before 8:00 a.m., Sev walked into a London police station and handed himself over. He didn't want anyone to know about his arrest and even tried to keep it a secret from his two children.

. . .

Arif prepared the best legal defense money could buy to avoid being extradited to stand trial in the United States. He hired Hugo Keith, an experienced lawyer who worked at the same chambers as Alexander Cameron, brother of the former prime minister David Cameron. Hugo's peers described him as silky smooth and extraordinarily clever. He had represented Queen Elizabeth II at the inquest into the death of Princess Diana and successfully defended an Algerian pilot accused of training terrorists involved in the September 11, 2001, attacks.

Hugo was at Westminster Magistrates' Court on the morning of April 18, 2019, to defend Arif. Judge Emma Arbuthnot was having a busy morning, with a succession of extradition cases. Romanians, Poles, Frenchmen, Italians, and Latvians appeared in person or via video link from jail to face charges of fraud, theft, and assault. In case after case, the wheels of global justice turned slowly.

"Next case," Judge Arbuthnot called.

"He's coming up," a clerk responded.

In a cell beneath the courts Arif stood up, walked out and ascended a staircase leading to the dock in the courtroom. A female prison guard followed behind. Thick glass panels separated Arif from the judge.

Arif was casually dressed in blue jeans, a T-shirt, and a dark bomber jacket. His swept-back hair was still as thick as in his youth but streaked with gray and white. He looked leaner than he'd been for a long time. There was a moment of stillness in the small public gallery where journalists had been jostling for seats with Fayeeza, her two sons, daughter-in-law, and half a dozen friends and advisers.

Fayeeza was calm. She swayed gently back and forth as she stood elegantly dressed in a dark trouser suit and neck scarf. Her left nostril was pierced with a small gold stud. Arif smiled and waved to her. She waved back, gently bending the fingers of her right hand.

Arif didn't speak during the brief hearing. The judge quickly scheduled another hearing for the following week. Hugo said substantial bail money would be offered.

Next up was Sev, who appeared via a video link from Wandsworth Prison.

"Could you bring Mr. Vi . . . viv . . . et . . . ti . . . pla . . . ," the court clerk asked the prison guards, struggling to pronounce the Sri Lankan surname Vettivetpillai.

Sev wore a burgundy sweatshirt and sat with his arms crossed in a small room with pale blue walls. He stood up as the judge addressed him, revealing gray sweat pants.

Judge Arbuthnot grappled with the details of the Abraaj case.

"Mr. Vettivetpillai is said to have been a managing partner, head of impact investments and member of the global investment committee," his lawyer said.

"Head of what?" the judge asked.

"Impact investments," the lawyer replied.

"Impact investments," the judge repeated, intrigued by what the term might mean.

Sev's lawyer explained that impact investments were supposed to create social and environmental improvements as well as profits and that Abraaj was an expert in the field. Sev was a pillar of his local

community and wasn't involved in any wrongdoing at Abraaj, the lawyer said. Sev was unhappy with Arif's dictatorial and despotic management style, the lawyer added.

To convince the judge to release Sev on bail, the lawyer explained
that he was a British citizen who owned nursing homes and properties in the United Kingdom. His son was at Oxford University and
had been head boy at an elite private school. His daughter was head
of her senior year at school. The children didn't know that their father was in prison.

"Both of them face serious exams soon," the lawyer said.

For bail money, Sev offered £500,000 kept in an account at Coutts,
the bank used by Queen Elizabeth II.

Rachel Kapila, the lawyer representing the U.S. government, said
Sev was a rung below Arif in the hierarchy of Abraaj and played an
instrumental role in the fraud.

"These are plainly very serious offenses," Rachel said.

Judge Arbuthnot granted Sev bail at £1 million on the assumption
that he hadn't gained personally from the fraud and had strong community ties. She ordered him to wear an electronic tag and to report
daily to a police station.

Arif and his lawyer were back in court a week later. The case was
heard after a Brazilian accused of smuggling drugs, an Indian jeweler accused of laundering money, and a Romanian accused of assault.
Arif was determined to be released from Wandsworth Prison on bail.
Some of his former colleagues feared he would flee.

"Arif will almost certainly escape with bail and use the most sophisticated methods to do so," Ali Shihabi wrote in a WhatsApp message.
"He will realize this is his only hope and will get the best operatives
even if he has to swim down the Thames!"

To illustrate his point, Ali sent a message with a link to a news
article titled "Killer on the Run Probably Sliced His Ankle Monitor
with Bolt Cutters."

"Mr. Naviq can come up now," called a clerk, mispronouncing his
name.

Arif entered the dock again. This time he was dressed smartly in a dark suit, tie, and light blue shirt.

"There is a strong concern he will flee to Pakistan," Rachel Kapila said. "There is a strong concern it will be impossible to get him back."

Arif offered £1.5 million for bail. The sum was far too small, Rachel said.

"The numbers are so huge here, ten times that amount would be a drop in the ocean," Rachel said. She estimated Arif's personal wealth at between $400 million and $1 billion.

"He is alleged to have played the leading role in a multimillion-dollar fraud to deceive investors," Rachel said. "Abraaj raised one billion dollars for a dedicated health fund. It was said to focus on impact investing in hospitals and clinics."

"So health-related?" the judge asked.

"Yes," Rachel replied.

The lawyer explained that between 2016 and 2018 Abraaj was raising money for a new $6 billion fund. Abraaj provided investors with fraudulently inflated valuations for its investments, thereby depriving them of accurate information on which to base their investment decisions. Abraaj was paid management fees as a percentage of assets under management, so inflating the valuations resulted in more income for Arif and other Abraaj executives. Abraaj inflated its assets by more than $500 million and Arif was the driving force behind the fraud, Rachel said.

"He traveled to the U.S. to participate in fundraising efforts," she said. "He was exchanging emails with others within Abraaj about the need to inflate the valuations of positions held by Abraaj funds, despite some resistance from more junior Abraaj employees."

Arif's sons, both wearing smart dark suits, shook their heads in disagreement when they heard this remark. The older son, Ahsan, had black, slicked-back hair in his father's style. The younger, slimmer son, Faaris, had a crew cut.

Investors were repeatedly given false assurances as to the whereabouts of their money, Rachel said. Arif was the sole A-level signatory for Abraaj bank accounts, which meant that his authorization was needed to move large sums of money, she said. Evidence of wrongdoing included voice recordings and emails in which discussions about the cover-up took place. Abraaj executives had supplied fabricated bank accounts to investors, accountants, and regulators, Rachel told the judge. U.S. government investigators had been following the money trail secretly for months. Rachel emphasized that Arif had powerful friends in Pakistan who might help him escape.

"He has a compound," she said. "He has substantial ties to Pakistan's current political leadership."

The lawyer suggested Arif had recently traveled to Pakistan by private jet and urged the judge not to grant him bail.

"There are no bail conditions that can mitigate that risk," Rachel concluded. She sat down. Hugo took the stand and tried to demolish the case.

"I need to challenge the whole basis on which the objections to bail have been made," he told the judge. "Public reporting says Mr. Naqvi is worth five hundred million to one billion dollars. It is arrant nonsense. This may refer to a few years ago when Abraaj was at its peak. He is not now.

"There was a reference to a private jet. The flight ticket shows Mr. Naqvi left the U.K. on April 5 on a PIA plane. Such is the level of suspicion in the mind of the DoJ.

"I have the boarding pass in my hand," Hugo said, waving a piece of paper for the Pakistan International Airlines flight. "It is, I am afraid, a terrible example of how on one view some basic facts about the matter of the case can be turned to make it look as if the situation is a great deal more terrible than it is."

Arif was a man of good character without a criminal record. He was a reputable CEO whose name had been blackened with allegations, Hugo said. Arif's character, reputation, and charitable donations made it inconceivable that he would break a court order, the lawyer said. Arif had, after all, been an honorary fellow of the London

School of Economics, a member of the United Nations Global Compact, a director of the Interpol Foundation, and a winner of the Oslo Business for Peace Award.

"He is absolutely deserving of the court's trust. He should not really be in custody at all," Hugo said.

Arif had strong ties to the United Kingdom. He had been a permanent resident in London for more than twenty years and lived there with his wife, younger son, and eighty-four-year-old mother, Hugo said. His older son lived next door with his pregnant wife. Arif's younger son squeezed his mother's hands as the lawyer reached the conclusion of his argument. Arif was the real victim, Hugo said.

"Great weight was placed by the U.S. press—some of whom are in the audience today—on the alleged misappropriation of money from American investors," Hugo said. "He has traveled on a multitude of occasions to Pakistan to try to get the Karachi Electric deal completed. He could have stayed. But he returned."

There was no wrongdoing at Abraaj, Hugo said.

"The funds it managed were hugely successful," he said.

Any mistakes Arif made were unintended.

"The spending at the group level ran ahead of the management fees, its income, and that resulted in a cash squeeze," Hugo said. "Banks lent the group money and withdrew their support in the light of the press reporting. There was a run on the group and that hastened the end."

Arif repaid money he owed Abraaj before he left the company, Hugo said.

"If anything, he is owed money."

"The DoJ sees what it sees," Hugo said. "The personal benefit allegation is wrong."

The bagful of passports Arif handed over when he was arrested was explained. One of the two Pakistani passports had expired. Arif and his family had Saint Kitts and Nevis passports to enable them to visit more countries. Carrying a Saint Kitts passport gave visa-free access to 156 countries, almost five times as many as a Pakistani passport. Arif received the Interpol travel document when he joined the board of the Interpol Foundation.

"As for access to funds, my learned friend said he has massive wealth," Hugo said, referring to Rachel. "His four bank accounts have been shut. Every bank in the world has read about him and no bank is going to let money go through his hands or his accounts."

Judge Arbuthnot asked Hugo about the junior Abraaj employees who had pushed back against the valuation fraud. Arif shook his head.

"The objections to bail simply do not carry the weight placed upon them," Hugo said. "You can indict a ham sandwich in front of a grand jury," he said, referring to the U.S. jury that had authorized Arif's arrest.

Hugo sat down.

"Mr. Keith has put forth a very persuasive case," Judge Arbuthnot said. But it wasn't persuasive enough. She denied bail at £1.5 million. "I am concerned he will go to Pakistan. I am not going to engage in horse trading."

In the following days the judge changed her mind. Perhaps proving money talks even more effectively than a lawyer, she accepted a £15 million bail offer on May 1, 2019, then the largest in British history. It would take most Pakistanis 14,800 years to earn such a sum. The judge ordered that Arif be fitted with an electronic tag to his ankle and that he should live in his South Kensington apartment under a twenty-four-hour curfew. The U.S. government immediately appealed the decision to the High Court.

Two days later, Arif's family, lawyers, and journalists descended on the Victorian warren of stone corridors and wood-paneled rooms at the gothic Royal Courts of Justice on Fleet Street, just around the corner from the London School of Economics, where Arif studied four decades earlier. Arif remained incarcerated in Wandsworth Prison as lawyers squared up for the final bail battle in the case of *The Government of the United States of America vs. Arif Naqvi*.

"There remain serious allegations of fraud that, if proved, will result in a lengthy sentence," said Judge Michael Supperstone, who wore a red gown.

Rachel wore a traditional white wig and black gown as she presented a letter to the judge that she'd received overnight. It was from Deloitte, one of the Abraaj liquidators, and it said that Arif had taken at least $250 million more than he was entitled to before Abraaj collapsed. Payments were sent to offshore companies including Silverline in the Cayman Islands to conceal the transfers.

"The respondent still has hundreds of millions in assets which he maintains though various corporate entities and personal trusts," Rachel said. "The entities in which Naqvi maintains his assets are said to be based in various jurisdictions that have strong banking secrecy laws."

Hugo also wore a white wig and black gown. He insisted all the allegations against his client were false. He listed Arif's scholarship programs and community projects, including funding a social center at a north London mosque near where his parents lived until his father died in 2009. To prove that Arif wouldn't flee if granted bail, Hugo said that Arif wanted to be buried in England.

"His ties to the U.K. are so deep rooted that his father, uncle, and other family members are buried at Carpenders Park Cemetery in Watford," Hugo said. Arif had purchased burial plots for himself and other family members to ensure that his final resting place would be in English soil with his father. It was only fair for Arif to get bail, Hugo said. After all, Sev and Mustafa had each been granted bail at £1 million and $10 million.

Rachel highlighted the extreme lengths Arif was taking to undermine the U.S. government's case.

"An oddity about this case is the respondent disputes not only the substance of the offending, that of course being a matter of trial, but even the fact that certain allegations are being made against him," she said. "It will be argued that substantial investor monies were diverted for personal use. Mr. Naqvi is the architect of this scheme."

To illustrate Arif's wrongdoing, she read out one of his emails to Rafique.

"'Take a deep breath, smile, say Alhamdolillah and proceed. To send $300,000 to Ahsan in his U.K. account and $300,000 to The Modist account. Both are broke, need the cash tomorrow.'"

She read Rafique's response.

"'As you are aware, I am under tremendous pressure re Abraaj cash as well, there is a serious cash crunch and currently I don't have the funds to pay essential payments like salaries for the month of June. You are fully aware of the situation. Please help me.'"

There was no evidence that anyone else at Abraaj had ordered money to be stolen.

Arif was the Key Man.

"When he said he only received sums according to contractual entitlement, that is in dispute, civilly and criminally," Rachel said.

Three of Arif's friends, including his schoolmate Javed Ahmed, had offered £650,000 as surety to the court, which they would lose if Arif fled. Rachel said the money was no guarantee against escape because Arif had access to large amounts of cash and could repay his friends if necessary.

Hugo argued that the money Arif took from Abraaj was legitimately his. He criticized Rachel for describing a house Arif owned in Pakistan as a compound, a word he suggested she used to conjure the ghost of Osama bin Laden, who was killed in a compound in Pakistan.

The judge asked how much Arif was worth.

"He is an extremely wealthy individual but not in liquid form?"

"Yes," Hugo replied.

"With trusts you don't know how liquid he is," the judge said. Trusts are secretive offshore bank accounts.

"He is a world-renowned global CEO," Hugo said. "He is entitled to the court's trust. He has strong ties to the jurisdiction. He was educated here. The majority of members of his family are here."

The court rose as the judge left the room to consider his decision.

He returned about an hour later to dismiss the U.S. government's appeal and granted Arif the £15 million bail.

Arif's victory was brief.

Less than a month later, U.S. prosecutors published a more detailed version of their case against him. If found guilty of all the charges Arif faced 291 years in jail. He was accused of running Abraaj as a criminal organization, like the mafia. Rafique, Waqar, and Ashish were also indicted to stand trial with Arif, Sev, and Mustafa.

. . .

In June 2019 Mustafa pled guilty in New York to seven charges of fraud and racketeering. His lawyer, Paul Schechman, said the Egyptian was a good man who had tried to rectify the madness that Arif created. Mustafa gave a statement to the judge.

"Put simply, money was commingled that should have been segregated, and investors were not told the truth.

"This was especially so with respect to Abraaj Private Equity Fund IV, which was launched in 2008 and included U.S.-based investors.

"In 2016, Abraaj began raising money for a new fund, Abraaj Private Equity Fund VI. We raised approximately three billion dollars from entities and individuals, including several U.S. based investors. We met with potential investors in Manhattan and sent emails into the United States. In raising those funds, potential investors were lied to about Abraaj's financial health.

"We painted a rosy picture of a prosperous firm, when, in fact, the firm was experiencing the severe liquidity issues that I have described. We also materially overstated Abraaj's track record: we led potential investors to believe that several of our prior investments were more successful than they actually were. To that end, I approved valuations that I knew were inflated, and, at Naqvi's urging, I resisted attempts by others in the firm to mark down those valuations.

"At meetings with potential investors, I stood by silently while Abraaj's track record was overstated and its financial health falsely portrayed. I was respected by investors and potential investors. By my presence, I lent credibility to statements that I knew were not true.

"Judge, the indictment charges a criminal enterprise and conspiracy counts. There was no formal agreement among Abraaj's leaders to commit illegal acts. Some of us pushed back at Arif's misconduct. Too often, however, we capitulated. We knew that, acting together, we were giving investors and potential investors—people to whom we owed a duty of candor—a less than candid account of the firm.

"I knew at the time that I was participating in conduct that was wrong. When things turned bad in 2014, I should have walked away. I considered it, but didn't. My commitment to Abraaj compromised the integrity of my judgment, and I ended up drifting from who I really am. For that, I am ashamed. I hoped that, if I stayed, I could help give investors what they were promised and entitled to. That hope was never realized. I share responsibility for what happened. I regret my involvement more deeply than anyone can imagine."

• • •

On Christmas Eve, 2019, Arif sent a text message to former colleagues and advisers:

> I wish you a peaceful holiday and my best wishes for the future. May God bless you and your family and allow his Grace to always wash over you and keep you safe. Please forgive me if I have ever caused you any sadness or pain; over the last year, I have truly understood what humility means and the importance of human ties; when all is black and bleak, God finds ways to give you hope and compassion, none more so than the kind word, love and forgiveness. Stay safe and happy, and my best wishes and regards, Arif Naqvi.

• • •

In April 2020, a year after Arif was arrested, he was still mostly confined to his South Kensington apartment. He was allowed out only to see lawyers, to walk around Hyde Park for two hours each afternoon, and to visit a nearby mosque on Fridays. He had told a psychiatrist that he had such dreadful nightmares he was afraid of falling asleep. Feeling humiliated and broken financially and emotionally, he had been taking antidepressants and Xanax but his mental health had worsened.

Shirish, his former friend and business partner, still lived just around the corner but they never met. Shirish had been successful enough with his new company to buy *Kalizma*, an elegant old yacht once owned by movie stars Richard Burton and Elizabeth Taylor. It's said that Burton presented Taylor with a sixty-nine-carat diamond on board. Shirish bought *Kalizma* from Vijay Mallya, an Indian billionaire who had fallen on hard times. Mallya also lived in the U.K. and was fending off attempts to extradite him to India, where he faced charges of fraud.

Arif's lawyers returned to Westminster Magistrates' Court in June 2020 for his extradition trial. Arif wasn't required to attend the trial in person because of changes to the court system that were introduced to help contain the coronavirus pandemic. Instead, he was allowed to participate via a video link from his apartment. But the video connection in Court One wasn't working, so Hugo called his client on a mobile phone. Arif's face peered out of the screen. His cheeks and chin were covered in white stubble and his white hair flopped uncharacteristically forward onto his forehead from a center parting.

"By law the court has to see you and you have to be able to see what is going on," Hugo told Arif.

Judge Arbuthnot entered. Hugo propped up the phone on a pile of books in the courtroom so Arif could see the judge and the judge could see Arif on the screen.

"We have put Mr. Naqvi on FaceTime," Hugo said.

Days earlier, Sev appeared in court and agreed to extradition. Prosecutors expected him to plead guilty. His lawyer declined to comment.

Arif was still resisting extradition. Hugo said his client was suffering from poor health after spending time in hospital with suspected coronavirus. He argued that Arif shouldn't be sent to New York for two reasons. First, Arif could be tried for his alleged crimes in London. Second, the prison conditions in New York's jails, where Arif might end up in pretrial detention, were so appalling they would violate Arif's human rights and increase the risk of him committing suicide.

"His unshakeable conviction is that he is entirely innocent," Hugo told Judge Arbuthnot. "There is certainly a risk that he will make an attempt on his own life."

Arif was severely depressed and had coronary artery disease, high blood pressure, high cholesterol, diabetes, gastritis, sinus tachycardia, sleep apnea, hives, and inflamed nerves, Hugo said. He was still traumatized from his time in Wandsworth Prison, and Fayeeza's close supervision was keeping her husband alive.

A former jail warden from the Metropolitan Correctional Center in Manhattan, where Mustafa had been held and Jeffrey Epstein had died, was called as a witness. Maureen Baird said the jail was dangerously overcrowded, understaffed, and infested with rats, mold, and criminal gangs. It was a gulag, she said.

"The facility is so disgusting it's like a prison in a third-world country," Ms. Baird said.

Suicidal inmates were placed in small single cells with concrete beds surrounded by windows so guards could see them. They wore suicide smocks, which were like blankets with Velcro straps, and their meals were served in paper bags with plastic utensils so they couldn't injure themselves.

"Staff attention gets diverted to whatever is going on, so even if they are aware of Mr. Naqvi he could easily be forgotten in a sea of everything else that's going on," Ms. Baird said. "The risk with his current condition is very high that something bad could happen."

An alternative jail—the Metropolitan Detention Center in Brooklyn—was just as bad. A federal judge had described the conditions there as third-world too, according to Arif's lawyers.

U.S. prosecutors said they wouldn't oppose bail for Arif in New York, so he could avoid being detained in either jail before his trial, but Hugo said their assurances weren't good enough.

"The offer of bail is simply not sufficient to discount the real risk of detention," he said.

Hugo's efforts to keep Arif out of New York's third-world jails paid off. U.S. prosecutors relented and agreed that Arif wouldn't be sent to either the Manhattan or Brooklyn jails for pretrial detention. They said they'd propose another jail instead.

"Make it Guantánamo," Hugo said bitterly to Rachel as the hearing ended. "Then we've really got an issue to argue about for ten years."

• • •

While Arif and his lawyers fought the extradition process in London, the shockwaves from the collapse of Abraaj were still rippling throughout the global financial system. In the summer of 2020, Abraaj's liquidators subpoenaed sixteen banks in a quest to find missing money. Arif had taken a total of $780 million from Abraaj in 3,700 transactions and $385 million was unaccounted for. Tens of millions of dollars had gone to Silverline in the Cayman Islands. Arif was Silverline's sole shareholder, according to the subpoenas. Its directors were Rafique, another Abraaj employee called Asim Hameed, and a Swiss banker called Alessandro Celano who managed Arif's private affairs.

The liquidators asked the banks to provide information about where Arif sent the missing millions. The banks they asked for assistance were the most prestigious institutions in the world's most important financial capitals, confirming just how much of a globalist insider Arif had become. The information requests went to Bank of America, Bank of New York Mellon, Citigroup, Goldman Sachs, JPMorgan Chase, and Wells Fargo in the United States; Barclays, HSBC, and Standard Chartered in Britain; Bank of Nova Scotia in Canada; Mashreq Bank in the UAE; UBS in Switzerland; Deutsche Bank and Commerzbank in Germany; and BNP Paribas and Société

Générale in France. They were asked to check for cash transfers to
Arif's sons, to his wife, Fayeeza, to his sister Fawzia, to his cousins
Shahid and Ovais, and to his brother-in-law Waqar.

New lawsuits were still sprouting. Abraaj liquidators sued the
$1 billion healthcare fund to claw back $109 million from the Gates
Foundation and other investors. Arif had used Hamid Jafar's loans to
replenish the healthcare fund in December 2017, and the liquidators
wanted that money back to pay off creditors. Hamid Jafar also sued
Abraaj and the healthcare fund to try to get some of his money back.

In July 2020 the lawyers returned to court in London again. U.S.
prosecutors offered to have Arif stay at the Essex County Correctional Facility, across the Hudson River from New York in New
Jersey, if pretrial detention was required. Former Abraaj employees
marveled that Arif was still fighting to get his own way, this time by
selecting his own American jail.

"Perhaps it's only rich people who get that affordance," one former
employee said. "Makes a mockery of justice. I'm all for being careful
with extradition processes but this is getting ridiculous."

• • •

Judge Arbuthnot called Arif back to court on January 28, 2021, to
hear her verdict. He stood before her in a dark suit and black turtle
neck sweater, his hands cupped in front of himself and his gaze fixed
on the floor. His sons sat at the back of the courtroom. Fayeeza wasn't
there. The judge approved his extradition and said he could appeal.
Arif raised his hand to speak.

"I just wanted to thank you for the compassion that you have shown
throughout the trial irrespective of the outcome," Arif said.

Upon leaving the court he sent a message to people in which he
appealed to a higher authority.

"Everything happens on Allah's will and time," Arif wrote, "and I
have complete faith that he will always choose the best path for me."

EPILOGUE

"Alrighty—I am out of here!" Suzanne Mager, a lawyer at the Washington State Investment Board wrote to us in May 2019. "This is my last email before I turn in my key card and id."

Suzanne was stepping down after years of public service. She had been handling our freedom of information request, in which we submitted questions about the Washington pension fund's investment in Abraaj. But her departure turned out to be brief and less than six weeks later she was back at work. The Washington State Investment Board rehired her to continue working on cases, including trawling through thousands of emails and documents about Abraaj and redacting them. She spent the best part of a year smothering page after page of text with thick black lines to cover commercially sensitive information about the pension fund's investments.

Suzanne was as friendly and helpful as she could possibly be as she searched for documents that might shed light on how and why Washington State pledged $250 million belonging to teachers and firefighters to a man accused of perpetrating a massive international fraud. By the time she had finished, there was very little information left of interest to us. The exercise was a waste of time. Our freedom of information request yielded only a few useful nuggets of information and cost the pension fund thousands of dollars to process.

The Washington State Investment Board was one of the most transparent institutions to which we spoke. The Teacher Retirement System of Texas offered to disclose documents about Abraaj on condition we paid $75,463. We declined.

At every turn our attempts to gather information were resisted. A rare opportunity to question important players in the Abraaj saga came up at an Emerging Markets Private Equity Association conference in London in late 2018. Sev, by then a former Abraaj partner working for an investment fund created by the royal family of Liechtenstein, was on stage with Nick O'Donohoe, the former JPMorgan impact-investing banker who had moved on to run the U.K. government's CDC. Frank Dunleavy, an adviser at the U.S. government's OPIC, sat alongside them. They talked about investing in emerging markets for the best part of an hour and never once mentioned Abraaj, which had collapsed just a few months earlier.

"There's an elephant in this room and it's called Abraaj," Simon said in a public question-and-answer session at the end of their discussion. "Nick, you are an investor; Frank, you are a lender; Sev, you were a senior partner. What happened at Abraaj? What are the lessons? How can you stop this happening again? How can you improve this industry?"

Sev and Nick stayed silent.

"No comment," Frank said.

CDC—created to do good without losing British taxpayers' money—refused to answer our freedom of information request. "The public interest in withholding this information outweighs the public interest in its disclosure," CDC said.

OPIC, which President Trump renamed the U.S. International Development Finance Corporation, didn't answer our freedom of information request either.

The silence of public institutions that were supposedly reliable stewards of public funds was maddening. We recognized that private companies were unlikely to cooperate with our requests for information but surely, we thought, public institutions managing taxpayer money and pensions had a duty to share information with the public on whose behalf they worked? Apparently not.

Arif had obtained funding from CDC, OPIC, the World Bank, and other public institutions by pledging to promote the global common good. He was an outspoken evangelist for helping the poor and vowed to behave in a transparent manner but now that his plans had ended in disaster neither he nor his investors wanted to talk.

Bankers, billionaires, and investors who had lavished praise on Arif in his glory days quickly dropped him. Hamilton Lane, the investment firm responsible for steering hundreds of millions of dollars in commitments from American public institutions into Abraaj, refused to answer questions. In the good times, Hamilton Lane's Erik Hirsch had sung Arif's praises in *Forbes* and elsewhere.

"We aren't able to comment," Hamilton Lane's spokeswoman Kate McGann said. "We do not comment on specific funds or firms."

Abraaj directors including the Harvard academic Jane Nelson, the Swiss billionaire Thomas Schmidheiny, and John Chipman, the head of London's International Institute for Strategic Studies, declined to talk about Abraaj.

"The facts are more likely to emerge from a proper investigation ordered by the court, or undertaken by a regulator, than from speculation shared with journalists," Sean Cleary, Abraaj's former chairman, told us. "That does not imply any disrespect for the media."

The positive academic case studies that Josh Lerner wrote about Abraaj were removed from Harvard's website. Lerner, a member of Abraaj's advisory board from 2008 to 2010 and a paid consultant to the firm until 2017, told us that he had made an "inadvertent mistake" when he wrote a report analyzing Abraaj's performance that endorsed how the firm valued its investments.

Regulators outside the United States did nothing until it was too late. Months after an American court issued a warrant for Arif's arrest, the Dubai Financial Services Authority fined the bankrupt Abraaj a record $315 million for deceiving investors and carrying out unauthorized activities. Abraaj didn't have the money to pay the fine.

In the Cayman Islands, where most of Abraaj's companies and funds were incorporated, regulators washed their hands of the whole affair. The Cayman Islands Monetary Authority said it wasn't responsible for monitoring Abraaj or its funds.

KPMG, which audited Abraaj and its funds for years, announced an investigation into the debacle in 2018 but never mentioned the probe again. Abraaj investors filed a lawsuit against KPMG in Dubai in 2020. KPMG required repeated reminders from us and twenty-five days to respond to a final request for comment. They passed our questions to a public relations firm, which declined to comment on their behalf.

"Mr. Bronfman is not available to speak with you," wrote the assistant of the billionaire who once described Arif as a gentleman who was a gentle man.

Public relations companies were paid small fortunes to groom Arif's and Abraaj's image by aggrandizing the good and obscuring the bad. They declined to comment publicly but one former adviser to Arif said people had believed in him because he was so charming.

. . .

The real purpose of Abraaj was to pay fat salaries and bonuses to its executives, and Arif's promises to make the world a better place now look like delusional propaganda. The poor people of the world who Arif said he wanted to help didn't stand a chance of benefiting because they weren't the true priority and they didn't have a say in how the firm was run or what it chose to do. And Arif misused money raised in the name of the poor to benefit himself and his colleagues.

Sure, Arif drew public attention in his speeches to the vast wealth inequality in the world—something other Davos plutocrats and private equity tycoons are reluctant to do. And he was a visionary in pointing out the genuine investment opportunities to be found in developing countries. But since his fine words only served as cover for devious deeds, it would have been better if he'd never mentioned the plight of the poor, because the loss of trust and sense of betrayal he left as his legacy have damaged the cause he championed.

Poor people would perhaps have benefited more if Arif had carried his millions to the top of a tall building in Karachi and thrown them into the sky, letting the wind blowing in from the Arabian Sea scatter dollar bills across the city.

Arif's downfall is a tragedy. As his old partner Ali Shihabi told him in 2002, his brilliance and energy were mixed with some serious flaws. He wanted to dispel a negative stereotype about corruption in Pakistan and other developing countries but his actions may have ended up reinforcing it. By 2020 he might have been leading Pakistan, his vibrant and chaotic homeland, into a bright and prosperous future, according to a scenario imagined by American academics in 2011. Instead, he faced 291 years in jail for being accused of running a criminal enterprise.

"This doesn't seem to have gone according to plan," said Daniel Markey, a professor at Johns Hopkins University's School of Advanced International Studies partly responsible for writing the Pakistan 2020 report back in 2011. "You know, at certain times people just are the poster child."

"I guess we didn't call that one right," said Michael Oppenheimer, a professor at New York University's Center for Global Affairs who oversaw the report. "We put our money on the wrong horse."

So how did Western academics, billionaires, politicians, and journalists get it so wrong? After all, Arif's meteoric rise was possible only because they promoted him. Arif invited them to believe in his mission to improve the world through capitalism. It was a story that Bill Gates, Edgar Bronfman, John Kerry, Prince Charles, Klaus Schwab, Bank of America, McKinsey, KPMG, Hamilton Lane, and the rest of the global elite wanted to believe. The World Bank and the governments of the United States, the United Kingdom and France weren't just funding Arif and Abraaj—they were funding an idea that they wanted to be true. Instead, they showed how a conspiracy of self-righteousness and self-interest could blind them to what the main financial risk really was and always has been.

Greed.

Can there be any other conclusion? It's an important question because plenty more billionaires and chief executives are making the same claims as Arif—that they can make money and make the world a better place at the same time. Perhaps they are sincere and perhaps they will do what they say. Or perhaps they won't.

On August 19, 2019, the Business Roundtable, a powerful group of 181 chief executives of America's largest companies, overturned a decades-old policy statement that defined the purpose of companies as maximizing shareholder returns. Their new purpose was "for the benefit of all stakeholders—customers, employees, suppliers, communities and shareholders." The language they used in the statement was very familiar to anyone who had listened to Arif's speeches because, more than fourteen years earlier, Arif had dedicated Abraaj to the purpose of promoting "the shared values of all our stakeholders." This was why he won the Oslo Business for Peace Award in 2013 and why Jeff Skoll put him on stage with Richard Branson in 2014.

As it becomes ever more fashionable for billionaires and CEOs to pledge to do good and start foundations, join Interpol and United Nations boards and team up with governments, universities, and schools to fulfill grand plans, it's worth remembering that there's already a system in place to fairly and justly manage human affairs in a way that values everyone equally, regardless of how much money they have.

It's called democracy.

Democratically elected governments are supposed to raise revenue by taxing companies and individuals and to spend that money on providing public services such as schools and hospitals. If people don't like the decisions a government makes about spending that revenue they can elect a new government at the next election.

Billionaires and CEOs who say they can do a better job than governments should surely be heard but they shouldn't have the right to silence those who question them or disagree with them with threats from expensive lawyers.

Billionaires and CEOs usually have their own agendas. They have successfully lobbied governments to reduce taxes, and claiming that they can do a better job than governments is in part an argument to keep taxes low. The U.S. corporate tax rate has halved since the 1950s, and some countries struggle to raise much tax at all—less than 2 percent of Pakistan's 216 million citizens paid income tax in 2019.

Accounting firms like KPMG—which are supposed to monitor the integrity of financial statements—also advise companies and the wealthy on how to minimize their tax bills. Offshore tax havens such as the Cayman Islands, where Abraaj was incorporated, help the rich to avoid taxes too. American billionaires can also reduce their taxes by making philanthropic donations to causes of their own choosing.

So when billionaires and CEOs meet politicians at Davos and talk publicly about improving the state of the world, it's fair to assume that improving the state of the world isn't necessarily the only thing they have in mind. It wasn't the only thing Arif had in mind. To address this problem, global debates about the economy and ending poverty must include people who live on a few dollars a day. Conferences about poverty and the global economy that don't include poor people have as much integrity as a room full of men discussing how to improve gender equality.

Our private pensions and state pensions are flowing into the $4 trillion private equity industry, where the money is used to buy companies all around the world, from New York and London to Istanbul, Accra, and Karachi. Private equity is an industry that enjoys more secrecy than it deserves. If accountants and regulators can't keep private equity firms on the right track then more people are going to have to take an interest in how they operate and whether they stick to their promises. Yörsan, the Turkish dairy, filed for bankruptcy, while Fan Milk, the dairy in Ghana, fared better and has been swallowed by Danone. Karachi Electric still languished in 2020 without a new owner.

Abraaj's healthcare fund was taken over by TPG. The American private equity firm also hired John Kerry as an adviser. But TPG has encountered problems of its own. Like Arif, Bill McGlashan, who cofounded TPG's Rise impact-investing fund with U2's Bono and Jeff Skoll, was a star of the finance industry. And like Kito, Bill picked London's Connaught Hotel for a meeting with us in January 2019 to talk about his work assisting poor people who lived far from the luxurious Mayfair venue. Bill was briefly in London when he met us, on his way to Davos, where he gave a talk with Bono. A few weeks later, Bill was arrested in the U.S. college admissions scandal. The Department of Justice accused him of bribing officials to get his son into the University of Southern California, forcing him to leave TPG. Another impact-investing star was in trouble with the law.

Abraaj's liquidators at Deloitte and PricewaterhouseCoopers and their lawyers at firms including Weil, Gotshal & Manges, which, incidentally, also worked for Arif, had charged more than $60 million in fees by 2020. The hourly rate the liquidators charged was as much as $945, more than most Ethiopians earn in a year.

How to build and fund a fair and just world isn't only a question for the key men and key women who work in business and finance and dine with prime ministers in Davos.

Most important, it's a question for you.

ACKNOWLEDGMENTS

We couldn't have written this book without the trust and cooperation of dozens of people around the world who were deeply affected by the events at Abraaj but couldn't speak out publicly. They wanted this story to be told, and we are very grateful for the testimony and evidence they shared with us.

Eric Lupfer, our agent at Fletcher & Co., had the idea for this book and proposed that we write it. His vision and support were vital. Hollis Heimbouch, our editor at HarperCollins, and Lydia Yadi, our editor at Penguin Random House, recognized the significance of the story and provided wise guidance about how to tell it. We are also grateful to Grainne Fox at Fletcher; Wendy Wong, Nicholas Davies, Penny Makras, Nikki Baldauf, and Andrew Jacobs at HarperCollins; and Celia Buzuk, Lucy Middleton, Leo Donlan, and Kayla Fuller at Penguin Random House.

This book evolved out of our journalism at the *Wall Street Journal*, where many colleagues helped shine a light on Abraaj. Foremost among them was Nicolas Parasie, our partner in the investigation. Nico's expertise and reporting on the ground in Dubai were extremely important. We would also like to acknowledge Anuj Gangahar, Ed Ballard, Michael Amon, Laura Kreutzer, Laura Cooper, Parminder Bahra, George Downs, Jovi Juan, Richard Boudreaux, Jacob Goldstein, Lisa Kalis, Alex Frangos, and Charles Forelle.

We're thankful to our friends and family for their support and advice.

Will thanks Colin, Julia, Clem, Harry, and Nick. He is also grateful for the guidance received from the Taylors, Guy McDonald, and Xander Fraser, as well as the residents of 10 Helix Road and 4 Coastguard Cottages.

Simon is grateful for helpful advice from Peter Koenig, Caroline Clark, Claudia Cerrina, Vivian Vignoles, Francis Robinson, and Zeb Lamb. Thank you to Ambra Clark, Oliver Clark, and Zahira Jaser for everything.

![NOTES]

PROLOGUE

1 "innumerable lives": Abraaj Group, "Scaling Impact Investing: Keynote—Arif Naqvi, Founder & Group Chief Executive, The Abraaj Group," published on October 9, 2017, YouTube video, www.youtube.com/watch?v=tJ_EL3qkyYc&t=53s

2 end global poverty by 2030: United Nations News, September 25, 2015, news.un.org/en/story/2015/09/509712-future-demands-us-critical-and-global-decisions-pope-francis-tells-un-general

2 were already providing: UNCTAD World Investment Report 2014, 11. unctad.org/system/files/official-document/wir2014_en.pdf

2 asking investors for $6 billion: Abraaj Private Equity Fund VI Private Placement Memorandum, March 3, 2017.

2 "better place": Abraaj Group, "Scaling Impact Investing: Keynote—Arif Naqvi, Founder & Group Chief Executive, The Abraaj Group," published on October 9, 2017, YouTube video, www.youtube.com/watch?v=tJ_EL3qkyYc&t=53s

3 Rafique told him: *United States Securities and Exchange Commission vs. Abraaj Investment Management Limited and Arif Naqvi*, United States District Court, Southern District of New York, Case 1:19-cv-03244-AJN, August 16, 2019, 39.

3 Arif had taken more than $780 million: Klestadt Winters Jureller Southard & Stevems LLP, "Application of Abraaj Investment Management Limited: For an Order to Obtain Discovery for Use in Foreign Proceedings Pursuant to 28 USC 1782," United States District Court, Southern District of New York, Case 1:20-mc-00229, June 12, 2020.

3 *Mission: Impossible* films: "Doing Well by Doing Good? Private Equity Investing in Emerging Markets," published by the London School of Economics, 2013, www.mixcloud.com/lse/doing-well-by-doing-good-private-equity-investing-in-emerging-markets-audio/

4 healthcare in poor countries: *United States of America vs. Arif Naqvi, Waqar Siddique, Rafique Lakhani, Mustafa Abdel-Wadood, Ashish Dave and Sivendran Vettivetpillai,*

S6 19 Cr. 233 Superseding Indictment, United States District Court, Southern District of New York, 2019.

4 Business for Peace Award: Business for Peace Foundation, May 14, 2013, businessforpeace.no/award/previous-hounorees/2013-honourees/

4 homeland to prosperity: Pakistan 2020, Center for Global Affairs, New York University, 2011.

6 front-page investigation: Simon Clark, Nicolas Parasie, and William Louch, "Private-Equity Firm Abraaj Raised Billions Pledging to Do Good—Then It Fell Apart," *Wall Street Journal*, October 16, 2018, www.wsj.com/articles/private-equity -firm-abraaj-raised-billions-pledging-to-do-goodthen-it-fell-apart-1539706575

6 arrested Arif: Simon Clark, William Louch, and Nicolas Parasie, "Abraaj Founder Accused of Fraud as U.S. Seeks Extradition," *Wall Street Journal*, April 12, 2019, www.wsj.com/articles/abraaj-founder-accused-of-fraud-as-u-s-seeks-extradition -11555086776

6 like the mafia: *United States vs. Arif Naqvi et al.*, Superseding Indictment, S6 19 Cr. 233, 2019.

7 holding on to $385 million: Simon Clark and William Louch, "Abraaj Liquidators Sue Fund Backed by Gates Foundation," *Wall Street Journal*, July 16, 2020, www.wsj.com/articles/abraaj-liquidators-sue-fund-backed-by-gates-foundation -11594922921

7 high-security jail: Simon Clark and William Louch, "Abraaj Founder Naqvi to Avoid Jail Where Epstein Died," *Wall Street Journal*, July 1, 2020, www.wsj.com /articles/abraaj-founder-naqvi-to-avoid-jail-where-epstein-died-11593630940

CHAPTER 1: THE BOY FROM KARACHI

9 "Wow": Richard Branson and Arif Naqvi in Conversation with Mindy Lubber, Skoll Foundation, published on April 24, 2014, YouTube video, 27:10, www.you tube.com/watch?v=M-rjVaPlZ4o

11 Empress Market: Qaseem Saeed, "Karachi's Empress Market—a Legacy Built upon the Ashes of Mutiny," Geo.tv, November 2018, www.geo.tv/latest/220009 -faded-glory-of-empress-empress-market-and-stains-on-history-history-of-empress

11 Karachi's population: World Bank Group, "Transforming Karachi into a Livable and Competitive Megacity," 2018, openknowledge.worldbank.org/bitstream /handle/10986/29376/211211ov.pdf

12 for a bond: Laura Cooper and Simon Clark, "Egyptian Billionaire Sawiris Backs Bail for Abraaj's Abdel-Wadood," *Wall Street Journal*, May 9, 2019, www.wsj.com /articles/egyptian-billionaire-sawiris-backs-bail-for-abraajs-abdel-wadood-115574 27009

12 the Bhatti Cousins: Staff reporter, "Pakistan: The Golden Boys," *Time*, June 15, 1959, content.time.com/time/magazine/article/0,9171,892658,00.html

13 "Good morning, God!": Arif Naqvi, "In Conversation with Arif Naqvi & Fadi

Ghandour," Step Conference, published on June 9, 2016, YouTube video, www.you tube.com/watch?v=GdQ2WVavcx4&fbclid

14   graduating in 1982: Paul Peachey, "British University Edits Out ex-Abraaj Boss Arif Naqvi from Recruitment Video," *National*, April 30, 2019, www.thenational.ae /business/british-university-edits-out-ex-abraaj-boss-arif-naqvi-from-recruitment -video-1.855703

16   "Well, I want your job": Arif Naqvi, "Arif Naqvi, Founder and Group Chief Executive, the Abraaj Group," Yale School of Management, published on September 24, 2014, YouTube video, www.youtube.com/watch?v=3OC6Y3NTLZo

18   "what I am looking for!": Imtiaz Hydari, *Leverage in the Desert: The Birth of Private Equity in the Middle East*, 2013, 31–38.

18   "Eastern culture": Imtiaz Hydari, *Leverage in the Desert: The Birth of Private Equity in the Middle East*, 2013, 51.

CHAPTER 2: A GLITTERING OASIS

22   were rumored: Imtiaz Hydari, *Leverage in the Desert: The Birth of Private Equity in the Middle East*, 2013, 72.

24   The organization: Neha Hirandani, "What It's Like to Belong to a Secretive Network of Ultra-rich Young Executives," *Quartz*, September 23, 2016, qz.com /655646/young-presidents-organization-inside-the-worlds-biggest-and-most -powerful-secret-network/

24   Arif first met Fadi: Abraaj Group, "The Abraaj Group: Arif Naqvi 2011 Endeavour Gala Address," published on February 25, 2013, YouTube video, 06:06, www.youtube.com/watch?v=z6zY7w3GZdY

25   "One of us": Endeavor Global, "Fadi Ghandour—Endeavor's 2011 High-Impact Entrepreneur of the Year," published on November 16, 2011, YouTube video, www.youtube.com/watch?v=Ww7BlnONmbk

25   over rocky paths: Melodena Stephens Balakrishnan, "Aramex PJSC: Carving a Competitive Advantage in the Global Logistics and Express Transportation Service Industry," Actions and insights—Middle East North Africa: East meets West, Emerald Group Publishing, Bingley, 2013, 15–67, doi.org/10.1108/EEMCS-03-2015-0036

25   a formidable business: Fadi Ghandour, "How I Did It: The CEO of Aramex on Turning a Failed Sale into a Huge Opportunity," *Harvard Business Review*, March 2011, hbr.org/2011/03/how-i-did-it-the-ceo-of-aramex-on-turning-a-failed-sale-into -a-huge-opportunity

26   terrorism, and civil disturbance: Aramex International Ltd., Securities and Exchange Commission Form F-1, November 6, 1996, www.sec.gov/Archives/edgar /data/1026459/0000912057-96-024866.txt

26   discuss a takeover: Aramex International Ltd, Securities and Exchange Commission Form 14D-9/A, January 29, 2002, www.sec.gov/Archives/edgar/data/1026459 /000095013302000290/0000950133-02-000290-index.htm

26   a confidential agreement: Aramex International Ltd., Securities and Exchange Commission Schedule 13E-3, January 29, 2002, www.sec.gov/Archives/edgar/data /1026459/000095013302000289/0000950133-02-000289-index.htm

CHAPTER 3: NOW WE RULE

32   "Caveat emptor": *Caveat emptor* is a Latin term that means let the buyer beware.

35   fund he had led: *The Public Institution for Social Security versus Mr. Fahad Maziad Rajaan al Rajaan & Others*, Royal Courts of Justice, November 2020, accessed via the British and Irish Legal Information Institute, bailii.org/ew/cases/EWHC /Comm/2020/2979.html#B1

37   The four companies: Abraaj Group, "The Abraaj Group Annual Review 2007," 40–47.

38   access to the system: Fadi Ghandour, "How I Did It: The CEO of Aramex on Turning a Failed Sale into a Huge Opportunity," *Harvard Business Review*, March 2011, hbr.org/2011/03/how-i-did-it-the-ceo-of-aramex-on-turning-a-failed-sale-into -a-huge-opportunity

38   Sales doubled: Aramex, Aramex Annual Report 2005, www.aramex.com /content/uploads/100/55/27272/2005%20-%20Annual%20Report.pdf

39   second private equity fund: Abraaj Group press release, "Abraaj Capital Announces Closing of Largest Private Equity Fund," December 17, 2005, wam.ae/en /details/1395227551237

39   $14 million payout: Thomas Friedman, *The World Is Flat: A Brief History of the Twenty-First Century*. New York: Farrar, Straus and Giroux, 2005, 150–216.

39   antidote for the terrorism: Thomas Friedman, *The World Is Flat: A Brief History of the Twenty-First Century*. New York: Farrar, Straus and Giroux, 2005, 150–216.

CHAPTER 4: THE GREAT SHOWMAN

41   "agents of change": Arif Naqvi, "Defining Future Trends: Entrepreneurship in the Arab World," September 2004.

42   Sinbad: Arif Naqvi, "Arif Naqvi of Abraaj Capital on Empowering Entrepreneurs and Fostering Innovation," SP Productions, published on February 16, 2016, YouTube video, 02:24, www.youtube.com/watch?v=rqQ5wZXsZ84

43   $100 million charitable organization: Aman Foundation Annual Report 2013–2015, www.theamanfoundation.org/wp-content/uploads/2017/08/01-Aman -Foundation-AR-Complete-Latest-20th-oct.pdf

45   consumer goods maker: "Unilever receives C K Prahalad Award for leadership in sustainability," Unilever, June 28, 2012, www.unilever.com/news/news-and -features/Feature-article/2012/12-06-28-Unilever-receives-C-K-Prahalad-Award -for-leadership-in-sustainability.html

49   $505 million: David Lanchner, "The Gulf's Buyout King," *Institutional Investor*,

July 15, 2008, www.institutionalinvestor.com/article/b150q7hfdfq8mp/the-gulf39s
-buyout-king

50   Abraaj sold in 2007: Abraaj Group Annual Review 2007, 40–47.

50   The article: Simon Clark, "Castles in the Sand," *Bloomberg Markets*, May 2008.

54   emptied the account again: Dubai Financial Services Authority, "Decision Notice to Abraaj Capital Limited," Dubai Financial Services Authority.

CHAPTER 5: KARACHI ELECTRIC

57   Arif recalled years later: Josh Lerner, Asim Ijaz Khwaja, and Ann Leamon, "Abraaj Capital and the Karachi Electric Supply Company," Harvard Business Publishing, Harvard, March 6, 2012.

58   reliable energy supply: Augustine Anthony and Ruma Paul, "Textiles on the Move: From Pakistan to Bangladesh," Reuters, August 30, 2011, uk.reuters.com /article/uk-pakistan-bangladesh-textiles/textiles-on-the-move-from-pakistan-to -bangladesh-idUKTRE77T11020110830

58   Daniel Pearl: Asra Q. Romani, "The Truth Left Behind," The Pearl Project, 2011, cloudfront-files-1.publicintegrity.org/documents/pdfs/The_Pearl_Project.pdf

59   blew himself up: Peter Wonacott and Jay Solomon, "Pakistan's Bhutto Is Killed in Attack," *Wall Street Journal*, December 27, 2007, www.wsj.com/articles /SB119875550729752531

59   bought 71 percent of the company: Karachi Electric Annual Report 2007, www.ke.com.pk/investor-relation/financial-data/

60   for a decade: Karachi Electric Annual Report 2009, www.ke.com.pk/down load/financial-data/KESC-Annual-Report-2009.pdf

61   Resolving these issues: Josh Lerner, Asim Ijaz Khwaja, and Ann Leamon, "Abraaj Capital and the Karachi Electric Supply Company," Harvard Business Publishing, Harvard, March 6, 2012, 2.

62   make a move: Josh Lerner, Asim Ijaz Khwaja, and Ann Leamon, "Abraaj Capital and the Karachi Electric Supply Company," Harvard Business Publishing, Harvard, March 6, 2012, 10–11.

63   U.S. Senate had cited him: Committee on Government Affairs, "Private Banking and Money Laundering: A Case Study of Opportunities and Vulnerabilities," U.S. Government Printing Office, 2000, www.govinfo.gov/content/pkg/CHRG-106 shrg61699/html/CHRG-106shrg61699.htm

63   the letter said: "Abraaj Goes Public with Some of Its Juicy Secrets," *News Pakistan*, October 30, 2008, www.thenews.com.pk/archive/print/660404-abraaj-goes -public-with-some-of-its-juicy-secrets

64   "seek Consulate Dubai's assistance": Wikileaks, "Encouraging Gulf Investment in Karachi's Power System," August 25, 2009, wikileaks.org/plusd/cables /09ISLAMABAD2022_a.html

65   adventure capitalism: Wikileaks, "Tuning out Politics, Abraaj Capital Tries

to Rebuild Karachi Electrical Supply Company," September 3, 2009, wikileaks.org /plusd/cables/09DUBAI367_a.html

65   U.S. politicians pledged: Peter Spiegel and Zahid Hussain, "U.S. Tries to Soothe Pakistan Worries on Aid," *Wall Street Journal*, October 15, 2009, www.wsj .com/articles/SB125548290488483937

67   running toward him: Nyla Aleem Ansari, "Downsize or Rightsize? KESC to K-Electric," Emerald Group Publishing, May 5, 2016, www.emerald.com/insight /content/doi/10.1108/EEMCS-01-2015-0014/full/html

68   jobs back: "Karachi Power Utility Reinstates Sacked Workers," BBC News, January 24, 2011, www.bbc.com/news/world-south-asia-12264297

68   hunger strike: "KESC Workers on Hunger Strike unto Death," *News International*, April 30, 2011, www.thenews.com.pk/archive/print/298387

68   "Who Wants to Be a Millionaire": Imdad Soomro, "Who Wants to Be a Millionaire with KESC?," *Pakistan Today*, May 20, 2011, www.pakistantoday.com.pk/2011 /05/20/who-wants-to-be-a-millionaire-with-kesc/

69   seventeen years: Karachi Electric, "Our History," www.ke.com.pk/our-company /our-journey/#:~:text=The%20Turnaround&text=Regaining%20Karachi's%20 Identity%3A%20Massive%20efforts,17%20years%20in%202011%2D12

CHAPTER 6: ARAB SPRING

71   a different approach: President Barack Obama, "President Obama Speaks to the Muslim World from Cairo, Egypt," The White House, YouTube video published on June 4, 2009, 54:56, www.youtube.com/watch?v=NaxZPiiKyMw

73   Riyada Ventures: Abraaj Capital, "Abraaj Acquires Riyada Ventures," November 25, 2009, www.privateequitywire.co.uk/2009/11/25/24801/abraaj-capital -acquires-venture-capital-firm-riyada

75   Arif's speech: Arif M. Naqvi, "Abraaj's Arif Naqvi at the Presidential Summit on Entrepreneurship," www.youtube.com/watch?v=V2YHQmOMKEo

78   a $6 million budget: Melodena Stephens Balakrishnan and Ian Michael, "Abraaj Capital: Celebration of Entrepreneurship," Emerald Group Publishing Limited, vol. 1 no. 4, 2011, 1–21.

80   "down to up": Jan Romany, "Naguib Sawiris Interviewed by Fadi Ghandour," published on April 23, 2015, YouTube video, 01:43, www.youtube.com/watch?v=l1y EIWjMVhc

81   within an hour: Melodena Stephens Balakrishnan and Ian Michael, "Abraaj Capital: Celebration of Entrepreneurship," Emerald Group Publishing Limited, vol. 1 no. 4, 2011, 19.

81   an enthusiastic article: Christopher Schroeder, "Dubai, a New Locus of Entrepreneurial Energy," *Washington Post*, November 26, 2010, www.washingtonpost .com/wp-dyn/content/article/2010/11/25/AR2010112502227.html

81   event in Dubai: Wikileaks, "Outcome of the Entrepreneurship Summit," November 29, 2011, wikileaks.org/clinton-emails/emailid/1057

81   sang his praises: Judith McHale, "Remarks at the Global Technology Symposium," Menlo Park, California, March 24, 2011, 2009-2017.state.gov/r/remarks/2011/159141.htm

84   modernize Pakistan: Pakistan 2020, Center for Global Affairs, New York University, 2011.

CHAPTER 7: IMPACT INVESTING

85   his Gospel: Andrew Carnegie, "The Gospel of Wealth, and Other Timely Essays," Carnegie Corporation of New York, 2017, first published in 1889, www.carnegie.org/publications/the-gospel-of-wealth/

86   women in Africa: Oxfam, "Time to Care," January 2020, oxfamilibrary.openrepository.com/bitstream/handle/10546/620928/bp-time-to-care-inequality-200120-en.pdf

86   129 Afghans: The World Bank, data.worldbank.org/indicator/NY.GDP.PCAP.CD?locations=PK

88   for shareholders: Milton Friedman, "A Friedman Doctrine—The Social Responsibility of Business Is to Increase Its Profits," *New York Times*, September 13, 1970, www.nytimes.com/1970/09/13/archives/a-friedman-doctrine-the-social-responsibility-of-business-is-to.html

89   "a new alternative": Nick O'Donohoe, Christina Leijonhufvud, and Yasemin Saltuk, "Impact Investments: An Emerging Asset Class," JP Morgan Global Research, November 29, 2010, thegiin.org/assets/documents/Impact%20Investments%20an%20Emerging%20Asset%20Class2.pdf

90   Sir Ronald Cohen: Catholic Relief Services, "2018 Impact Investing—Welcoming Remarks," published on September 6, 2018, YouTube video, https://www.youtube.com/watch?v=cerAZXusft0

90   Turkson saw impact investing: Simon Clark interviewed Cardinal Turkson about impact investing in Vatican City in December 2018.

91   blue sweater: Jacqueline Novogratz, *The Blue Sweater: Bridging the Gap Between Rich and Poor in an Interconnected World*, Penguin Random House, 2010.

92   Acumen's annual meeting: Acumen, "An Empathetic Evolution: The 2009 Acumen Fund Investor Gathering," November 21, 2009, acumen.org/blog/press-releases/an-empathetic-evolution-the-2009-acumen-fund-investor-gathering/

92   CDC was founded: CDC, "Our history," www.cdcgroup.com/en/about/our-history/

96   agreed to buy: Stefan Wagstyl, Kiran Stacey, and Simeon Kerr, "Abraaj Targets SMEs with Aureos Deal," *Financial Times*, February 20, 2012, www.ft.com/content/2e1c2fd6-5be9-11e1-bbc4-00144feabdc0

98   OPIC agreed: Karachi Electric, "K-Electric Secures up to $250 Million in Financing from OPIC," October 22, 2015, www.ke.com.pk/k-electric-secures-upto-us-250-million-financing-opic/

98   pledged $24 million: USAID, partnerships.usaid.gov/partnership/pakistan-private-investment-initiative-ppii-abraaj-capital

98   UN Global Compact: Arif Sharif, "Abraaj's Arif Naqvi Appointed to UN Advisory Body Global Compact," Bloomberg News, May 1, 2012, www.bloomberg .com/news/articles/2012-05-01/abraaj-s-arif-naqvi-appointed-to-un-advisory-body -global-compact

98   the Clinton Global Initiative: Clinton Foundation, www.clintonfoundation.org /contributors?category=%24500%2C001+to+%241%2C000%2C000

99   a Business for Peace Award: "Arif Naqvi Receives 2013 Oslo Business for Peace Award," published on May 16, 2013, YouTube video, 43:21, www.youtube.com/watch ?v=9r_rsDFtees

100   Linda Rottenberg: endeavor.org/team/linda-rottenberg/

101   "great wealth comes great responsibility": Endeavour Global, "2014 Endeavor Gala: Honoree Arif M. Naqvi's Remarks," published on November 12, 2014, YouTube video, 16:14, www.youtube.com/watch?v=YPorSJlhsWg

CHAPTER 8: THE CULT OF ABRAAJ

108   visa-free access to: Henley & Partners Passport Index, "Global Ranking 2020," www.henleypassportindex.com/passport

CHAPTER 9: TURKS WILL ALWAYS DRINK MILK

117   Abraaj bought Yörsan: Anne-Sylvaine Chassany and Daniel Dombey, "Dubai's Abraaj Buys Majority Stake in Turkey's Yörsan Group," *Financial Times*, January 21, 2014, www.ft.com/content/e0ede9c6-8282-11e3-8119-00144feab7de

118   an attractive target: Abraaj Group, "Abraaj Private Equity Fund IV, Report of the General Partner for the Period Ended September 30, 2017."

119   Abraaj invested $142 million: Abraaj Group, "Abraaj Private Equity Fund IV, Report of the General Partner for the Period Ended September 30, 2017."

119   Turkey's $3.6 billion dairy industry: Svitlana Pyrkalo, "EBRD and Abraaj Acquire Majority Stake in Turkish Dairy Producer, Yörsan," European Bank for Reconstruction and Development, June 21, 2014.

119   the deal was announced: "Abraaj Group Acquires Majority Stake in Turkish Dairy Business Yörsan Group," *Private Equity Wire*, January 21, 2014, www.private equitywire.co.uk/2014/01/21/196124/abraaj-group-acquires-majority-stake-turkish -dairy-business-yörsan-group

120   remain in charge: "Şerafettin Yörük: 'Abraaj Did Not Purchase, Yörsan Becomes a Partner!'" June 7, 2015, www.milliyet.com.tr/yerel-haberler/istanbul/serafettin -yoruk-the-abraaj-yorsan-i-satin-almadi-ortak-oldu-10870558

121   coup d'état: Dion Nissenbaum, Adam Entous, and Emre Peker, "Turkish President Foiled Coup with Luck, Tech Savvy," *Wall Street Journal*, July 17, 2016, www .wsj.com/articles/coup-plotters-targeted-turkish-president-with-daring-helicopter -raid-1468786991

122   profits kept falling: Abraaj Group, "Abraaj Private Equity Fund IV, Report of the General Partner for the Period Ended September 30, 2017."

123 Emborg started: Fan Milk Ghana, "Our History," 41.189.183.5/history.php

123 against fierce competition: Rob Minto, "Abraaj: A Fan of Milk," *Financial Times*, June 19, 2013, www.ft.com/content/a1b37a61-b61d-3138-8bfd-9c08f1efafac

125 price of gold: Joe Bavier and Matthew Mpoke Bigg, "Gold Price Drop Jolts West Africa from Mining Dreams," Reuters, October 25, 2013, www.reuters.com /article/us-africa-investment-gold-analysis/analysis-gold-price-drop-jolts-west -africa-from-mining-dreams-idUSBRE99O0S320131025

125 worst-performing currency: Moses Mozart Dzawu and Robert Brand, "World's Worst Currency Drops as Ghana Pulls Back from IMF Aid," Bloomberg News, July 30, 2014, www.bloomberg.com/news/articles/2014-07-30/world-s-worst-currency -drops-as-ghana-pulls-back-from-imf-aid

126 40 percent of its value: Carolyn Cui and Julie Wernau, "Naira Plunges After Nigeria Ends Dollar Peg," *Wall Street Journal*, June 20, 2016, www.wsj.com/articles /naira-plunges-after-nigeria-ends-dollar-peg-1466440618#:~:text=Nigeria's%20 currency%20plummeted%20more%20than,some%20major%20oil%2Dproducing %20nations.&text=Nigeria%20introduced%20the%20fixed%2Dcurrency,effort %20to%20stabilize%20the%20naira

126 sliding toward bankruptcy: Abraaj Group, "Abraaj Private Equity Fund IV, Report of the General Partner for the Period Ended September 30, 2017."

127 impartial case studies: Josh Lerner, Asim Ijaz Khwaja, and Ann Leamon, "Abraaj Capital and the Karachi Electric Supply Company," Harvard Business Publishing, Harvard, March 6, 2012.

127 Abraaj as extraordinary: Abraaj Group, "The Abraaj Academy: A Talk with Professor Josh Lerner," published on February 25, 2013, YouTube video, 00:56, www.youtube.com/watch?v=xeryFvdGVIw

128 the only person involved: Karl Shmavonian, "Arabia-Asia: Business Is Personal for Abraaj Capital's Omar Lodhi," *Forbes Asia*, October 2012, www.forbes.com/sites /forbesasia/2012/10/11/arabia-asia-business-is-personal-for-abraaj-capitals-omar -lodhi/

CHAPTER 10: CASH CRUNCH

129 "reason we're all here": Skoll Foundation, "Skoll World Forum 2014 Opening Plenary," published on April 9, 2014, YouTube video, www.youtube.com/watch?v =Ry9sVvfQIHg

130 a finance manager wrote: *United States of America vs. Arif Naqvi, Waqar Sid-dique, Rafique Lakhani, Mustafa Abdel-Wadood, Ashish Dave and Sivendran Vettivetpillai*, S6 19 Cr. 233 Superseding Indictment, United States District Court, Southern District of New York, 2019, 12.

130 U.S. Department of Justice later concluded: *United States of America vs. Arif Naqvi, Waqar Siddique, Rafique Lakhani, Mustafa Abdel-Wadood, Ashish Dave and Sivendran Vettivetpillai*, S6 19 Cr. 233 Superseding Indictment, United States District Court, Southern District of New York, 2019, 1–78.

131   in an Abraaj fund: *United States of America vs. Arif Naqvi, Waqar Siddique, Rafique Lakhani, Mustafa Abdel-Wadood, Ashish Dave and Sivendran Vettivetpillai*, S6 19 Cr. 233 Superseding Indictment, United States District Court, Southern District of New York, 2019, 12–13.

132   Panama in March: World Economic Forum, "World Economic Forum on Latin America: Opening Pathways for Shared Progress," April 1–3, 2014.

132   "that's just a fact": World Economic Forum, "Panama 2014—Middle Class Matters," published on June 5, 2014, YouTube video, www.youtube.com/watch?v =l3_Zkn0QL18

132   appeared on the screen: Skoll Foundation, "Skoll World Forum 2014 Opening Plenary," published on April 9, 2014, YouTube video, www.youtube.com/watch?v =Ry9sVvfQIHg

134   "double espresso": Skoll Foundation, "Skoll World Forum 2014 Opening Plenary," published on April 9, 2014, YouTube video, www.youtube.com/watch?v =Ry9sVvfQIHg

136   Arif's team devised: Dubai Financial Services Authority, "Decision Notice to Abraaj Investment Management Limited," July 29, 2019, 40.

136   Abraaj's funds: *United States of America vs. Arif Naqvi, Waqar Siddique, Rafique Lakhani, Mustafa Abdel-Wadood, Ashish Dave and Sivendran Vettivetpillai*, S6 19 Cr. 233 Superseding Indictment, United States District Court, Southern District of New York, 2019, 14–15.

137   was plundering: *United States of America vs. Arif Naqvi, Waqar Siddique, Rafique Lakhani, Mustafa Abdel-Wadood, Ashish Dave and Sivendran Vettivetpillai*, S6 19 Cr. 233 Superseding Indictment, United States District Court, Southern District of New York, 2019, 14–16.

138   a scholarship program: Royal College of Art, "Abraaj RCA Innovation Scholarship Programme to Support Five Outstanding Students," September 16, 2014, www .rca.ac.uk/news-and-events/news/abraaj-rca-innovation-scholarship-programme/

138   he interviewed Arif: Jeffrey Garten, "Interview with Arif Naqvi," Yale School of Management, published on September 24, 2014, YouTube video, som.yale.edu /blog/interview-with-arif-naqvi

142   Interpol plugged Arif: Interpol Foundation, "INTERPOL Foundation for a Safer World Appoints Arif Naqvi, Founder of the Abraaj Group, to its Global Board of Trustees," November 19, 2014, www.zawya.com/mena/en/press-releases/story /INTERPOL_Foundation_for_a_Safer_World_Appoints_Arif_Naqvi_Founder _of_The_Abraaj_Group_to_its_Global_Board_of_Trustees_-ZAWYA20141119 131426/

142   Ghosn was later arrested: Nick Kostov and Sean McLain, "Carlos Ghosn Flees Trial in Japan for Lebanon," *Wall Street Journal*, December 31, 2019, www.wsj.com /articles/carlos-ghosn-arrives-in-lebanon-after-fleeing-japan-11577741238

142   "benefit from globalization": Abraaj Group, "Partnership Policing for the Future," published on April 3, 2017, YouTube video, 03:04.

143   To conceal the deficit: *United States vs. Arif Naqvi et al.*, Superseding Indictment, S6 19 Cr. 233, 2019, 13.

144   deprived his investors: Dubai Financial Services Authority, "Decision Notice to Abraaj Investment Management Limited," July 29, 2019, 23.

144   Arif paid himself: *United States Securities and Exchange Commission vs. Abraaj Investment Management Limited and Arif Naqvi*, United States District Court, Southern District of New York, No. 19-cv-3244, April 11, 2019.

144   40,000 years to earn: Pakistan's GDP per capita was $1,284.70 in 2019, according to the World Bank, data.worldbank.org/indicator/NY.GDP.PCAP.CD?locations=PK

145   around the time: *United States Securities and Exchange Commission vs. Abraaj Investment Management Limited and Arif Naqvi*, United States District Court, Southern District of New York, No. 19-cv-3244, April 11, 2019.

145   $168 million: *United States Securities and Exchange Commission vs. Abraaj Investment Management Limited and Arif Naqvi*, United States District Court, Southern District of New York, Case 1:19-cv-03244-AJN, August 16, 2019, 12.

145   BNP Paribas: BNP Paribas Wealth Twitter account, June 25, 2015, twitter.com/bnpp_wealth/status/614127815663984640

146   Arif's personal finances: *United States Securities and Exchange Commission vs. Abraaj Investment Management Limited and Arif Naqvi*, United States District Court, Southern District of New York, No. 19-cv-3244, April 11, 2019, 19.

146   Rafique asked: *United States Securities and Exchange Commission vs. Abraaj Investment Management Limited and Arif Naqvi*, United States District Court, Southern District of New York, Case 1:19-cv-03244-AJN, August 16, 2019, 38.

CHAPTER 11: DREAM WEAVERS

147   United Nations Secretary General: Ban Ki-moon, "Remarks to the General Assembly on the Occasion of the Visit by His Holiness Pope Francis," United Nations General Assembly, September 25, 2015, www.un.org/sg/en/content/sg/speeches/2015-09-25/remarks-general-assembly-occasion-visit-his-holiness-pope-francis

147   "for a better world": United Nations Secretary General, "Remarks at Summit for the Adoption of the Post-2015 Development Agenda," United Nations General Assembly, September 25, 2015, www.un.org/sg/en/content/sg/speeches/2015-09-25/remarks-summit-adoption-post-2015-development-agenda

148   $2.5 trillion annual shortfall: United Nations Conference on Trade and Development, "Developing Countries Face $2.5 Trillion Annual Investment Gap in Key Sustainable Development Sectors, UNCTAD Report Estimates," June 24, 2014, unctad.org/en/pages/PressRelease.aspx?OriginalVersionID=194

148   the fifth time: Speech by Pope Francis to the United Nations, September 25, 2015, www.vatican.va/content/francesco/en/speeches/2015/september/documents/papa-francesco_20150925_onu-visita.html

149   "do them effectively": Abraaj Group, "Abraaj Week 2017: Setting the Scene," published on March 28, 2017, YouTube video, www.youtube.com/watch?v=G8u0qvS U6nA

150   birthday celebration: Jordan Fabian, "Obama Golfs with Old Friends on Pre-Birthday Weekend," *The Hill*, August 1, 2015, thehill.com/homenews/administration /250003-obama-golfs-with-old-friends-on-pre-birthday-weekend

150   Egyptian minister of trade: World Economic Forum biography, Tarek Kabil, www.weforum.org/people/tarek-kabil-327c0e46-a34a-4b58-be76-d0784c8fafc3

150   "Global Private Equity": Elizabeth MacBride, "The Story Behind Abraaj Group's Stunning Rise in Global Private Equity," *Forbes*, November 4, 2015, www .forbes.com/sites/elizabethmacbride/2015/11/04/the-story-behind-abraajs-stun ning-rise/

151   lose $100 million: PricewaterhouseCoopers, "Abraaj Holdings: First Report of the Joint Provisional Liquidators to the Grand Court of the Cayman Islands," FSD Cause No: 95 of 2018, July 11, 2018, 21.

152    $238.5 million be paid: *United States Securities and Exchange Commission vs. Abraaj Investment Management Limited and Arif Naqvi*, United States District Court, Southern District of New York, Case 1:19-cv-03244-AJN, August 16, 2019, 16.

152   spend on other purposes: *United States Securities and Exchange Commission vs. Abraaj Investment Management Limited and Arif Naqvi*, United States District Court, Southern District of New York, Case 1:19-cv-03244-AJN, August 16, 2019, 17.

152   A $5.4 million slice: *United States Securities and Exchange Commission vs. Abraaj Investment Management Limited and Arif Naqvi*, United States District Court, Southern District of New York, Case 1:19-cv-03244-AJN, August 16, 2019, 16–20.

152   to find a buyer: David French, "Abraaj to Sell Pakistan K-Electric Stake to Shanghai Electric for $1.77 bln," Reuters, October 30, 2016, www.reuters.com /article/k-electric-ma-sh-elec-power/abraaj-to-sell-pakistan-k-electric-stake-to -shanghai-electric-for-1-77-bln-idUSD5N1CO012

153   accused Karachi Electric: Salman Masood, "Pakistani Taliban Blame Electric Company for Heat Wave Deaths," *New York Times*, June 26, 2015, www.nytimes .com/2015/06/27/world/asia/pakistani-taliban-blame-electric-company-for-heat -wave-deaths.html

153   His devotion: Angela Shah, "Arabia-Asia: Business Is Personal for Abraaj Capital's Omar Lodhi," *Forbes*, October 11, 2012, www.forbes.com/sites/forbesasia/2012/10 /11/arabia-asia-business-is-personal-for-abraaj-capitals-omar-lodhi/

153   the Punjab: www.dawn.com/news/1427542

154   election fund kitty: *United States vs. Arif Naqvi et al.*, Superseding Indictment, S6 19 Cr. 233, 2019, 23–25.

155   Network International: Dubai Financial Services Authority, "Decision Notice to Abraaj Investment Management Limited," July 29, 2019, 20–30.

155   The buyers of Network International: *United States Securities and Exchange Com-*

mission vs. Abraaj Investment Management Limited and Arif Naqvi, United States District Court, Southern District of New York, Case 1:19-cv-03244-AJN, August 16, 2019, 17–18.

158   Rafique wrote to Arif: *United States Securities and Exchange Commission vs. Abraaj Investment Management Limited and Arif Naqvi,* United States District Court, Southern District of New York, Case 1:19-cv-03244-AJN, August 16, 2019.

158   a second installment: *United States Securities and Exchange Commission vs. Abraaj Investment Management Limited and Arif Naqvi,* United States District Court, Southern District of New York, Case 1:19-cv-03244-AJN, August 16, 2019, 18.

159   Abraaj received $185 million: Dubai Financial Services Authority, "Decision Notice to Abraaj Investment Management Limited," July 29, 2019, 26.

159   Cayman Islands: *United States Securities and Exchange Commission vs. Abraaj Investment Management Limited and Arif Naqvi,* United States District Court, Southern District of New York, Case 1:19-cv-03244-AJN, August 16, 2019, 21.

159   $219 million was transferred: *United States Securities and Exchange Commission vs. Abraaj Investment Management Limited and Arif Naqvi,* United States District Court, Southern District of New York, Case 1:19-cv-03244-AJN, August 16, 2019.

159   the Pearl Initiative: "Pearl Initiative board of governs' meeting highlights five-year achievements," *Gulf Times,* March 9, 2016, www.gulf-times.com/story /483985/Pearl-Initiative-board-of-governors-meeting-highlights-five-year-achieve ments

160   A New York–based investor: *United States Securities and Exchange Commission vs. Abraaj Investment Management Limited and Arif Naqvi,* United States District Court, Southern District of New York, Case 1:19-cv-03244-AJN, August 16, 2019.

160   "Noise makers": *United States Securities and Exchange Commission vs. Abraaj Investment Management Limited and Arif Naqvi,* United States District Court, Southern District of New York, Case 1:19-cv-03244-AJN, August 16, 2019, 22–23.

161   "needs no introduction": Abraaj Group, "Navigating Global Growth Markets— Keynote by Arif Naqvi, the Abraaj Group," published on June 5, 2016, YouTube video, 38:28, www.youtube.com/watch?v=MpYnoZc8Sf0

161   $47 million more: *United States Securities and Exchange Commission vs. Abraaj Investment Management Limited and Arif Naqvi,* United States District Court, Southern District of New York, Case 1:19-cv-03244-AJN, August 16, 2019.

162   "This must be on your mind": *United States vs. Arif Naqvi et al.,* Superseding Indictment, S6 19 Cr. 233, 2019.

162   Amazingly, they agreed: *United States Securities and Exchange Commission vs. Abraaj Investment Management Limited and Arif Naqvi,* United States District Court, Southern District of New York, Case 1:19-cv-03244-AJN, August 16, 2019, 25–26.

162   "Yes, Professor": *United States Securities and Exchange Commission vs. Abraaj Investment Management Limited and Arif Naqvi,* United States District Court, Southern District of New York, Case 1:19-cv-03244-AJN, August 16, 2019.

CHAPTER 12: HEALTHY LIVES

163   Africa for the first time: Bill Gates, "Giving the Mandela Lecture," Gates Notes, July 17, 2016, www.gatesnotes.com/Development/Nelson-Mandela-Annual -Lecture

163   organized the trip: Joss Kent, as told to Charlotte Metcalf, "Bill Gates and Me," *The Spectator*, July 18, 2009.

164   "we couldn't ignore": Bill Gates, "Giving the Mandela Lecture," Gates Notes, July 17, 2016, www.gatesnotes.com/Development/Nelson-Mandela-Annual-Lecture

164   Bill wrote: Bill Gates, "Warren Buffett's Best Investment," GatesNotes, February 14, 2017, www.gatesnotes.com/2017-annual-letter

165   health at the center: Nicholas D. Kristof, "For Third World, Water Is Still a Deadly Drink," *New York Times*, January 9, 1997, www.nytimes.com/1997/01/09 /world/for-third-world-water-is-still-a-deadly-drink.html

165   "Dad": Gates Foundation, "Who We Are," www.gatesfoundation.org/Who -We-Are/General-Information/History

165   Bill explained: Bill Gates, "Giving the Mandela Lecture," Gates Notes, July 17, 2016, www.gatesnotes.com/Development/Nelson-Mandela-Annual-Lecture

166   young Indian girl: "Abraaj Growth Markets Health Fund Impact Report for 2017," Abraaj investor report, May 2018.

167   "The Business of Health": International Finance Corporation, "The Business of Health in Africa: Partnering with the Private Sector to Improve People's Lives," World Bank Group, 2008.

168   "Blind Optimism": Oxfam International, "Blind Optimism: Challenging the Myths about Private Healthcare in Poor Countries," February 12, 2009, oi-files-d8 -prod.s3.eu-west-2.amazonaws.com/s3fs-public/file_attachments/bp125_Blind%20 optimism%20paper_SUMMARY%20FINAL%20ENGLISH_3.pdf

168   Sev, responded: Aureos Capital, "Aureos Capital: Proposal to Manage the Equity Vehicle for Health in Africa," December 3, 2008.

169   first investment opportunities: "A Middle Way," *The Economist*, November 16, 2013, www.economist.com/middle-east-and-africa/2013/11/16/a-middle-way

170   The Microsoft founder explained: Abu Dhabi Media Summit, "Bill Gates at Abu Dhabi Media Summit 2012," published on October 9, 2012, YouTube video, 38:58, www.youtube.com/watch?v=ruvFS2rNLfk

171   Bill was quoted: "Gates Foundation, Aman Vow to Work Together," *Trade Arabia*, www.tradearabia.com/news/HEAL_223608.html

172   global medical industry: John Burn-Murdoch and Katarina Stankovic, "Who Is Going to Davos 2013? Get the Full List of Attendees," *The Guardian*, January 22, 2013.

173   sound so simple: Abraaj Group, "Abraaj Growth Markets Health Fund," Private Placement Memorandum, July 31, 2016.

175   Khawar's rise: Khawar Mann LinkedIn profile, www.linkedin.com/in/khawar -mann/?originalSubdomain=ae

175   Aly's curriculum vitae: McKinsey & Co, "Our people," www.mckinsey.com /our-people/aly-jeddy

177   he joined the Communist Party: Randeep Ramesh, "Sir David Nicholson: The 'Stalinist' NHS Chief Who Showed Loyalty to Tory Boss," *The Guardian*, May 22, 2013, www.theguardian.com/society/2013/may/22/sir-david-nicholson-nhs -chief

177   forced to apologize: Rebecca Smith, "Mid Staffs: David Nicholson Apologises for Scandal as 'a Human Being and a CEO,'" *Daily Telegraph*, January 31, 2013, www.telegraph.co.uk/news/health/news/9837374/Mid-Staffs-David-Nicholson -apologises-for-scandal-as-a-human-being-and-as-CEO.html

178   "first close": Abraaj Group, "Abraaj Growth Markets Health Fund," Private Placement Memorandum, July 31, 2016.

179   bidding war: Bobby Kurian and Reeba Zachariah, "Temasek-TPG, Abraaj Vie for Care," *The Times of India*, October 8, 2015, timesofindia.indiatimes.com/business /india-business/Temasek-TPG-Abraaj-vie-for-Care/articleshow/49266091.cms

179   competed: Indulal PM, "Thomson Medical Emerges Top Bidder for Advent International's 72% Stake in CARE Hospitals," *Economic Times*, October 20, 2015, economictimes.indiatimes.com/industry/healthcare/biotech/healthcare/thomson -medical-emerges-top-bidder-for-advent-internationals-72-stake-in-care-hospitals /articleshow/49459866.cms

180   The deal was signed: Karen Rebelo and Zeba Siddiqui, "Dubai's Abraaj Group to Buy Majority Stake in India's Care Hospitals," Reuters, January 13, 2016, www .reuters.com/article/care-hospitals-ma-abraaj-group/update-1-dubais-abraaj-group -to-buy-majority-stake-in-indias-care-hospitals-idUSL3N14X34U20160113

180   Arif took to the stage: World Economic Forum, "Davos 2016—Press Conference: Health as a Global Challenge," published on January 20, 2016, YouTube video, 32:56, www.youtube.com/watch?v=N2OhdkODg_w

182   for himself and his staff: *United States vs. Arif Naqvi et al.*, Superseding Indictment, S6 19 Cr. 233, 2019, 17–19.

CHAPTER 13: BREATHE, SMILE, SAY ALHAMDULLILAH, AND PROCEED

186   Omar prepared a $20 million: *United States vs. Arif Naqvi et al.*, Superseding Indictment, S6 19 Cr. 233, 2019, 24–25.

188   The deal promised: Syed Raza Hassan, "China's Shanghai Electric to Buy $1.77 Billion Stake in Pakistani Power Company," Reuters, October 30, 2016, www .reuters.com/article/pakistan-energy-china/chinas-shanghai-electric-to-buy-1-77 -billion-stake-in-pakistani-power-company-idINKBN12U0IS

189   siphoned $140 million: *United States Securities and Exchange Commission vs. Abraaj Investment Management Limited and Arif Naqvi*, United States District Court, Southern District of New York, No. 19-cv-3244, April 11, 2019, 34.

189   $3.2 million: *United States of America versus Arif Naqvi, Waqar Siddique, Rafique Lakhani, Mustafa Abdel-Wadood, Ashish Dave and Sivendran Vettivetpillai*, S6 19 Cr. 233

Superseding Indictment, United States District Court, Southern District of New York, 2019, 18.

189 $73 million: Dubai Financial Services Authority, "Decision Notice to Abraaj Investment Management Limited," 31.

189 Hepsiburada: Abraaj Group, "Eric Schantz @Medtronic & CEOs of Abraaj Partner Companies @Hepsiburada @CapaDeOzonoZ & @Kudu SA Talking Growing Businesses in #GrowthMarkets," Twitter, December 14, 2016, twitter.com /abraajgroup/status/809133967672803330?s=20

189 "the same culture": Abraaj Group, "E-commerce in Turkey: A Growth Opportunity," published on July 4, 2017, YouTube video, www.youtube.com/watch?v =ZuONatb57fk

189 $85 million: *United States Securities and Exchange Commission vs. Abraaj Investment Management Limited and Arif Naqvi*, United States District Court, Southern District of New York, No. 19-cv-3244, April 11, 2019, 8.

189 $173 million: *United States Securities and Exchange Commission vs. Abraaj Investment Management Limited and Arif Naqvi*, United States District Court, Southern District of New York, No. 19-cv-3244, April 11, 2019, 9.

191 "shut down the business": *United States Securities and Exchange Commission vs. Abraaj Investment Management Limited and Arif Naqvi*, United States District Court, Southern District of New York, No. 19-cv-3244, April 11, 2019, 9.

191 Arif was in top form: *The Economist*, "From Poverty to a Thriving Global Middle Class: A Conversation with Arif Naqvi," published on March 1, 2017, YouTube video, 23:55, www.youtube.com/watch?v=v2Dpe4Hewlk&t=15s

192 Abraaj needed $4.2 million: *United States Securities and Exchange Commission vs. Abraaj Investment Management Limited and Arif Naqvi*, United States District Court, Southern District of New York, Case 1:19-cv-03244-AJN, August 16, 2019, 35.

192 Project Dido: *United States Securities and Exchange Commission vs. Abraaj Investment Management Limited and Arif Naqvi*, United States District Court, Southern District of New York, Case 1:19-cv-03244-AJN, August 16, 2019, 28–29.

192 send $115 million more: *United States Securities and Exchange Commission vs. Abraaj Investment Management Limited and Arif Naqvi*, United States District Court, Southern District of New York, Case 1:19-cv-03244-AJN, August 16, 2019, 36.

192 used to buy clinics and hospitals: Abraaj Group, "Abraaj Growth Markets Health Fund: Report of the Manager," September 30, 2017, 11.

193 Ghizlan said: The Modist, "The First Global Online Destination for Luxury Modest Fashion Launches on International Women's Day," PR Newswire, March 8, 2017, www.prnewswire.com/in/news-releases/the-first-global-online -destination-for-luxury-modest-fashion-launches-on-international-womens-day-8th -march-2017-615649393.html

193 lectured the crowd: SuperReturn TV, "Arif Naqvi: When Will This Rollercoaster Stop?" published on March 8, 2017, YouTube video, 22:51, www.youtube.com /watch?v=bjgfbFjCqio

193   "out of control": *United States Securities and Exchange Commission vs. Abraaj Investment Management Limited and Arif Naqvi*, United States District Court, Southern District of New York, Case 1:19-cv-03244-AJN, August 16, 2019, 37.

194   sitting down with: World Economic Forum, World Economic Forum on the Middle East and North Africa: Regional Agenda, May 19–21, 2017, www3.weforum.org/docs/WEF_MENA17_Meeting_Overview.pdf

194   coolly responded: *United States vs. Arif Naqvi et al.*, Superseding Indictment, S6 19 Cr. 233, 2019, 22.

194   "Both are broke": Simon Clark, Nicolas Parasie, and William Louch, "Private-Equity Firm Abraaj Raised Billions Pledging to Do Good—Then It Fell Apart," *Wall Street Journal*, October 16, 2018, www.wsj.com/articles/private-equity-firm-abraaj-raised-billions-pledging-to-do-goodthen-it-fell-apart-1539706575

194   his expense account: *United States Securities and Exchange Commission vs. Abraaj Investment Management Limited and Arif Naqvi*, United States District Court, Southern District of New York, Case 1:19-cv-03244-AJN, August 16, 2019, 38.

195   "As you are aware": *United States vs. Arif Naqvi et al.*, Superseding Indictment, S6 19 Cr. 233, 2019, 19.

195   "I will sort it out": *United States Securities and Exchange Commission vs. Abraaj Investment Management Limited and Arif Naqvi*, United States District Court, Southern District of New York, Case 1:19-cv-03244-AJN, August 16, 2019, 38.

195   fill the hole: *United States Securities and Exchange Commission vs. Abraaj Investment Management Limited and Arif Naqvi*, United States District Court, Southern District of New York, Case 1:19-cv-03244-AJN, August 16, 2019, 40–42.

196   He asked airline executives: *United States Securities and Exchange Commission vs. Abraaj Investment Management Limited and Arif Naqvi*, United States District Court, Southern District of New York, Case 1:19-cv-03244-AJN, August 16, 2019, 41–42.

196   "playing poker": *United States of America versus Arif Naqvi, Waqar Siddique, Rafique Lakhani, Mustafa Abdel-Wadood, Ashish Dave and Sivendran Vettivetpillai*, S6 19 Cr. 233 Superseding Indictment, United States District Court, Southern District of New York, 2019, 34.

CHAPTER 14: AMERICA FIRST

199   Kito told a journalist: Afshin Molavi, "The Veteran McKinsey Pioneer Reflects on His Journey from Delhi to Dubai—and Now, East Jerusalem," emerge85, March 17, 2017, emerge85.io/Insights/the-veteran-mckinsey-pioneer-reflects-on-his-journey-from-delhi-to-dubai-and-now-east-jerusalem/

200   Arif's arguments: "Remarks at the U.S. Institute of Peace's Passing the Baton 2017: America's Role in the World," January 10, 2017, https://2009-2017.state.gov/secretary/remarks/2017/01/266778.htm

201   putting America first: The White House, "The Inaugural Address," January 20, 2017, www.whitehouse.gov/briefings-statements/the-inaugural-address/

201   Xi said: State Council Information Office, People's Republic of China, "Full

Text: Xi Jinping's Keynote Speech at the World Economic Forum," April 6, 2017, www.china.org.cn/node_7247529/content_40569136.htm

202   in Berlin: SuperReturn TV, "Arif Naqvi: When Will This Rollercoaster Stop?" published on March 8, 2017, YouTube video, 22:51, www.youtube.com/watch?v=b jgfbFjCqio

CHAPTER 15: DOUBLING DOWN

205   "helping you make money": *The Economist*, "From Poverty to a Thriving Global Middle Class: A Conversation with Arif Naqvi," published on March 1, 2017, YouTube video, 14:00, www.youtube.com/watch?v=v2Dpe4Hewlk

206   raising $6 billion: Abraaj Group, "Abraaj Private Equity Fund VI Private Placement Memorandum," March 3, 2017.

206   annual returns: Abraaj Group, "Abraaj Private Equity Fund VI Private Placement Memorandum," March 3, 2017, 23.

206   low loss ratio: Abraaj Group, "Abraaj Private Equity Fund VI Private Placement Memorandum," March 3, 2017, 23.

207   nominated Matt: U.S. Senate Committee on Foreign Relations, "Statement of Matthew McGuire, Nominee for United States Executive Director," May 14, 2014, www.foreign.senate.gov/imo/media/doc/McGuire_Testimony.pdf

209   Arif's turn to speak: Milken Institute, "Framework for Investing in the Long Term," published on June 26, 2017, YouTube video, 1:01:45, www.youtube.com /watch?time_continue=3364&v=JTrHX7RjmKQ&feature=emb_title

209   the supreme court removed: Salman Masood, "Nawaz Sharif, Pakistan's Prime Minister, Is Toppled by Corruption Case," *New York Times*, July 28, 2017, www.nytimes .com/2017/07/28/world/asia/pakistan-prime-minister-nawaz-sharif-removed.html

210   The dairy company: Abraaj Group, Abraaj Private Equity Fund IV Investor Report, September 30, 2017.

210   increased Yörsan's valuation: Abraaj Group, Abraaj Private Equity Fund IV Investor Report, September 30, 2017.

210   mark up the value: *United States vs. Arif Naqvi et al.*, Superseding Indictment, S6 19 Cr. 233, 2019, 36.

210   "the safe zone": *United States vs. Arif Naqvi et al.*, Superseding Indictment, S6 19 Cr. 233, 2019, 37.

211   junior Abraaj employee: *United States vs. Arif Naqvi et al.*, Superseding Indictment, S6 19 Cr. 233, 2019, 38.

CHAPTER 16: PEAK ABRAAJ

215   managed $2 billion: Gates Foundation, "Who We Are: Andrew Farnum Biography," www.gatesfoundation.org/zh/Who-We-Are/General-Information/Leadership /Operations/Andrew-Farnum

217   His patience snapped: Abraaj healthcare fund investors, "The Partnership," letter to Weil, Gotshal & Manges, July 9, 2018, 194.

217   some of the biggest names: Milken Institute, "Investment Titans: Dispelling the Myth of Emerging Markets," published on September 26, 2017, YouTube video, 57:13, www.youtube.com/watch?v=-1l4RQhqZjg

220   Raj Morjaria told Andrew: Abraaj healthcare fund investors, "The Partnership," letter to Weil, Gotshal & Manges, July 9, 2018, 194.

220   Ashish had a better plan: *United States vs. Arif Naqvi et al.*, Superseding Indictment, S6 19 Cr. 233, 2019, 29–30.

221   On stage he claimed: Arif Naqvi, keynote speech at the forum "Scaling Impact Investing," published on September 18, 2017, YouTube video, www.youtube.com/watch?v=tJ_EL3qkyYc&t=53s

222   Rafique had emailed: *United States Securities and Exchange Commission vs. Abraaj Investment Management Limited and Arif Naqvi*, United States District Court, Southern District of New York, Case 1:19-cv-03244-AJN, August 16, 2019, 39.

222   "Is there a tradeoff": Bloomberg, "Business Leaders, Sustainable Development Goals Good for Business," published on September 20, 2017, YouTube video, 26:48.

223   Arif told Hamilton Lane: *United States vs. Arif Naqvi et al.*, Superseding Indictment, S6 19 Cr. 233, 2019, 28.

224   U.S. government fund: *United States vs. Arif Naqvi et al.*, Superseding Indictment, S6 19 Cr. 233, 2019, 20.

225   Ashish suggested: *United States vs. Arif Naqvi et al.*, Superseding Indictment, S6 19 Cr. 233, 2019, 33.

228   "actual bank statements": Abraaj healthcare fund investors, "The Partnership," letter to Weil, Gotshal & Manges, July 9, 2018, 195.

228   "make it work?": *United States vs. Arif Naqvi et al.*, Superseding Indictment, S6 19 Cr. 233, 2019, 31.

228   Arif borrowed $140 million: Dubai Financial Services Authority, "Decision Notice to Abraaj Investment Management Limited," 37.

229   operated like a company: *United States vs. Arif Naqvi et al.*, Superseding Indictment, S6 19 Cr. 233, 2019, 32.

230   "It's fraud. Simple": *United States vs. Arif Naqvi et al.*, Superseding Indictment, S6 19 Cr. 233, 2019, 40.

230   Mark Bourgeois agreed: *United States vs. Arif Naqvi et al.*, Superseding Indictment, S6 19 Cr. 233, 2019, 41.

CHAPTER 17: DON'T MAKE NICE WITH A FRAUDSTER

234   He laughed quietly: *United States vs. Arif Naqvi et al.*, Superseding Indictment, S6 19 Cr. 233, 2019, 43.

237   "Bill was instrumental": World Economic Forum, "A New Era for Global Health," published on January 26, 2018, YouTube video, 1:00:51, www.youtube.com/watch?v=tOlcV04C-KU

239   Abraaj's carefully cultivated public image: William Louch, Ed Ballard, and Simon Clark, "Abraaj Investors Hire Auditor to Trace Money," *Wall Street Journal*,

February 2, 2018, www.wsj.com/articles/abraaj-investors-hire-auditor-to-trace
-money-1517598630

239   *New York Times*: Landon Thomas, Jr., "Leading Private Equity Firm Accused of Misusing Funds," *New York Times*, February 2, 2018, www.nytimes.com/2018/02/02 /business/abraaj-naqvi-world-bank.html

240   "media reports": Email obtained through Freedom of Information Act request to the Washington State Investment Board.

241   Abraaj sent out: Reuters, "Abraaj Group Says KPMG Has Completed Audit of Healthcare Fund," February 7, 2018, uk.reuters.com/article/brief-abraaj-group -says-kpmg-has-complet/brief-abraaj-group-says-kpmg-has-completed-audit-of -healthcare-fund-idUKFWN1PX1FN

243   limit the damage: William Louch, Simon Clark, and Nicolas Parasie, "Abraaj Halts Investment Activities at Fund-Management Business," *Wall Street Journal*, February 23, 2018, www.wsj.com/articles/abraaj-founder-steps-down-from-fund -management-business-1519390019

243   Rafique warned Arif: *United States vs. Arif Naqvi et al.*, Superseding Indict- ment, S6 19 Cr. 233, 2019, 44–45.

243   fundraising was canceled: Joshua Franklin, Saeed Azhar, and Hadeel Al Sayegh, "Embattled Abraaj Frees Private Equity Investors from Capital Commitments," Reuters, March 7, 2018, www.reuters.com/article/us-abraaj-funds/embattled-abraaj -frees-private-equity-investors-from-capital-commitments-idUSKCN1GJ0C0

243   borrowed $150 million: PricewaterhouseCoopers, "Abraaj Holdings: First Re- port of the Joint Provisional Liquidators to the Grand Court of the Cayman Islands," FSD Cause No: 95 of 2018, July 11, 2018, 27.

244   Ashish told Reuters: Hadeel Al Sayegh, Tom Arnold, and Stanley Carvalho, "CFO Says He Left Dubai-Based Private Equity Firm Abraaj," Reuters, March 12, 2018, www.reuters.com/article/us-abraaj-funds-executives-exclusive/exclusive-cfo -says-he-left-dubai-based-private-equity-firm-abraaj-idUSKCN1GO1NA

247   "you will have zero balance": *United States vs. Arif Naqvi et al.*, Superseding Indictment, S6 19 Cr. 233, 2019, 45.

248   won the final: Alex Greenberger, "Lawrence Abu Hamdan Wins 2018 Abraaj Group Art Prize," *Art News*, October 4, 2017, www.artnews.com/art-news/news /lawrence-abu-hamdan-wins-2018-abraaj-group-art-prize-9105/

249   Arif told Mark: *United States vs. Arif Naqvi et al.*, Superseding Indictment, S6 19 Cr. 233, 2019, 45–46.

CHAPTER 18: KEYS TO THE KINGDOM

254   He appointed: Deloitte, "Abraaj Investment Management Limited: Joint Pro- visional Liquidators' First Report," July 11, 2018, 3.

255   Federal Reserve banned: "Federal Reserve Board announces it is permanently barring senior executive at Goldman Sachs from banking industry," Federal Re-

serve, February 4, 2020, federalreserve.gov/newsevents/pressreleases/enforcement 20200204a.htm

257 Arif had told investors: Simon Clark, William Louch, and Nicolas Parasie, "Abraaj, Already Under Scrutiny, Tapped Another Client Fund to Finance Itself," *Wall Street Journal*, May 23, 2018, www.wsj.com/articles/abraaj-already-under-scrutiny-tapped-another-client-fund-to-finance-itself-1527089842

260 Kuwaiti pension fund: Nicolas Parasie, "Kuwait Pension Fund Tries to Force Abraaj into Bankruptcy," *Wall Street Journal*, May 30, 2018, www.wsj.com/articles/kuwait-pension-fund-tries-to-force-abraaj-into-bankruptcy-1527717453

261 Cerberus offered $125 million: Nicolas Parasie and William Louch, "Cerberus Bids $125 Million for Abraaj's Private-Equity Business," *Wall Street Journal*, June 5, 2018, www.wsj.com/articles/cerberus-bids-125-million-for-abraajs-private-equity-business-1528146632

262 transferred his loan: Nicolas Parasie and William Louch, "Abraaj Pushed to Restructure $1 Billion Debt," *Wall Street Journal*, June 11, 2018, www.wsj.com/articles/abraaj-pushed-to-restructure-1-billion-debt-1528749673

262 A judge appointed: Simon Clark, Nicolas Parasie, and William Louch, "Private-Equity Firm Abraaj Raised Billions Pledging to Do Good—Then It Fell Apart," *Wall Street Journal*, October 16, 2018, www.wsj.com/articles/private-equity-firm-abraaj-raised-billions-pledging-to-do-goodthen-it-fell-apart-1539706575

264 last desperate offer: Deloitte, "Abraaj Investment Management Limited: Joint Provisional Liquidators' Third Report," November 6, 2018, 7.

267 Our investigation was published: Simon Clark, Nicolas Parasie, and William Louch, "Private-Equity Firm Abraaj Raised Billions Pledging to Do Good—Then It Fell Apart," *Wall Street Journal*, October 16, 2018, www.wsj.com/articles/private-equity-firm-abraaj-raised-billions-pledging-to-do-goodthen-it-fell-apart-1539706575

267 Arif ranted: Arif Masood Naqvi, "Fourth Affidavit of Arif Masood Naqvi: In the Grand Court of the Cayman Islands Financial Services Division," Cause No. FSD 95 of 2018 (RMJ), November 14, 2018.

267 Reham wrote: Reham Khan, *Reham Khan*, HarperCollins India, July 10, 2018.

CHAPTER 19: FLIGHT RISK

269 had to stay out: Nicolas Parasie, "Abraaj Founder Faces Arrest Warrant in U.A.E.," *Wall Street Journal*, June 25, 2018, www.wsj.com/articles/abraaj-founder-faces-arrest-warrant-in-u-a-e-1529956791

270 issued an arrest warrant: Simon Clark, William Louch, and Nicolas Parasie, "Abraaj Founder Accused of Fraud as U.S. Seeks Extradition," *Wall Street Journal*, April 12, 2019, www.wsj.com/articles/abraaj-founder-accused-of-fraud-as-u-s-seeks-extradition-11555086776

271 1,600 inmates: U.K. Government, "Wandsworth Prison," www.gov.uk/guidance/wandsworth-prison

271   judge denied bail: Simon Clark, "U.K. Judge Blocks Bail in Arif Naqvi Extradition Case," *Wall Street Journal*, April 26, 2019, www.wsj.com/articles/u-k-judge-blocks-bail-in-arif-naqvi-extradition-case-11556298117

272   He never did: Simon Clark and William Louch, "Third Abraaj Executive Arrested," *Wall Street Journal*, April 18, 2019, www.wsj.com/articles/third-abraaj-executive-arrested-11555585989#:~:text=A%20third%20former%20Abraaj%20Group,equity%20firm%20in%20emerging%20markets.&text=Abraaj%20founder%20Arif%20Naqvi%20was,criminal%20case%20against%20the%20firm

277   Pakistani passports: Henley & Partners Passport Index, "Global Ranking 2020," www.henleypassportindex.com/passport

281   U.S. prosecutors published: *United States vs. Arif Naqvi et al.*, Superseding Indictment, S6 19 Cr. 233, 2019.

281   291 years in jail: Simon Clark and William Louch, "Abraaj Liquidators Sue Fund Backed by Gates Foundation," *Wall Street Journal*, July 16, 2020, www.wsj.com/articles/abraaj-liquidators-sue-fund-backed-by-gates-foundation-11594922921

281   Mustafa pled guilty: Laura Cooper and Simon Clark, "Ex-Abraaj Executive Pleads Guilty to Racketeering, Fraud," *Wall Street Journal*, June 28, 2019, www.wsj.com/articles/ex-abraaj-executive-pleads-guilty-to-racketeering-fraud-11561742457

283   antidepressants: Emma Arbuthnot, *Judgment in the matter of a request for Extradition under Part 2 of the Extradition Act 2003 between The United States of America and Arif Masood Naqvi*, Westminster Magistrates' Court, London, January 28, 2021.

285   Abraaj's liquidators subpoenaed: Klestadt Winters Jureller Southard & Stevens LLP, "Application of Abraaj Investment Management Limited: For an Order to Obtain Discovery for Use in Foreign Proceedings Pursuant to 28 USC 1782," United States District Court, Southern District of New York, Case 1:20-mc-00229, June 12, 2020.

286   "the best path for me.": Atika Rehman, "Footprints: Arif Naqvi - The Man Who Flew Too Close to The Sun," *Dawn*, February 1, 2021, www.dawn.com/news/1604796

EPILOGUE

293   in 2019: "FBR Achieved 17% Revenue Growth Till January, 2020," Federal Board of Revenue, March 8, 2020, www.fbr.gov.pk/pr/fbr-achieved-17-revenue-growth-till-january-2/152289

294   $60 million in fees: Abraaj Joint Official Liquidators' Second Report, September 11, 2020.

INDEX

ABOUT THE AUTHORS

SIMON CLARK is a *Wall Street Journal* reporter based in London. His investigative reporting has led him to the poppy fields of Afghanistan, the copper mines of Congo, and many banks in the City of London. He was nominated for a Pulitzer Prize in 2016. He lives in Lewes, England.

WILL LOUCH is at law school in London. He was previously a *Wall Street Journal* reporter covering private equity in London and New York. Previously he was based in Brussels, where he wrote about European politics. He lives in London.